INTERDISCIPLINARY PERSPECTIVES ON HUMAN DIGNITY AND HUMAN RIGHTS

INTERDISCIPLINARY PERSPECTIVES ON HUMAN DIGNITY AND HUMAN RIGHTS

EDITED BY

HODA MAHMOUDI AND MICHAEL L. PENN

emerald
PUBLISHING

United Kingdom – North America – Japan – India – Malaysia – China

Emerald Publishing Limited
Howard House, Wagon Lane, Bingley BD16 1WA, UK

First edition 2020

Reprints and permissions service
Contact: permissions@emeraldinsight.com

British Library Cataloguing in Publication Data
A catalogue record for this book is available from the British Library

ISBN: 978-1-78973-822-3 (Print)
ISBN: 978-1-78973-821-6 (Online)
ISBN: 978-1-78973-823-0 (Epub)
ISBN: 978-1-78973-824-7 (Pbk.)

INVESTOR IN PEOPLE

Contents

About the Contributors

Editors

Hoda Mahmoudi has held the Bahá'í Chair for World Peace at the University of Maryland, College Park since 2012. As Chair, she studies structural racism, gender equality, global governance, and globalization and the environment. As Director of this endowed academic program, Professor Mahmoudi collaborates with a wide range of scholars, researchers, and practitioners to advance interdisciplinary analysis and open discourse on global peace. Before joining the University of Maryland Faculty, Professor Mahmoudi served as Coordinator of the Research Department at the Bahá'í World Centre in Haifa, Israel. Prior to that, Dr Mahmoudi was Dean of the College of Arts and Sciences at Northeastern Illinois University, where she was also a Faculty Member in the Department of Sociology. Professor Mahmoudi is Co-editor of *Children and Globalization: Multidisciplinary Perspectives* (Routledge, 2019).

Michael L. Penn is a Clinical Psychologist and Professor of Psychology at Franklin & Marshall College. His research interests and publications explore the application of psychological research and theory to human rights, the interpenetration of psychology and philosophy, and the epidemiology of gender-based violence.

Contributing Authors

Sania Anwar, J.D., is the Chief Executive Officer of Global Scholars Project, Inc., a non-profit organization which develops educational opportunities for young girls in remote areas of Pakistan. She has given talks in Pakistan and in the US on topics related to law and human dignity. She is also an Attorney and prior to private practice served as a Judicial Appellate Clerk at the Colorado Court of Appeals. She resides in New York City.

The late **Suheil Bushrui** was a distinguished author, poet, and translator whose extensive publications in both English and Arabic brought him renown as an authority on W.B. Yeats and Kahlil Gibran. Over the long arc of his six-decade career, he taught at leading universities in Europe, Africa, the Middle East, and North America. In 2015, Suheil Bushrui retired as Professor Emeritus at the University of Maryland, where he had founded and directed two endowed peace chairs and taught an award-winning course on the Spiritual Heritage of the Human Race.

Justin de Leon, Ph.D., is a Researcher with Vanderbilt University's *Global Feminism Research Collaborative* and was previously a full-time Lecturer at UC San Diego teaching courses on race, gender, and critical media production. De Leon served as Director of the 2018 Pilot Program for the Native Film and Storytelling Institute, a residential program combining feminist and Indigenous approaches to storytelling and representation with professional filmmaking. His most recent film collaboration, *More Than a Word* (2018), is a documentary on native mascots in professional sports.

Jack Donnelly is the Andrew Mellon Professor in the Josef Korbel School of International Studies at the University of Denver. He has written extensively on the theory and practice of human rights, including *Universal Human Rights in Theory and Practice* (3rd ed., Cornell University Press, 2013).

Barbara Finkelstein is Professor Emerita, Distinguished-Scholar Teacher, and Founding Director of the International Center for Transcultural Education at the University of Maryland. She is a Cultural Historian who has received an array of prestigious awards and fellowships for work that examines the historical and transcultural dimensions of education policies, processes, and practices as they impinge on the lives of children, youth, and minority groups, shaping the quality of education available to them.

Michael J. Haslip, Ph.D., is Assistant Professor of Early Childhood Education at Drexel University. His research investigates how to develop the character strengths of teachers and children. Previously, he has explored how teachers can use positive guidance strategies to improve children's social-emotional learning and improve teacher–child relationships. At Drexel, he coordinates the expansion of the early childhood program. He is a former first- and second-grade teacher.

Michael Karlberg is a Professor of Communication Studies at Western Washington University. He examines prevailing conceptions of human nature, power, social organization, and social change – and their implications for the pursuit of peace and justice. His book *Beyond the Culture of Contest* (George Ronald, 2014) examines the consequences of organizing social institutions as contests of power. He is working on a second book reconciling perennial tensions between truth and relativism, as well as knowledge and power.

Tri Nguyen is a Doctoral Candidate in Psychology at Arizona State University. His current research explores the effect of modern technologies on human cognition and perception.

Introduction

Hoda Mahmoudi

Human Dignity: A Notion Defined, A Defining Notion

Human dignity defines us. It shapes a narrative of who we are, who we were, and who we may become. It grapples with ideas of autonomy, spirituality, rights, responsibilities, and the individual versus the collective. Defining human dignity provides a means of defining the basic nature of our humanity – a way of answering the "big" questions. The search for these answers has captivated every tribe, culture, and nation, and continues to do so today.

But though it is one of the most important topics of our age – and of ages past – it is also one of the most difficult subjects to discern, describe, or define. It can be elusive and squishy. But though it's meaning and messages are challenging to enumerate, its importance is beyond question. This is because the concept of human dignity lies at the fault line of our greatest moral and ethical challenges. The idea that there is something indivisible and irreducible about the human species, and the concomitant demands and responsibilities that this idea confers on individuals, communities, and states surrounds the debate of every critical societal challenge. Though we may not always view it as such, human dignity – the sense of what is right, decent, proper, moral, and ethical about how we relate to one another – frames all the great questions about our human experience.

Human Dignity: A History

In the Western world prior to 1900, human dignity was associated with the works of Kant, the writings of the French Revolution, and Catholic social thought[1] (particularly the papacy of Leo XIII 1878–1903; Beitz, 2013). To Kant, human dignity and freedom were intrinsic to all human beings – a status that placed human beings above all others. In this sense human dignity is inviolable – it cannot be taken away based on one's actions. In the writings of the French Revolution dignity was a responsibility enacted, a code lived-out, and an inner garden

---

[1]See Rerum Novarum, Encyclical of Pope Leo Xiii on Capital And Labor. http://w2.vatican.va/content/leo-xiii/en/encyclicals/documents/hf_l-xiii_enc_15051891_rerum-novarum.html.

Interdisciplinary Perspectives on Human Dignity and Human Rights, 1–14
Copyright © 2020 by Emerald Publishing Limited
All rights of reproduction in any form reserved
doi:10.1108/978-1-78973-821-620191001

cultivated. To Catholics, the intrinsic dignity of all human beings was a God-given attribute – its presence was always in line with God's gift and God's providence.

Before the twentieth century, the word dignity was not a part of the language of law or jurisprudence. Dignity was originally mentioned in the Constitutions of the Weimar Republic (1919), Portugal (1933), and Ireland (1937). After World War I, human dignity was still mostly absent from human rights documents. Dignity does not appear in the H. G. Wells' famous influential work, *The Rights of Man*, nor is it mentioned in Franklin Roosevelt's "Four Freedoms" speech. However, between 1943 and the post-World War II period, human dignity begins to appear in a variety of documents describing human rights. But, as the scholar Charles Beitz explains,

> it seems more realistic to regard the project of producing a conception of human dignity, understood as a ground or feature of human rights, as a matter of constructive interpretation rather than as an effort to give an account of an idea of human dignity implicit in the framing of postwar human rights.

In the 1945 Charter of the United Nations, human dignity was linked to human rights:

> We the peoples of the United Nations determined to reaffirm faith in fundamental human rights, in the dignity and worth of the human person, in the equal rights of men and women and of nations large and small ....[2]

Human dignity was invoked in the *Universal Declaration of Human Rights* by the United Nations General Assembly in 1948. Here, dignity was given the following dual attributes: inherent *dignity*, *dignity* and worth, *dignity* and equality, *dignity* and rights, *dignity* and freedom, and *dignity* and personality.[3]

Defining Dignity, Defining Rights: Vectors and Geographies of Dignity

Human dignity can be examined from a perspective of history, philosophy, politics, law, or religion. It can be researched by historians, sociologists, philosophers, anthropologists, and judges. It can be considered by individuals working in conflict zones. It can be pondered by ordinary citizens facing their own lives and challenges. It can be studied by psychologists, psychotherapists, and social workers. It can be invoked by pastors, imams, and rabbis.

Human dignity's form, once defined, can give rise to its function. One's conception of human dignity will shape whether one believes it to be a universal

---

[2]http://www.un.org/en/sections/un-charter/un-charter-full-text/.
[3]Italics are added. http://www.un.org/en/universal-declaration-human-rights/.

need, a fundamental human characteristic, a state of mind, an emotional condition, or a political right. These forms lead to functions that emphasize dignity as a philosophy of thinking, a prescription for action, a form of human capital, a political principle, a strategy of economic redistribution, or a fundamental driver of human capability.

Within the academy, some scholars have suggested that the concept of human dignity is indefinable. Others argue that human dignity is an abstract concept with multiple possible meanings. Some scholars locate human dignity as a prerequisite human right. Still, other scholars claim that human dignity is conferred on people by law and is, therefore, a legal status.

Yet nowhere are discussions about human dignity more animated than when exploring its meaning in relation to human rights. Take, for example, Remey Debes' (2009) argument about human rights and human dignity.

> [T]he difference between rights-denial and dignity-denial is a chasm. We bandy about the claim that slavery was an insult to human dignity, but we must realize that if it was, it was not the "mere" denial of rights to some group of people. That is not the relevant sense of "inhumanity" at stake, as if there was simply a problem of discrete (albeit vast in number) moral misjudgments about the value of persons. Slavery was an insult to dignity because it arguably *obliterated* persons: it erased them from the *space* of value. This is not only wrong, but vile. Similarly, in the case of Jewish genocide … what began as a demonizing depression of Jewish agency and corresponding suppression of rights ended in a more radical depersonalization. It became something different, something not explicable in conventional moral terms, but needing new conceptual powers that "dignity" and its "annihilation" perhaps provide.

To enlarge on the problematic nature of linking human dignity to human rights, Debes draws upon Alexander Hamilton's criticism of the United States Bill of Rights. "One could argue," Debes (2009, p. 55) points out, "that more power is actually reserved for persons by *not* specifying what powers they have – or in the case of dignity, what accounts for those powers."

> For, as Hamilton noted, once you specify, you create 'handles' for the forces of zeal. In particular, precedent is created in thinking that the specification is all there is – all the rights that *are*, or all that dignity *is*. Thus, Hamilton argued, if nothing is surrendered then everything is retained and there is 'no need of particular reservations. (Hamilton, 1788)

The moral philosopher Doris Schroeder (2012) has noted how apart from the 1966 International Covenant on Civil and Political Rights (recognition that these rights derive from the inherent dignity of the human person), there is no other legal document that makes a distinction made between human dignity and human rights. But, as Hamilton argued, a lack of specification does not necessarily indicate a lack of importance.

Other scholars are dubious about the connection between human rights and human dignity[4]; for many scholars and practitioners, the linking of dignity to human rights remains problematic at best. Bagaric and Allan are two of several scholars who raise major objections to using human dignity as a foundation for human rights. They argue that since human dignity is not clearly defined, "it is not at all clear how one can attempt to prove (or disprove) the worth of such a concept" (Bagaric & Allan, 2006). Accordingly, they argue, it difficult to uphold dignity as a foundation of human rights. This "empty nature of the concept of dignity" (Bagaric & Allan, 2006, p. 266), they argue, can be shown through the problem of euthanasia.

Opponents of euthanasia argue that deliberately killing a person violates their dignity. Proponents of euthanasia argue that not allowing a patient to die violates their dignity. Beyleveld and Brownsword (2001) maintain that:

> the right to choose is a basic expression of one's dignity and there is no more fundamental expression of one's dignity than the right to make life-saving or life-terminating choice. Dignity ... is embedded in the right to choose itself, irrespective of the particular choice that one makes.

In this example, dignity is used "both as a vehicle to justify something as being important and as a means to extinguish it and thereby detract from its importance in the most direct fashion possible" (Bagaric & Allan, 2006, p. 267) The authors thus conclude that dignity "should be discarded as a potential foundation for rights claims unless, and until, its source, nature, relevance and meaning are determined" (Bagaric & Allan, 2006, p. 269). Others have concluded that the term dignity generates confusion since its meaning can be interpreted from a variety of perspectives; religious, philosophical, political, legal, or pragmatic (Schroeder, 2012). Michael Ignatieff (2001) finds the concept of dignity difficult to accept because of its multiple cultural expressions.

> Rituals of sexual initiation, like genital cutting, for example, are linked to an idea of womanly dignity and worth. Likewise, ultra-Orthodox Judaism imposes a role on women that secular women find oppressive, but that religious women find both fulfilling and respectful of their dignity. So ideas of dignity that are supposed to unite different cultures in some shared attachment to human rights actually divide us.

---

[4]See, Beitz (2013), Kretzmer and Eckart (2002), Bagaric and Allan (2006), Dworkin (2011), Waldron (2012, 2013), Kateb (2012), McCrudden (2008), Margalit (1996), Rosen (2012), Donnelly (1982), and Schroeder (2012).

For Ignatieff (2001, p. 165), the relationship between dignity and human rights stems from the classical European model of

> republican citizenship, from the political conception of human beings as entitled to participate in the making of the laws that rule them, to deliberate freely over their meaning, and to be protected from the arbitrary exercise of power.

From this Western outlook, human rights declarations and agreements govern the relationship between citizens and the states within a democratic system. Ignatieff points out that those individuals who represent non-Western traditions may not identify with the Western conception of dignity. For example, identity with one's religion or tribe presents a challenge to individualistic notions of dignity.

Christopher McCrudden (2008) also believes that the concept of human dignity lacks a clear definition. Yet, he contends that this is not accidental. In his estimation, because the drafters of human rights covenants could not agree on what language to use, they purposely selected philosophical language like dignity to elide more difficult choices.

The theistic philosopher Andrew Gleeson (2014) argues that human dignity is "something very different from what we get if we focus on sentience, rational autonomy, flourishing and so on". According to Gleeson, reverence for human life is not simply about autonomy, sentience, or flourishing, but should include the unborn, babies, the disabled, and those adults who have suffered terribly or experienced appalling humiliation.

> And when we do focus on adult humans in a way that brings out the moral demands they make upon us, it is *not* their rationality, flourishing, sentience or even their moral qualities that bears the weight of those demands, but simply their *mortal vulnerability*, the very opposite of rational, autonomous flourishing. (Gleeson, 2014)

To expound on his perspective regarding human dignity, Gleeson turns to an example made by the philosopher Cora Diamond. Diamond in turn describes a scene from Dickens' *Our Mutual Friend*. Rogue Riderhood, our anti-hero, is collectively loathed. Pulled from the river Thames and presumed drowned, the townspeople gather around him in interest. Yet, Dickens describes a sense of empathy, amazement, and concern. Gleeson (2014, pp. 372–373) notes:

> it seems little more plausible that his life and his death are the momentous things they are for them because of his capacities for rational autonomy or for flourishing or even the moral qualities. The discourse of these theories sit ill with the sense of solemn awe in face of the mysteries of life and death, the sense of being bound to Riderhood – this terrible man who normally so disgusts them – by a common condition, predicament or fate, that Dickens puts

front and center: 'If you are not gone for good, Mr. Riderhood, it would be something to know where you are hiding at present .... If you are gone for good, Rogue, it is very solemn, and if you are coming back, it is hardly less so. Nay in the supreme and mystery of the latter question, involving that of where you may be now, there is a solemnity even added to that of death.

Gleeson (2014, p. 373) concludes that:

"[...] the awe that Dickens describes here is something very different from that excitement we can feel towards high intelligence and healthy flourishing, and other kinds of worldly success, an awe liable to resentment and envy and superiority, among other things. It is a sense of awe before something sublime, something uncanny, something humbling, and it is one very important instance of inter-human bonds of sympathy and fellow-feeling *that are among what I have called the moral qualities.* Before death, we are all equal. To shut someone out from companionship in the face of that enemy is the ultimate (moral) sanction."

Herbert Spiegelberg (1971) elucidates the distinction to be made between "the ultimate dignity in man and the claims issuing from it, which can be violated in the sense of not being fulfilled, though they can never be annihilated." Human dignity is not something that is achievable, rather it is inherent. Spiegelberg (1971) explains that "'Losing one's dignity' in the sense of becoming deprived of it ... [is] something which the thesis of universal human dignity considers impossible." Even when individuals lose their dignity through their own undignified actions, this does imply the loss of their dignity as a human being. Human dignity is an unchanging condition that applies equally to all human beings. Spiegelberg (1971) calls attention to the distinction that must be made between "the ultimate dignity in man and the claims issuing from it, which can be violated in the sense of not being fulfilled, though they can never be annihilated."

The philosopher Doris Schroeder (2012) identifies no less than five different meanings for human dignity.

A. Inviolable dignity
   (1) Traditional Catholic dignity – Dignity is an inviolable property invested by God in all human beings, which makes each life sacred.
   (2) Kantian dignity – Dignity is an inviolable property invested in all rational beings due to their capacity for moral self-legislation. As dignity holders, rational beings have the right to exact always respect for their sense of purpose and self-worth.

B. Aspirational dignity
   (3) Aristocratic dignity – Dignity is the quality of a human being who has been invested with superior rank and position and acts accordingly.

(4) Comportment dignity – Dignity is the outwardly displayed quality of a human being who acts in accordance with society's expectations of well-mannered demeanor and bearing.

(5) Meritorious dignity – Dignity is a virtue, which subsumes the four cardinal virtues and one's sense of self-worth (p. 332).

Schroeder (2012) explains, "If we want to use dignity as the foundation of human rights *and* accord *all* human beings human rights, then only the Traditional Catholic[5] understanding of dignity is appropriate" (p. 332). Kantian dignity, Schroeder (2012) explains "excludes those who will never (re)gain rational faculties." She objects to the use of dignity as the grounds for universal human rights and concludes, "proponents of universal human rights are better off looking for alternative frameworks to justify human rights rather than relying on the concept of dignity. However, there is one proviso." This, according to Schroeder, would require the reversal of the relationship between rights and dignity such that dignity "informs the content of human rights. Those who formulate, pronounce and try to protect human rights would turn to empirical instances of dehumanization as experienced, for example, in Nazi Germany, or during the Cultural Revolution, or in Abu Ghraib, to refine their efforts" (Schroeder, 2012, pp. 333–334).

From this perspective, the real value in linking human dignity to human rights lies in our capacity to describe instances where human beings are subjected to humiliation and degradation; using empirical evidence to describe dehumanizing experiences suffered by individuals or groups allows advocates of human rights to develop measures to protect said individuals (Schroeder, 2012, see also Rao, 2008, 2011). Dignity may be conceived as an antidote to the destructive power of humiliation, dehumanization, and stereotyping. Yet, it may not be an antidote that works in all cases. There may occur moments so horrendous, so unimaginable, so unspeakable, that they challenge not only our concept of human dignity, but also our concept of humanity itself.

Outside the Lines: Human Dignity and Human Evil

Examining the notion of human dignity when faced with unspeakable evil can be instructive. The horror of the Holocaust and its system of mechanized torture and murder challenges us and forces us to come face to face with the nature of human experience. One of the most uncomfortable questions the Holocaust raises – and there are many – is the following. Does it make sense to speak of positive human values any longer? Or to paraphrase Theodore Adorno – is discussing poetry after Auschwitz wrong? Are some evils so grand that its perpetrators permanently forgo any claim of humanity? Are there any moral victories in the face of incomprehensible destruction?

---

[5]Schroeder notes that "other religions are likely to have equally tenable justifications at their disposal, as long as the justification is used only amongst believers." Footnote, p. 332.

The Italian writer and Holocaust survivor Primo Levi describes the "at once stupid and symbolic violence" executed against those forced into concentration camps. He describes the

> iniquitous use that was made (not sporadically but with method) of the human body as an object, an anonymous thing belonging to no one, to be disposed in an arbitrary manner. (Levi, 1986)

He reminds us of the "chosen individuals" – well-fed prisoners destined for the torture table – who needed to be healthy for the vile Nazi experiments.

> This cruelty, typical and devoid of apparent purpose but highly symbolic, was extended, precisely because symbolic, to human remains after death: those remains which every civilization, begin-ning with remotest prehistory, has respected, honored, and some-times feared. (Levi, 1986, p. 124)

He reckoned that "these were not human remains but indifferent brute matter, in the best of cases good for some industrial use" (Levi, 1986, p. 124).

> The human ashes coming from the crematoria, tons daily, were easily recognized as such, because they often contained teeth and vertebrae. Nevertheless, they were employed for several purposes: as fill for swamp lands, as thermal insulation between the walls of wooden buildings, and as phosphate fertilizer; and especially notable, they were used instead of gravel to cover the paths of the SS village located near the camp, whether out of pure callousness or because, due to their origins, they were regarded as material to be trampled on, I couldn't say. (Levi, 1986, p. 125)

What is one to make of such conditions? Does it make sense to discuss "dig-nity" when human beings burn other human beings? What is human dignity to the butchers butchered alike? These extreme conditions challenge the very nature of our definitions. But if it is difficult to imagine dignity in such con-ditions, it is also difficult to imagine *rights* in these circumstances as well. In imagining the Holocaust, what haunts us in not so much the loss of *rights*, but the total absence of the ability to preserve one's *dignity*. The hellish nature of its poison is rooted not in the loss of constitutional order, but in the loss of moral order – in the scabrous nature of evil on display when all concern for human dignity is devoured.

But the Holocaust is not our only example of a grotesque system so horrid that it challenges our fundamental understandings of human nature. America's history of slavery is rife with not only unpalatable incidents, but occurrences that drive a stake into what we understand about human dignity and humanity itself.

In 1856, more than a decade before Emancipation, Margaret Garner, an escap-ing slave, murdered her two-year-old daughter with a butcher knife. Her pursuers at the door, she committed an unimaginable act so that her daughter would not be re-enslaved. *The Cincinnati Gazette* read "Arrest of Fugitive Slaves: A Slave Mother Murders her Child rather than see it Returned to Slavery."[6]

Was Margaret Garner preserving her children's dignity? Did she sacrifice her own? Is murder ever permissible to preserve the dignity of others? If so, who determines the intrinsic moral value of such an act? Can there be dignified murder? Our usual definitions escape us. And yet, it is precisely these extreme situations that open a back door for us to examine these critical issues. As is the case in our conception of the Holocaust, it is clear that Margaret Garner was not so much worried about her *rights*. But for her own *dignity*, or for the *dignity* of her child, she was willing to murder. Such actions should give us pause, and force us to reexamine human motivation and the need for human dignity.

Toward A Universal Dignity: Human Dignity as Foreshadowing Human Rights

When examined more closely, human dignity foreshadows human rights. It provides rights with a moral bearing – a covenant to its contract. It locates legal rights in something much higher, an idea of an endowment, of a likeness to something much greater. Human Dignity is a spiritual herald to the more corporal reality of Human Rights.

Though it is a difficult concept, human dignity's ability to rationally describe human concerns, human agency and human need remains unparalleled. Human dignity suggests that there is a spirit to human life that cannot be explained or fully understood through jurisprudence or human rights. This unique aspect of dignity concerns the lives of human beings beyond their individual rights and freedoms. It touches on the sacred nature of human beings, and suggests that human dignity can be better achieved through spreading knowledge of human abilities, motivations, and understanding.

Scholars rightly criticize certain aspects of human dignity, yet many scholars mistake healthy argument for unhealthy confusion. For though there was once a vigorous debate concerning the nature of slavery, debates about slavery are not invalid because there are differing courses of opinion. Healthy arguments about human dignity's role in complex subjects like euthanasia are not examples of human dignity's conceptual weakness.

The Kantian, secular view of human dignity – "human capacity for moral self-legislation" – fails to justify the universal notion of human rights (Levi, 1986, p. 333). The writings of the French revolution rightly locate human dignity as a rallying point but fail to place bounds around its use and practice. The Catholic perspective of human dignity as the foundation of human rights leaves out a secular understanding of dignity.

---

[6]An interpretation of Margaret Garner's story is the basis of for Toni Morrison's Pulitzer Prize-winning novel *Beloved*.

Human dignity is not something that can be destroyed by assault or acts of violence against a person. This side of dignity echoes Martin Luther King's conception of dignity. "One's dignity may be assaulted, vandalized, cruelly mocked, but it can never be taken away unless it is surrendered."

The Structure of the Book

To explore the meaning of human dignity in a rapidly changing and turbulent twenty-first century world, it must be addressed through an interdisciplinary lens. The collection of timely chapters in this book provides this perspective. The authors offer insights, questions, and recommendations that outline a pursuable human dignity agenda. They identify challenges and opportunities in education, international law, social discourse, religion, and media, seeking ways to define, broaden, and protect human dignity. The contributors also address the need for reconstituting the current discourses on dignity to align them more effectively with the intellectual, moral, emotional, and spiritual nature of human beings. This book moves generally from a broad outline of human dignity to specific iterations and examples of human dignity in diverse communities in the world. Part 1 is concerned with *Defining Human Dignity*, while Part 2 is concerned with *Delineating Human Dignity.*

Chapters

In the chapter "Universal Consciousness of Human Dignity," Hoda Mahmoudi outlines the range of definitions of dignity offered by scholars of various disciplines and addresses the characteristics of human nature, as well as the struggles and opportunities for the "highly-interdependent global society" toward which humanity has evolved. Regarding human nature, Mahmoudi asserts the critical importance of a moral and spiritual framework for defining what it means to be human and what might be required if we are to honor all with dignity. Her chapter acknowledges the extreme state of worldwide inequality on a multitude of levels and contends that the old model of top-down intervention has failed humanity. She argues for the creation of an inclusive global community that seeks to eliminate and move beyond the faulty conceptual framework of "us versus them." Mahmoudi claims that the promotion of spiritual and ethical values will contribute to the safeguarding of human honor and dignity for all people.

Suheil Bushrui offers an exploration of related themes in his contribution, "Toward a Principle of Human Dignity." He asserts that, above all, the educational institutions provide the most crucial venues for creating and disseminating a principle of human dignity and cautions against the current trend among many institutions of higher learning to approach their work more like corporations that prioritize profitability above other values. For Bushrui, religion also offers a means to strengthen and promote human dignity through the values it inculcates, the ways it shapes people's understanding of their identity and purpose, and the learning communities it builds. Bushrui reflects on the possibility of religious cooperation in response to human dignity and maintains that such a collaborative achievement would address some of the struggles that remain as barriers to peace. He proposes the creation of an interfaith parliament that would engage all religious communities in a moral dialog to establish common understandings of dignity and promote increased cooperation among diverse faith communities.

This volume continues with Michael Karlberg's chapter, "Reframing Human Dignity." Karlberg outlines the shift in social frames regarding human nature from the perspective that it is inevitably self-interested and competitive, to the frame that humanity, as a species, may be likened to a human body where the "well-being of each depends upon the well-being of the body as a whole." He also explains that the maturation of human dignity requires the reframing of human consciousness at the level of social discourse. All social institutions – families, schools, media corporations, and the state – have a responsibility to cultivate and protect the development of human potential and direct it toward the betterment of society. He highlights how education is both a process of learning how to respect others and treat them with dignity and a tool to cultivate the capacity to respond to violations of dignity with "constructive resilience." Only then can we break the vicious cycle of indignities being met with further indignities and violence.

Michael L. Penn, with assistance from Tri Nguyen in "Promoting Human Rights and Human Dignity in an Axial Age," asserts that current approaches to the protection of human dignity are limited by the human rights and development discourse that

> is focused almost exclusively on humanity's material concerns while neglecting consideration of those capacities of consciousness that animate the human spirit, that provide the basis for human dignity, and upon which the future of civilization, in all of its forms, ultimately depends.

This chapter explores the relationship between human rights law and dignity by identifying how human dignity has served as a basis for human rights claims. Some examples they discover include condemning all forms of discrimination as a basis for the equal treatment of all people, providing equal access to basic needs like healthcare and education, ensuring the protection of cultural identity, and upholding standards for how the media represents different groups.

Jack Donnelly also explores the linkages between human dignity and human rights in his chapter "How Does Dignity Ground Human Rights?" He asserts that "human dignity is the foundational concept of the global human rights regime." He claims that "human rights go beyond the *inherent* dignity of the human person to provide mechanisms for realizing a *life of dignity.*" His chapter explains that human dignity is a concept that links human rights to what philosopher John Rawls calls "comprehensive doctrines" – an overlapping consensus approach where there may be different foundations for why people believe human dignity is valuable. He argues that this approach stresses dialog among societies, cultures, religions, and regions, and it enables the possibility of local interpretation and implementation of universal human rights.

Sania Anwar's chapter, "Honor-based Violence in Pakistan and Its Eradication through the Development of Cultural and Jurisprudential Ethos of
Human Dignity," provides an extensive overview of rural Pakistani cultural
beliefs, norms, and habits regarding honor, sexuality, shame, guilt, and gender, and how they interact to produce and often legitimize honor killings. She
also offers powerful and creative solutions to eliminate this destructive practice.
Focusing on Islamic religious communities and building on Karlberg's discussion of customized frames and Penn and Donnelly's discourse on human rights,
Anwar contends that one of the main ways to eliminate honor killings is to
use more persuasive and socially acceptable arguments that employ Pakistan's
own ideals and values to improve women's rights. In this case, this means using
Islam to establish the unconditional right to human dignity. Like Karlberg who
asserts that vehicles for developing human dignity require customized frames
for different cultures, Anwar explains that framing human rights demands in
religious language and concepts is necessary to build support from the majority of women in Pakistan, for whom Islamic values are foundational to their
society.

Justin de Leon's chapter on documentary filmmaking, "(In)dignity via (Mis)
representation: Politics, Power, and Documentary Film," explores how the choices
of documentary filmmakers to utilize certain frames through which individuals
and groups are represented can either dignify or dehumanize. He argues that
the conceptual and ideological considerations of filmmaking require conscious
reflection or "reflexivity," so that concerns about how individuals and cultures
are perceived, who is considered capable of expert knowledge, and how a story
is appropriated can be carefully addressed in a manner that dignifies those being
represented. His hope is that documentary film and media can help fashion new
ways of connection across differences.

Barbara Finkelstein's chapter, "Dignifying Education: The Emergence of
Teachers as Transcultural Messengers," envisions educators as "dignity workers"
who "view the world as a seedbed of opportunity for construction of more inclusive global communities, permeable boundaries of nation state, and more expansive and culturally empowering transcultural educational worlds." She focuses on
the role of educators in offering dignifying experiences to children and youth of
various minorities, making space for and valuing their voices, languages, and cultural experiences, and providing an "equal distribution of dignity across boundaries of race, class, gender, ethnicity, generation, and spiritual belief." Finkelstein
highlights the histories and achievements of four specific transcultural educators
who themselves experienced dignity violations based on prejudice in their school
environments. She then goes on to establish learning atmospheres that honor and
value the contributions of diverse cultures.

Michael J. Haslip and Michael L. Penn's "Cultivating Human Rights by Nurturing Altruism and a Life of Service: Integrating UN Sustainable Development
Goals into School Curricula" examines how a concept like *moral identity formation* can assist in the development of a worldwide consciousness of human
dignity, specifically around the issues of sustainability. Both scholars utilize their

backgrounds in child development and psychology to suggest possibilities of societal growth, maturation, and moral achievement. The authors argue that the vaunted precepts of the United Nations Sustainable Development Goals should be integrated in academic curricula throughout the world and convincingly suggest that in order to address such a looming and complex challenge as the world's ecological and environmental success, nothing less than a broad sea change will be effective. They rightly argue that education is the proper methodology for such an undertaking.

I hope that the diverse contributions in this volume will inspire continued and rigorous effort in diverse fields of study and practice. The protection of human dignity is a means of ensuring that each member of the human race is able to realize their human potential and be protagonists in their own development. The understanding of human dignity is a means of ensuring that each community in the world is able to realize its potential to promote better relations among its members. The consciousness of human dignity provides a path for all of us to first view the true nature of our being, and afterward view the true nature of our fellow man.

References

Bagaric, M., & Allan, J. (2006). The vacuous concept of dignity. *Journal of Human Rights, 5,* 257–270.

Beitz, C. R. (2013). Human dignity in the theory of human rights: Nothing but a phrase? *Philosophy and Public Affairs, 41*(3), 262, 259–290.

Beyleveld, D., & R. Brownsword, R. (2001). *Human dignity in bioethics and biolaw* (p. 242). New York, NY: Oxford University Press.

Debes, R. (2009). Dignity's gauntlet. *Ethics, 23,* 55, 45–78.

Dworkin, R. (2011). *Justice for the hedgehogs.* Cambridge, MA: Harvard University Press.

Gleeson, A. (2014). The limits of dignity. *Philosophical Investigations, 37*(4 October), 371.

Hamilton, A. (1788). *The Federalist*, No. *84,* May 28. Retrieved from https://founders. archives.gov/documents/Hamilton/01-04-02-0247. Accessed on July 18, 2019 .

Ignatieff, M. (2001). *Human rights as politics and idolatry* (p. 164). Princeton, NJ: Princeton University Press.

Kateb, G. (2012). *Human dignity.* Cambridge, MA: Harvard University Press.

Kretzmer, D., & Eckart, K. (2002). *The concept of human dignity in human rights discourse.* Hague, The Netherlands: Kluwer.

Levi, P. (1986). *The drowned and the saved* (p. 123). New York, NY: Summit Books.

Margalit, A. (1996). *The decent society.* Cambridge, MA: Harvard University Press.

McCrudden, C. (2008). Human dignity and judicial interpretation of human rights. *European Journal of International Law, 19,* 655–724.

Rao, N. (2008). On the use and abuse of dignity in constitutional law. *Columbia Journal of European Law, 14,* 201.

Rao, N. (2011). Three concepts of dignity in constitutional law. *Notre Dame Law Review, 86,* 183.

Rosen, M. (2012). *Dignity: Its history and meaning.* Cambridge, MA: Harvard University Press.

Schroeder, D. (2012). Human rights and human dignity: An appeal to separate the con-
joined twins. *Ethical Theory and Moral Practice, 15*(3, June), 323–335.

Spiegelberg, H. (1971). Human dignity: A challenge to contemporary philosophy. *World Future, 9*(1–2), 54.

Waldron, J. (2012). Dignity, rank, and rights. In *Tanner lectures at the University of California, Berkeley, 2009*. New York, NY: Oxford University Press.

Waldron, J. (2013). *Is dignity the foundation of human rights*. New York University Public Law and Legal Theory Working Papers. Paper 374. Retrieved from http://lsr.nellco.org/nyu_plltwp/374

Section One

Theory/Discourse

Chapter 1

Universal Consciousness of Human Dignity

Hoda Mahmoudi

Introduction

Human dignity is receiving much attention in scholarship and the media. As a widely discussed concept, it concerns how social relationships and structures treat or mistreat, honor or humiliate the individual. Explored through the lens of a wide range of disciplines, the meaning of dignity has been conveyed as respect, choice, agency, rights, freedom, personal dignity, honor, self-respect, and as a status not belonging solely to the elite. The attention paid and aspiration to better understand human dignity are indicators of the importance of this concept in a rapidly changing and fragile contemporary society.

As ongoing processes of globalization evolve, succession of social problems are making their impact at the international level rather than being confined to local or regional sectors. Among the social ills reflecting this trend are the globalization of the capitalist economic system, the ever-widening economic gap, and large international migrations stemming from violent conflicts, unemployment, and poverty. The rapidly changing world is unable to socially regulate itself. Yet, at the same time, it has become apparent that humanity as a whole now represents a highly interdependent global society in which a greater awareness has emerged about the significance of human dignity.

The aim of this chapter is to explore human dignity as a fundamental prerequisite for the advancement of the emerging global community. From the standpoint of the Bahá'í Chair for World Peace, human dignity is an essential component of the achievement of the equality of all peoples and the development of processes that will lead to a more peaceful world.

Presented in three sections, the chapter will first consider human dignity's place in a post-Westphalian world, where exclusive sovereign statehood has shifted toward a disaggregated state as a consequence of the dynamic force of globalization (McGrew, 2011). In this context, the connection between human

Interdisciplinary Perspectives on Human Dignity and Human Rights, 17–26
Copyright © 2020 by Emerald Publishing Limited
All rights of reproduction in any form reserved
doi:10.1108/978-1-78973-821-620191002

dignity and a humanity that is now viewed as a single, global society residing in a highly interconnected world is examined. The second section provides a review of the current thinking among a selected group of scholars regarding the meaning of human dignity. The final section will address several lines of research that are intended to explore the possibility of advancing a universal consciousness about human dignity as a spiritual basis for the making of a better global society.

One People

Although residing on a single planet for millions of years, human beings only gradually and over the centuries discovered the entireness of the world. Throughout the twentieth century and particularly toward its latter half, the world began to experience an intensifying acceleration in both "concrete global interdependence and consciousness of the global whole" (Robertson, 1992). These momentous changes shaping the present social order are described by sociologist Roland Robertson (1992, p. 8) as, "the compression of the world and the intensification of the consciousness of the world as a whole, as a single place."

Sociologist Gören Therborn (2011) observes,

> while we go on being, say, Chinese or American, Muslims or Hindus, workers or bankers, African women or European men, young or old, we have also become members of a common humankind and stakeholders in the same planet.

Sociologist George Ritzer (2010) defines globalization as

> a transplanetary *process* or set of *processes* involving growing multidirectional *flows* of increasingly *liquid* people, objects, places, and information and the *structures* they encounter and create that are *barriers* to, or *expedite*, those flows.

Globalization has brought about, according to sociologist Frank Lechner (2004), the growth of "a shared global consciousness."

In his comprehensive analysis of the transformations occurring in the world today, *The World: A Beginner's Guide*, Therborn uses terms such as "a common humankind," or a planetary human society, in portraying these unprecedented changes. More and more, the arena of social interaction encompasses the entire world. We now live, according to Therborn (2011, p. ix) on "a finite planet of enormous variety, interdependent and intercommunicating." For him, globalization is "the new interdependence of humankind, through capital flows, commodity chains, foreign penetration of domestic markets, migration flows picking up and cultural exchange intensifying and cross-fertilizing" (Therborn, 2011, p. 2).

Accepting Therborn's analysis of a "new interdependence of humankind," it can be said that a globalizing world has brought about a greater integration in certain segments of the world community. For example, many diverse groups from throughout the world are working together. Some of these groups, representing multiple nations and peoples, cooperate successfully in scientific, social, cultural, and economic matters. At the same time, it is important to acknowledge that social fragmentation, division, and breakdown is widespread within the global social order and accelerating at an alarming rate. This process includes, among others, cultural conflicts with religious, racial, ethnic, tribal, and national roots. Likewise, the crisis of a failed and inequitable global economic system, as well as the tensions and conflicts stemming from the many crises in the political realm, contribute to the forces of disintegration. This brings about violent exchanges between people and governments, leads to the destruction of the environment, and becomes the source of untold social and economic havoc. As the people become more interdependent, a vast majority find themselves victims of increasing disparity, social injustice, and untold misery.

The challenges before us, especially those involving the forces of destruction and conflict, stem, in large part, from continued reliance on age-old norms and outdated strategies which, over time, have become barriers to the resolution of social harms. For example, there is ample evidence showing that simply generating more laws to protect human rights, as crucial as this may be, is not sufficient to achieve the goal. An important question that requires serious study is whether increasing the consciousness of human dignity among the peoples of the world would, over time, facilitate a greater spirit of cooperation and reciprocity of action in an effort to make a better society. Ultimately what is needed in order to advance a greater consciousness of the worth of every person is a moral framework and internalized values which safeguard the dignity that is the essential right of all.

Human Dignity

What follows is a brief and non-exhaustive overview of different conceptions and accounts of human dignity.

A comprehensive work titled *Understanding Human Dignity*, edited by Christopher McCrudden, offers multidisciplinary and intra-disciplinary examination of human dignity. The volume starts with dignity's history, discussing the various meanings in different historical periods. This includes the idea of natural rights in the Middle Ages, the late eighteenth-century French and American Revolutions, and the *Universal Declaration of Human Rights* in the 1940s. McCrudden points out that "[m]ost recently, several scholars have emphasized the 1970s 'as marking a decisive shift in the embedding of human rights theory and practice.'" McCrudden (2013) states that "Samuel Moyn sees developments in the 1970s as marking a significant break from the past." Other sections of the work include dignity critiques; theological, philosophical, and judicial perspectives; applications of dignity; and a final section on the future discourse on dignity.

Donna Hicks (2001), an associate at the Weatherhead Center for International Affairs at Harvard University, states: "Dignity is a birthright." All deserve to be treated with dignity "no matter what they do" (Hicks, p. 4–5). Hicks makes the following distinction between a person who deserves respect and a person's actions that may not be worthy of respect. She says:

> Human beings often behave in ways that are harmful to others, making it difficult to respect them for what they have done. I make the distinction between a *person*, who deserves respect, and a person's *actions*, which may or may not deserve respect. (Hicks)

Political theorist George Kateb (2011) speaks of dignity as extending beyond the individual to the human species. When compared to other species, what is uniquely human, according to Kateb (2011, p. x), is that the "human species achieves a partial break with nature which is the reason" why the human species is the "highest of all." As the highest species on the planet, Kateb (2011, p. 5) notes, humans carry a greater responsibility and should direct their energies "to the stewardship of nature."

Legal philosopher Jeremy Waldron (2013) has examined the relationship between dignity and human rights. He views dignity as both the ground and content of rights, suggesting that in terms of their status, all human beings are equal, should be treated as noble, and as having rights against degrading treatment (Waldron, 2012).

Michael Rosen (2012), a professor of government and a philosopher, who has examined the numerous meanings and definitions of dignity over time, suggests that a sense of dignity is the right of everyone to be treated *with dignity*, or proper respect. He states that "[i]n protecting the individual from degradation, insult, and contempt we are requiring that people act towards [the individual] in ways that are substantively respectful." Rosen elaborates, "[t]o respect their dignity in this sense means to treat them *with respect*" Waldron (2012, p. 95).

According to Rosen, "dignitary harms are harms of a special kind." He suggests that "expressive or symbolic harms," such as degradation, insult, and contempt, all have one thing in common – their failure to acknowledge "the elevated status of human beings" (Rosen, 2012). From this analysis, Rosen then proceeds with the following insightful observation in relation to the "humiliation and symbolic degradation of the victims" of the "Nazi concentration camps, the Soviet gulag, the killing Fields in Cambodia, or the Balkans ethnic cleansing." He observes:

> It seems to be a fact about human nature that human beings are able more easily to engage in the most violent behavior towards one another if at the same time they can expressively deny the humanity of their victims. If this is so then the preservation of our fellow human beings from dignitary harm is also fundamental to the defense of their humanity. (Rosen, 2012, p. 97)

Philosopher K. Anthony Appiah (2001) offers a more broad view about human dignity, stating:

We do not need to argue that we are all created in the image of God, or that we have natural rights that flow from our human essence, to agree that we do not want to be tortured by government officials, that we do not want our lives, families, and property forfeited. And ordinary people almost everywhere have something like the notion of dignity – it has different names and somewhat different places – and desire something like respect from their fellows and believe they merit it unless they do evil.

Finally, the philosopher Avishai Margalit (2002) states that "we recognize dignity by the way we react to humiliation." Humiliation, according to Margalit, is the treatment of humans as nonhumans (i.e., the infliction of insult, injury, pain, humiliation, or torture) (Lindner, 2007). "Dignity, unlike social honor," writes Margalit (2002, p. 114),

> is not a positional good. It is supposed to be accorded to everybody, even to the one who is nobody, by virtue of the most universal common denominator of being human.

He states that "[a]nybody should be recognized as a bearer of human dignity."

To summarize these accounts of human dignity, it is apparent that the concept of human dignity is all-inclusive. It aspires to recognize everybody, encompasses all peoples, humankind as a whole, and acknowledges and welcomes the diversity of the peoples of the world.

The final section explores social and structural arrangements that serve as major barriers to treating all human beings with dignity. A few examples are provided in relation to processes and lines of action that may facilitate advancement of a universal acceptance of the intrinsic human dignity for all people.

Collective Consciousness of Human Dignity

The great rupture of the twentieth century, the Holocaust, was a breaking point – an end to civilization. It exposed the complete evil that humanity is capable of committing and the gruesome consequences of racism unleashed as anti-Semitism, with all of the typecasting and stereotyping that form the architecture of the blight of prejudice. The Holocaust was a force of tyranny that inflicted indescribable human cruelty and an unthinkably efficient program for the systematic demolition of human life. Some six million Jews perished in the course of about four years. Over the same period, estimates suggest that 60 million people were killed in the Second World War, or approximately 2.5 percent of the world's population at the time.

As a result of the immense devastation of the Second World War, a shift in human consciousness had become apparent. The magnitude of the destruction from the combination of both World Wars had ended the great European empires and their antiquated systems of colonial rule and other forms of political oppression. Therefore, it is not entirely surprising that in 1945, the nations of the world displayed a willingness to create a new system of international order with provision for a peacekeeping authority.

The creation of the United Nations and its Charter in 1945 and the adoption of the *Universal Declaration of Human Rights* three years later established for the first time in history, the right of every person to challenge unjust state law or oppressive practices irrespective of race, gender, age, religion, or nationality. Prior to the Declaration, only nation states had rights under international law. However, in the preamble of the Declaration, human dignity is expressed as an inherent, an inborn human condition. It reads:

> Whereas recognition of the inherent dignity and of the equal and inalienable rights of all members of the human family is the foundation of freedom, justice and peace in the world …."

The United Nations also established a medium by which all people could voice their concerns and begin to gradually envision their role, and that of humanity as a whole, in deciding their own future.

As a result of the formation of the United Nations, important progress has been made in raising greater awareness about the protection of the rights and dignity of all people. However, the United Nations has not yet achieved what its mission set out to accomplish in relation to the promotion of the security, happiness, and prosperity of the entire human community. Throughout the world, entrenched prejudice and unchecked and widespread corruption impair efforts to alleviate economic disparity and protect civilian populations from harm while, unfortunately intensifying the violation of people's dignity whether manifested as ethnic, religious, and racial oppression; systematic violence against and exploitation of women and children; economic inequality, corruption, discrimination, and prejudice, the violation of human dignity and rights is rife throughout the world.

Regarding such dysfunctional patterns that permeate the global order and their potential impact on human dignity, sociologist Joe R. Feagin (2011) observes:

> […] social injustice can be examined not only in terms of the maldistribution of goods and services, but also in regard to the social relations responsible for that maldistribution. These social relations, which can range from centrally oppressive power relations to less central mechanisms of discrimination, determine whether individuals, families, and other groups are excluded from society's important resources and decision making processes. They shape the development of group and individual identities and the sense of personal dignity.

Feagin's statement points to those social relations which give rise to oppressive power relationships, mechanisms of discrimination, and forces that marginalize groups and populations from the processes of decision making and access to resources. Such patterns of social injustice will need to be conceptualized such that the whole of humanity is given the opportunity to determine its future.

Lines of action that aim to promote human dignity will need to inevitably address human values. Feagin (2011, p. 12) makes the observation that "In everyday practice all sociology is a moral activity." This, of course, applies to any discipline. Feagin (2011) points out that in an effort to measure the status quo one must "step outside of the frame of the existing society and/or nation state." Referring to it as "countersystem" approach to research, Feagin notes that this form of study creates

> a broad human rights framework in which each person is entitled to fair treatment and justice simply because they are human beings, not because they are members of a particular nation-state. (Feagin, 2011)

With this research perspective in mind, a few examples are presented below in an effort to explore the role of research and its application in the promotion of human dignity and the potential for creating more just social order.

Rethinking Relationships that Sustain the Social Order

It is evident that while social problems and injustices violate human rights, they also dishonor human dignity. For this reason, we cannot overlook the value of applying scientifically based knowledge and the wide-ranging expertise generated in all fields of endeavor in an attempt to develop a better understanding of such problems and ultimately arrive at their resolution. However, such a strategy, as important as it is, has not and cannot advance a moral consciousness regarding the centrality of human dignity among the peoples of the world. Humanity's social and moral life, together, requires cultivation in an effort toward the eventual achievement of a universal consciousness of human dignity.

Toward this end, a research agenda should be pursued that aims to explore the lines of action that lead to developing approaches to human relationships and institutional capacities capable of creating more peaceful and sustainable societies. What follows are a few broad examples of research endeavors focused on, as stated by Feagin (2011, p. 13), "the possibility of a world moral community."

Among the fundamental research questions to be explored is whether human relationships can develop, perhaps by the design of educational interventions with built-in service components, to the extent where problem solving does not require constructing an "enemy" or "other" that is blamed for the source of the problems. Repeating this pattern of thinking and behavior serves to perpetuate further the current prejudices and stereotypes. The elimination of groundless views and attitudes about other people requires a system of education that opens minds to embrace human beings as a single species. This is by no means an easy task in a world where misconceptions are readily accepted as facts and differences among individuals lead to their further disaggregation from one another. In an interconnected and interdependent world, education and learning should value diversity as a source of strength. Teaching and learning that every person is a full member of humanity with capacities that contribute to the common weal is an important measure toward dissolving the fallacious notion that for there to be an "us" there must always also be a "them," and promoting the honor and dignity of all people.

Another research question involves our overall limited image, or conception, of the world and humanity's place within it. Here, the analogy of humankind as an interconnected organic body, likened to the human body, is useful. If one part of the body is injured or malfunctioning, the entire system suffers. In a planetary community where social problems such as environmental and economic crises, inequalities, consumerism, poverty, pandemics, and other such issues impact humanity on a global scale, research should analyze humanity as a single highly interconnected body that suffers from multiple injuries. In other words, what aspects of the global community would have to undergo transformation in order to better address matters that impact humanity and the planet as a whole?

The final research question concerns the approaches that are pursued in the areas of social and economic development. Many development agendas appear to focus on approaches that lead to material prosperity with little attention given to the moral and ethical dimensions. Sometimes, development efforts are engaged in the application of a uniform set of usually ethnocentric procedures and policies – whether economic models, governmental practices, or social norms – to different regions of the world. Over the past decades, social and development programs and interventions applied throughout the world have shown the futility of traditional models of development including the "top-down" approach. In many instances, development decisions imposed from the outside ultimately fail to meet the needs of the population they are designed to benefit. Those from outside a community, although well-intentioned, cannot succeed in implementing or imposing methods of development that are foreign and unfamiliar to native populations. The native population itself navigates the process of social and economic development aimed at empowering community members to make decisions on their own behalf.

A different approach to development is called for. Here, it is vital to investigate and learn from those processes of sound development that provide all members of the global community the right of participation, especially in matters that impact their own lives. This approach begins at the local level, engaging the members of the local community who take responsibility for the future of their society. In other words, for any population to pursue its own course of development, it must take responsibility for its own institutions and structures. Likewise, if people are to take responsibility of their own development, they must engage in the process of life-long learning.[1] The sustainability of a sound social and economic

[1] For further reading see, *For the Betterment of the World: The Worldwide Bahá'í Community's Approach to Social and Economic Development*, Bahá'í International Community, http://www.bahai.org/documents/osed/betterment-world.pdf?b6e03266.

development implies that all people in every land have an obligation to contribute their share to the construction of a flourishing global community.

These are a few research questions that are proposed for consideration as we explore the means by which the human dignity of every person can be supported and a better understanding of how to create a peaceful global society may gradually become more apparent.

Conclusion

By any measure, the day has come when humanity must be regarded as one people living in a highly interdependent world. But adjusting to the fact of humanity as one organic entity presents formidable challenges to outdated ways of thinking patterns of behavior, and institutional structures. New ideas and principles for the betterment of the condition of all people and safeguarding of their dignity are essential steps for a world that can no longer afford to overlook its oneness.

In May 2000, UN Secretary-General Kofi Annan invited over one thousand non-governmental organizations representing more than one hundred countries to the Millennium Summit in New York City. The goal of the summit was to formulate a new vision for the new century with specific emphasis on the role of the United Nations and civil society in relation to peace, poverty eradication, human rights, the environment, globalization, and the revitalization of the United Nations. That gathering drafted and adopted a declaration outlining a vision as well as practical measures for its implementation. The goal to which these civil leaders and their organizations committed themselves was the following:

> In our vision we are one human family, in all our diversity, living on one common homeland and sharing a just, sustainable and peaceful world, guided by universal principles of democracy, equality, inclusion, voluntarism, non-discrimination and participation by all persons, men and women, young and old, regardless of race, faith, disability, sexual orientation, ethnicity or nationality.

Today, the image of one diverse human family living in one common global community is a reality. The complex task that lies ahead concerns the promotion of values that can become the source of respect in safeguarding the human honor and dignity of all people. There is urgency in pursuing pathways that lead to the recognition of human dignity on a universal basis. In this regard, the significant role of education, knowledge, and research are paramount.

References

Anthony Appiah, K. (2001). Grounding human rights. In M. Ignatieff & A. Guttman (Eds.), *Human rights as politics and idolatry* (p. 106). Princeton, NJ: Princeton University Press

Bahá'í International Community. (2018). For the Betterment of the World: The Worldwide Bahá'í Community's Approach to Social and Economic Development, Retrieved from http://www.bahai.org/documents/osed/betterment-world.pdf?b6e03266.

Feagin, J. R. (2011). Social justice and sociology: Agendas for the twenty-first century. *American Sociological Review, 66*(February), 11.

Hicks, D. (2011) *Dignity: Its Essential Role in Resolving Conflict.* New Haven, CT: Yale University Press.

Kateb, G. (2011), *Human dignity* (p. 95). Cambridge, MA: Harvard University Press.

Lechner, F. (2004). "Globalization," cited in George Ritzer. In *The globalization of nothing* (p. 72). Thousand Oaks, CA: Pine Forge Press.

Lindner, E. G. (2007). In times of globalization and human rights: Does humiliation become the most disruptive force? *Journal of Human Dignity and Humiliation Studies, 1*(1, March). Retrieved from http://www.humiliationstudies.org/documents/evelin/HumiliationandFearinGlobalizingWorldHumanDHSJournal.pdf

Margalit, A. (2002). *The ethics of memory* (p. 115). Cambridge, MA: Harvard University Press.

McCrudden, C. (Ed.). (2013). *Understanding human dignity* (p. 4). Oxford: Oxford University Press.

McGrew, A. (2011). Globalization and global politics. In J. Baylis, S. Smith, & P. Owens (Eds.), *The globalization of world politics: An introduction to international relations* (pp. 16–31). Oxford: Oxford University Press.

Ritzer, G. (2010), *Contemporary social theory: Its classical roots* (p. 270). New York, NY: McGraw-Hill.

Robertson, R. (1992). *Globalization: Social theory and global culture* (p. 8). London: SAGE Publications.

Rosen, M. (2012). *Dignity: Its history and meaning.* Cambridge, MA: Harvard University Press.

Therborn, G. (2011). *The world: A beginner's guide* (p. 1). Malden, MA: Polity.

Waldron, J. (2012). Dignity and Rank. In M. Dan-Cohen (Ed.), *Dignity, Rank and Rights* (pp. 13–46). New York, NY: Oxford University Press.

Waldron, J. (2013, January). *Is dignity the foundation of human rights.* New York University School of Law, Public Law & Legal Theory Research Paper Series, Working Paper No. 12-73. Retrieved from http://papers.ssrn.com/sol3/papers.cfm?abstract_id=2196074. Accessed on April 1, 2013.

Chapter 2

Toward a Principle of Human Dignity

Suheil Bushrui

What is a Principle of Human Dignity?

In his 1972 inaugural lecture at the University of Oxford, the Canadian scholar Alastair Buchan (1973) anticipated both the strength and challenge of our present world order when he spoke of his belief "in the validity of a plural international system [composed] of many different kinds and sizes of nations and civilizations … difficult though it may be to manage." Forty years later, US analyst Charles Kupchan (2012) emphasized the intricacy of "fashioning consensus and compromise in an increasingly diverse and unwieldy world … in which multiple versions of order and modernity coexist …."

In the twenty-first century, in an age of global interdependence, every civilization, every culture, every society, every community, every institution, and indeed, every individual, should enjoy the right and ability to articulate an understanding of the principle of human dignity. And perhaps, in this age of individual empowerment and profound interconnectedness, it would not be going too far to declare that we all labor under an *obligation* to do so.

The preamble to the *Universal Declaration of Human Rights*, which espouses a profound belief "in the dignity and worth of the human person," also asserts "recognition of the inherent dignity and … equal and inalienable rights of all members of the human family is the foundation of freedom, justice and peace in the world …"(United Nations, 1948).

A few years after the *Universal Declaration* was proclaimed, Swedish diplomat and then-UN Secretary-General Dag Hammarskjöld articulated his own understanding of human dignity. In an address titled "The International Significance of the Bill of Rights," Hammarskjöld (1956) said, "recognition of human dignity means to give others freedom from fear …." This elegantly simple but spiritually profound understanding "to give others freedom from fear" is especially appealing and constructive because it places the burden of upholding human dignity on every individual and not for themselves but rather for the benefit of others.

Interdisciplinary Perspectives on Human Dignity and Human Rights, 27–34
Copyright © 2020 by Emerald Publishing Limited
All rights of reproduction in any form reserved
doi:10.1108/978-1-78973-821-620191003

Expressing a similar sentiment, William Shakespeare's *Hamlet* remarks on the nobility of man in terms that inspire us to transcend our own narrow interests in favor of the betterment of all humankind:

> What a piece of work is a man!
> How noble in reason! How infinite in faculties!
> In form and moving, how express and admirable!
> In action how like an angel!

If Hammarskjöld's universal and other-directed definition of human dignity is widely accepted and applied as a principle, it would create a vast reciprocal web of responsibility that could humanize and civilize the world on various levels: family, community, nation, and international society. It could help engender a new culture; namely, a culture of peace. The concept of culture, like that of dignity, has many meanings and permutations. Half a century ago, professors L. F. Brosnahan and J. W. Spencer (1962) offered a definition of culture that still resonates:

> The word [culture] as it is used by the social anthropologists ... refers to the total complex of modes of acting, of ways of thinking and of habits of speaking which are characteristic of a community; and to the products or results of those ways of thinking and acting, namely, the ideas, the beliefs, the conceptions of that community, and what the anthropologists call the institutions that they have built up – that is, the religions, the forms of government and administration, the agricultural system, the language and so on. In short, by the culture of a community we mean all the learned and shared activities of that community and the results of such activities.

In their discussion of culture, Brosnahan and Spencer focus on key elements that could help activate a principle of human dignity. Specifically, they mention "modes of acting...ways of thinking and...habits of speaking ...." These three factors – acting, thinking, and speaking – are, perhaps, what Dag Hammarskjöld (1956, p. 9) had in mind when he declared, "recognition [of human dignity] cannot be simply a question of passive acceptance. It is a question of the positive action that must be taken in order to kill fear."

In the twenty-first century, we must discover ways and means of utilizing a principle of human dignity in order to banish fear itself. In the process of moving from an age of mutual fear to an era of reciprocal dignity, the question of justice is vital, for individuals and groups will never be liberated from fear without the operation of fair standards and systems of justice. In order to transform a principle of human dignity from a conceptual abstraction into a living reality, the establishment of universal standards of justice is a preeminent issue, for justice is the essential basis of unity, and without unity, there can be no peace. The construction of a peaceful global society is a progressive task: first, justice is established; second, unity is realized; and finally, peace prevails. This process cannot be reversed or otherwise reconfigured. And at each of the three stages, a functional principle of human dignity, in Hammarskjöld's sense, is essential.

Why is the Principle of Human Dignity Needed?

We need human dignity because thinking deeply about principles of peace is a necessary prelude to actions for peace. As the German analyst Karl Kaiser (2005) has said, "[p]olicy always begins with concepts and words." From this perspective, identifying the words that can enhance our understanding of human dignity is an act of peacebuilding.

Similarly, while there can be no doubt that practical steps to ensure material well-being and physical security are essential to achieving peace, creating peace on the level of the inner self is no less necessary. The importance of principles to this endeavor is captured in the following passage taken from a statement called *The Promise of World Peace*, issued in 1985 by the Universal House of Justice (2013), the governing authority of the Bahá'í International Community:

> [...] the primary challenge in dealing with issues of peace is to raise the context to the level of principle, as distinct from pure pragmatism. For, in essence, peace stems from an inner state supported by a spiritual or moral attitude, and it is chiefly in evoking this attitude that the possibility of enduring solutions can be found.

If a principle can help place the issue of dignity on the international agenda, then it will help us acquire a more subtle and, therefore, comprehensive understanding of current events and alternative futures. And a principle of human dignity can serve the cause of knowledge in another, broader fashion. In his book, *The Social Animal*, *New York Times* columnist David Brooks wrote (2011):

> The rationalism method has yielded many great discoveries, but when it is used to explain or organize the human world, it does have one core limitation. It highly values conscious cognition – what you might call Level 2 cognition – which it can see, quantify, formalize, and understand. But it is blind to the influence of unconscious – what you might call Level 1 cognition – which is cloudlike, nonlinear, hard to see, and impossible to formalize. Rationalists have a tendency to lop off or diminish all information that is not calculable according to their methodologies.

Finally, a principle of human dignity can help us imagine new perspectives for looking at our world and novel ways of diagnosing its myriad problems and challenges. In his book, *Eunomia* – a Greek word denoting the smooth and harmonious ordering of society – the international law expert Philip Allott (1990) identifies the need for a new model upon which to build a peaceful international society:

> It is impossible to imagine a world completely free of war. Or is it? In an age when the search for peaceful cohabitation between nations of the world has taken on a new and vibrant urgency, when what is needed is a model from which to fashion an international society that will hold firm in peace for generations to come, the tragic truth is that the ambitions of twentieth century peace-makers have been thwarted by a system of international diplomacy which mocks the idea of peace .... Generations of children are being brought up to believe that there are no rational social processes beyond the seemingly natural processes of politics, no values of truth and justice beyond the seemingly natural values of the market-place.

Allott's vision of a world free from war may be dismissed on grounds that it lacks realism, but in such a case the English poet Robert Browning has provided a suitable rejoinder:

> [...] a man's reach should exceed his grasp,
> Or what's a heaven for?

How Can a Principle of Human Dignity Be Created?

Without question, rich provision for a principle of human dignity can be found within the various spiritual and religious traditions. In the first instance, they all claim that human beings are created in the image of God. If humans, by dint of their very humanity, enjoy a direct relationship with a supreme being, then it follows that to degrade, to humiliate, or to inspire fear in any individual is unacceptable before God. In a religious-spiritual context, the universal and other-directed nature of human dignity, as we have defined this concept, finds powerful expression in the celebrated "Golden Rule" articulated consistently – albeit in different forms – within various traditions that have emerged over the long course of human history:

- Do not to another what is disagreeable to yourself (Hinduism).
- In the beginning, were the Instructions. They are to love and respect all living creatures and Mother Earth (American Indian).
- Hurt not others in ways that you yourself would find harmful (Buddhism).
- That nature alone is good which shall not do unto another whatever is not good for its own self (Zoroastrianism).
- What is hateful to you, do not to your fellow man. That is the entire Law, all the rest is commentary (Judaism).
- Do unto others as you would have them do unto you (Christianity).
- None of you is a believer until he desires for his brother what he desires for himself (Islam).
- Blessed is he who preferreth his brother before himself (Bahá'í Faith).

The essential message of the Golden Rule – whatever it's exact phrasing – is that extending respect and honor to others is the surest means of promoting one's own respect and honor. A hundred years ago, the American poet Edwin Markham understood this when he wrote:

> He drew a circle that shut me out –
> Heretic, a rebel, a thing to flout.
> But Love and I had the wit to win:
> We drew a circle that took him in!

The Golden Rule is an obvious starting place from which to explore the wealth of common ground that exists among the religions, beginning with their mutual assertion of shared human dignity. By focusing on such powerful commonalities, a path to peaceful coexistence among the religions can be traced. Ultimately, it is conscientious interfaith dialog that could enable the genesis, plausibility, diffusion, and, finally, global application of a principle of human dignity.

Amid the discord and commotion of contemporary international relations, recognition of shared human dignity could serve as a means for managing and even resolving certain conflicts, especially those with a prominent cultural dimension. In his book, *The Clash of Civilizations and the Remaking of World Order*, Samuel Huntington (1996) included this much-ignored conclusion:

> [...] as many have pointed out, whatever the degree to which they divided humankind, the world's major religions – Western Christianity, Orthodoxy, Hinduism, Buddhism, Islam, Confucianism, Taoism, Judaism – also share key values in common. If humans are ever to develop a universal civilization, it will emerge gradually through the exploration and expansion of these commonalities.

Huntington (1996) continues: "Peoples in all civilizations should search for and attempt to expand the values, institutions, and practices they have in common with people of other civilizations." Yet a search for common ground of the kind Huntington called for has not taken place – at least not in a sustained, systematic fashion. One reason for this is the lack of an institution that could sponsor such a continuous process of dialog.

In the second half of the twentieth century, numerous multilateral institutions, many directly subordinate to the United Nations, were created to deal with a broad range of issues. Organizations like the World Bank, the International Monetary Fund, the World Health Organization, United Nations Children's Emergency Fund (UNICEF), and United Nations Educational, Scientific and Cultural Organization (UNESCO) have helped create a more cooperative and civilized world order. But we must ask: What global body promotes systematic cooperation between the faith communities? The answer, of course, is that no such standing forum exists.

At the level of international relations, such an interfaith parliament could offer a framework within which to conduct a moral dialog – that is, a dialog among diverse moral systems, cultures, and faith communities – in order to first, create a principle of human dignity and second, resolve at least some of the conflicts that threaten peace. Harold James (2006), a professor of international relations at Princeton University, has called for dialog as a means of preventing conflicts between cultures:

> Instead of thinking that technical development will automatically produce prosperity and thus solve, as it were by a kind of magic, the problem of [conflicting] values, policymakers in the industrialized world need to think and talk explicitly about values and traditions. What does Islamic tradition have in common with western traditions that respect human dignity; and how can modern America show that it respects these values too?

In the Western world, perhaps the most important venue for creating, inculcating, and diffusing a principle of human dignity is educational institutions. For example: after decades of teaching, I have learned the importance of practicing, sometimes silently, the virtues of courtesy, kindness, caring, compassion, love, honesty, justice, self-discipline, humility, and of genuine belief in the sanctity of life. In the same way that I teach my students, they teach me, and we create a partnership of the spirit that remains sacred and enduring. Yet in the last two decades or so across the English-speaking world, the "corporate model" of education – meaning an approach that elevates business goals and market logic above all else – has permeated far and wide.[1]

Today, many in academia extol the transformative virtues of the internet and the ability of web-based teaching to enhance university profitability. Yet, even while educators utilize the internet in pedagogy, we must be aware that the cyber world could contribute to a degradation of educational standards. The internet might, for example, further devalue the written word in favor of the electronic image. Reading books, as we all know, is a slow and sometimes laborious process. Yet the great virtue of reading is that it places a premium on contemplation and reflection. The internet has now joined television as a pervasive influence on American society, including politics, and so it has increasingly fallen to educators to uphold traditional forms of learning, discourse, and civility. Fulfilling this conservative role – and I use the word "conservative" in its meaning of adhering to traditional methods – may be the greatest challenge and contribution of education in the twenty-first century.

---

[1] An excellent treatment of this phenomenon – a danger call, really – can be found in Mary Gallagher's (2012) study.

Conclusion

If we are to move beyond an international community composed of quarrel-some nation states and feuding faith communities, then we must not under-estimate the need for a large-scale, long-term educational effort to inculcate a principle of human dignity. Not only foreign policy elites but also the general public, in all regions of the world, should be involved in this process of educa-tion. People everywhere must be convinced they are members of a world con-stituency advocating a form of dignity that confers global rights and carries global responsibilities.

Only by focusing on our common spiritual heritage can we hope to mend the wounds of divisiveness and instead establish what is at the heart of every spiritual tradition, namely peace. Mahatma Gandhi (1941) expressed this idea when he said: "There will be no lasting peace on earth unless we learn not merely to toler-ate but even to respect the other faiths as our own." Even for those who adhere to a secular viewpoint, the question of interfaith dialog is critical. For, as the Swiss scholar and Catholic theologian Hans Küng (1991) has cautioned, "[t]here can be no peace among the nations without peace among the religions."

In the twenty-first century – the age of interdependence – the world has become one country, and all human beings are its citizens. If this global country is to produce a more perfect – meaning more peaceful – union, then it must be built on a principle of human dignity that enshrines respect for others, without reservation or exception. The time has come when we must all recognize that our own dignity is linked, symbiotically, to the dignity of others.

References

Allott, P. (1990). *Eunomia: New order for a new world*. Oxford: Oxford University Press (front jacket flap copy).

Brooks, D. (2011). *The social animal: The hidden sources of love, character, and achievement* (p. 226). New York, NY: Random House.

Brosnahan, L. F., & Spencer, J. W. (1962). Language and culture. In *Language and Society* (p. 9). Ibadan, Nigeria: Ibadan University Press (four talks given for the Nigerian Broadcasting Corporation in February 1962).

Buchan, A. (1973). Can international relations be professed? In *An inaugural lecture deliv-ered before the University of Oxford on November 7, 1972* (p. 26). Oxford: Oxford University Press.

Gallagher, M. (2012). *Academic Armageddon: An Irish requiem for higher education*. Dublin, Ireland: Liffey Press.

Gandhi, M. (1941). Introduction to Allama Sir Abdullah Al-Mamun Al-Suhrawardy. In *The sayings of Muhammad*. London: John Murray (Reprint, Boston, MA: Charles E. Tuttle Company, 1920, p. 7).

Hammarskjöld, D. (1956). Prelude to independence: The international significance of the bill of rights. Address delivered at Colonial Williamsburg, Virginia, May 15.

Huntington, S. P. (1996). *The clash of civilizations and the remaking of world order* (p. 320). New York, NY: Simon and Schuster.

James, H. (2006). Modern America in a Roman predicament. *Financial Times*, February 20. Retrieved from http://www.ft.com/cms/s/1/f9236d6e-a24c-11da-9096-0000779e2340. html#axzz1iuPWxnOw. Accessed on January 8, 2012.

Kaiser, K. (2005). Interview by Ray Suarez on the Public Broadcasting Service. *NewsHour with Jim Lehrer*, February 23. Retrieved from http://www.kqed.org/tv/programs/archive/index.jsp?pgmid=6376&date=20050201

Küng, H. (1991). *Global responsibility: In search of a new world ethic* (p. 105). New York, NY: Crossroad.

Kupchan, C. A. (2012). America's place in the new world. *New York Times,* April 7. Retrieved from http://www.nytimes.com/2012/04/08/opinion/sunday/americas-place-in-the-new-world.html. Accessed on April 7, 2013.

The Universal House of Justice. (2013). *The promise of world peace* (p. 75). College Park, MD: University of Maryland (Reprinted in Hoda Mahmoudi, *Vision and Prospects for World Peace*).

United Nations. (1948, December 10). *The universal declaration of human rights*. Retrieved from http://www.un.org/en/documents/udhr/index.shtml. Accessed on March 27, 2013.

Chapter 3

Reframing Human Dignity

Michael Karlberg

Introduction

The concept of *human dignity* is invoked within many significant public discourses today, ranging from discourses on human rights to discourses on conflict resolution to discourses on bioethics. Yet little agreement exists regarding the meaning or practical implications of the concept. One of the reasons for this is that the concept of dignity – like all concepts – takes on different meanings within different interpretive frames. This chapter examines three contrasting interpretive frames within which the concept of human dignity can be understood. After outlining each of these frames and exploring what meanings the concept of human dignity takes on within each of them, the chapter argues that the social body frame offers the most mature and fruitful understanding of the concept. The chapter concludes by exploring some of the practical implications of this insight, including the need to reframe significant discourses according to the logic of the social body frame.

Meaning and Discourse

To discuss the meaning of a phrase like "human dignity," it is helpful to consider, at the outset, the nature of *meaning* itself. The field of semiotics examines the relationship between meanings and signifiers. One of the most basic insights of semiotics is that meanings do not reside in words. Rather, words are associated with meanings largely through cultural codes – or socially constructed rules of correspondence between signifiers and meanings. Culturally encoded meanings can be widely shared or widely contested among diverse people and they can be relatively fixed or relatively fluid across time.

These culturally coded relationships are an essential substrate of social existence. They shape human perceptions, attitudes, and behaviors, and they inform social norms, institutions, and practices, in profound ways. Indeed, it can be

Interdisciplinary Perspectives on Human Dignity and Human Rights, 35–48
Copyright © 2020 by Emerald Publishing Limited
doi:10.1108/978-1-78973-821-620191004

argued that cultural codes are to social evolution what genetic codes are to biological evolution. In an overarching sense, our cultural codes determine how well adapted we are to changing conditions or environments (Karlberg, 2004).

Cultural codes are generated, altered, and transmitted largely through *discourse*. A discourse can be conceptualized as the evolving way people think and talk about a given aspect of reality, which influences their perceptions and social practices in relation to that aspect of reality. We can thus conceive of discourses on race, on gender, on the environment, or on any other significant aspect of reality. Most efforts to conceptualize discourse rest on the underlying premise that language, and language use, do not merely reflect or represent our social and mental realities, they also play a role in constructing or structuring these realities. This conception of language, and by extension discourse, as structuring agents is now widely accepted across the social sciences and humanities. However, this broad conception of discourse encompasses diverse approaches to inquiry (refer to discussions in McKinlay & McVittie, 2008; Phillips & Hardy, 2002; Schiffrin, Tannen, & Hamilton, 2001). Among these approaches is *critical discourse analysis*, which is especially relevant to the discussion at hand. Critical discourse analysis examines discourse in its broad social and historical context and is concerned with the ways that power dynamics produce, and are reproduced by, dominant discourses (van Dijk, 2001).

In this regard, critical discourse analysis reminds us that discourses can embody and perpetuate the perspectives, values, and interests of privileged segments of society who, through their social positions, exert disproportionate influence on the articulation of discourses. Such influence need not be consciously exerted. Rather, people often have an unconscious affinity for ideas that align with their own interests (Howe, 1978). Therefore, segments of society who have disproportionate access to the means of cultural production tend, to some extent, consciously or unconsciously, to shape dominant discourses according to self-interested ideas and perspectives. Discourses can thereby help to construct "a social reality that is taken for granted and that advantages some participants at the expense of others" (Phillips & Hardy, 2002, p. 15).

The Role of Interpretive Frames Within Discourse

In discourse analysis, discourse is viewed as a phenomenon that has distinct internal properties (McKinlay & McVittie, 2008). These properties include systems of categorization, metaphors, narratives, frames, and other interpretive devices that can influence cognition, perception, and action within communities of shared discourse. From among these properties, the discussion at hand is concerned primarily with interpretive frames.

Bateson (1954) is often credited for the initial concept of an interpretive frame. He pointed out that discrete communicative acts are rendered meaningful within larger interpretive frames. For example, an apparently "hostile" communicative act can take on completely different meanings when interpreted through the frame "this is play" or the frame "this is war." Building on these insights, Goffman (1974) conceptualized frames as cognitive schemata or mental frameworks that shape our perceptions, interpretations, and representations of reality; mentally organize our experience; and provide normative guides for our actions.

Following this work by Bateson and Goffman, the concept of *frames* and *framing* has been conceptualized with different nuances across the social and psychological sciences. What unifies these conceptions is the understanding that people must rely on acquired structures of interpretation to sift, sort, and make sense out of the otherwise overwhelming universe of information and experience they encounter in their daily lives (Tannen, 1993). Frames are, in effect, a form of "conceptual scaffolding" that we rely on to construct our understanding of the world (Snow & Benford 1988, p. 213). As Ryan and Gamson (2006) explain,

> Like a picture frame, an issue frame marks off some part of the world. Like a building frame, it holds things together. It provides coherence to an array of symbols, images, and arguments, linking them through an underlying organizing idea that suggests what is essential – what consequences and values are at stake. We do not see the frame directly, but infer its presence by its characteristic expressions and language. Each frame gives the advantage to certain ways of talking and thinking, while it places others 'out of the picture.' (p. 14)

Such frames are often acquired unconsciously. They influence not only how we interpret specific phenomena but also which phenomena we notice. They are composed of tacit explanations and expectations regarding "what exists, what happens, and what matters" (Gitlin, 1980, p. 6). In this regard, a given "fact" will become more or less salient, or take on different meanings, within different frames (Ryan & Gamson, 2006). Indeed, any given word can take on different meanings within different interpretive frames (Lakoff, 2006a).

Interpretative frames can be conceptualized in terms of *surface frames* and *deep frames*. For the discussion at hand, deep frames are particularly relevant because they shape, among other things, our deepest assumptions about human nature and the social order. Or, as Lakoff (2006a) explains,

> Deep frames structure your moral system or your worldview. Surface frames have a much smaller scope .... Deep frames are where the action is ... they characterize moral and political principles that are so deep they are part of your very identity. Deep framing is the conceptual infrastructure of the mind: the foundations, walls, and beams of that edifice. Without the deep frames, there is nothing for the surface message frames to hang on. (p. 12)

Deep Frames

With these insights in mind, we can examine three deep frames that bear directly on the concept of *human dignity* because they embody foundational assumptions regarding human nature and social reality and, in the process, they lend structure to different moral worldviews. These frames, which have been elaborated in more detail elsewhere (Karlberg, 2012), are the *social command frame*, the *social contest frame*, and the *social body frame*.

The Social Command Frame

The social command frame is a legacy of patriarchal and authoritarian modes of thought. Within the social command frame, human nature tends to be conceived in terms of strength and weakness, and the social order tends to be conceived in terms of dominance and submission. Society is thus understood in strongly hierarchical terms and power is conceived in terms of control and coercion. The frame suggests that society and all the social institutions within it need to be governed by powerful individuals who have the strength to impose order and discipline. According to this logic, most segments of the population are naturally inclined toward ignorance, moral weakness, or other forms of dependency, and are thus incapable of governing themselves effectively. Governance and leadership should, therefore, be the prerogative of exceptional individuals or groups that are in some way superior to others.

One of the metaphors that is invoked to support this frame is the metaphor of the "alpha male" who dominates and leads the pack. Another metaphor that is invoked toward similar ends is the military metaphor of a General in relation to his (rarely her) troops. Within the social command frame, these and similar metaphors suggest the normalcy and efficacy of a strongly hierarchical and authoritarian social order.

In the latter part of the twentieth century, democratic societies tended to reject the social command frame as an oppressive construct invoked by self-interested elites seeking to buttress their power and privilege in society. Yet the frame is still widely invoked in authoritarian societies, and it even appears to be resurgent in some democratic societies today. It can also be seen in strongly hierarchical organizations and patriarchal families.

The Social Contest Frame

The social contest frame became an influential interpretive frame with the ascendancy of Western-liberal thought where it emerged, in part, in response to the acute injustice and oppression associated with the social command frame. Within the social contest frame, human nature is conceived primarily in terms of egoistic, self-interested, and competitive instincts. Society is thus understood as a competitive arena in which self-maximizing individuals or groups pursue divergent interests in a world characterized by scarce resources and opportunities.

One widely invoked metaphor that encapsulates this frame is the metaphor of biological evolution, as interpreted through the lens of social Darwinism. Even though evolutionary biologists are increasingly recognizing the fundamental role that mutualism and symbiosis play as an evolutionary dynamic, a competitive understanding of evolution has dominated public consciousness since social Darwinism was consolidated as one of the ideological underpinnings of laissez-faire capitalism. According to this metaphor, society is just another arena of evolutionary competition in which only the strongest will survive. In the process, society as a whole will be strengthened. In addition to this social Darwinist metaphor, the social contest frame is also characterized by war metaphors, fight metaphors, sports metaphors, and market metaphors – all of which are widely invoked today to make sense out of virtually every aspect of social reality.

This interpretive frame has become embedded in a wide range of institutional structures, from partisan models of democratic governance, to advocacy-based models of justice, to grade-based models of education. What all these institutions share is the underlying normative assumption that the best way to organize society is to harness everyone's self-interested and competitive energy and attempt to channel it toward the maximum social benefit (Karlberg, 2004). This is attempted by organizing social relations and institutions as contests that allegedly reward truth, excellence, innovation, efficiency, and productivity. Such contests inevitably produce winners and losers but, in the long run (surviving) populations are allegedly better off.

The Social Body Frame

Though the social body frame has deep roots in diverse traditional cultures, it has been reemerging in a modern form over the past century in response to the ever-increasing social and ecological interdependence humanity is now experiencing on a global scale. At the core of this frame is an understanding of society as an integrated organic body. No other metaphor captures the logic of interdependence more effectively than this social body metaphor.[1]

In an interdependent social body, the well-being of every individual or group depends upon the well-being of the entire body. This collective well-being cannot be achieved through oppressive power hierarchies, as suggested by the social command frame. Nor can it be achieved by structuring every social institution as a contest of power, as suggested by the social contest frame. Rather, collective well-being can only be achieved by maximizing the possibilities for every individual to realize their latent potential to contribute to the common good, within empowering social relationships and institutional structures that foster and canalize human capacities in this way.

The social body frame requires a sober re-examination of prevailing assumptions about human nature. In this regard, the human sciences are now demonstrating that human beings are wired for both competition and cooperation, egoism and altruism, and which of these potentials is more fully realized depends in large part on our cultural environment, our education and training, our opportunities for moral development, and the institutional structures we act within (Axelrod, 1984; Becker, 1976; Bowles & Gintis, 2011; de Waal, 2009; Fellman, 1998;

---

[1]It is important to note that the social body metaphor has occasionally been invoked in the past, in cynical and oppressive ways, within the logic of the social command frame. For a full discussion of this theme refer to Karlberg (2012).

Henrich, Heine, & Norenzayan, 2010; Henrich & Henrich, 2007; Keltner, 2009; Kohn, 1990; Leaky & Lewin, 1977; Lewontin, 1991; Lunati, 1992; Margolis, 1982; Margulis, 1998; Monroe, 1996; Rose, Lewontin, & Kamin 1987; Scott & Seglow, 2007; Seville, 1987; Sober & Wilson, 1998; Tomasello, 2008).

In light of this emerging understanding of human nature and human potential, the social body frame brings into focus one of the most urgent challenges facing humanity today: At a time when over seven billion people must learn how to live together on an increasingly crowded planet, it is imperative that we learn how to cultivate – widely, systematically, and effectively – every individual's latent capacity for cooperation and altruism. The success of such efforts will depend, at least in part, on fostering a consciousness of the oneness of humanity (Karlberg, 2008, 2004; Kohn, 1990; Monroe, 1996). Such a consciousness entails a radical reconception of the relationship between the individual and society, the implications of which are conveyed in a compelling manner by the social body metaphor.

Reframing Human Dignity

The three frames outlined above are ideal-types (Weber, 1904). In other words, they are analytical constructs which, like all analytical constructs, never correspond perfectly with reality. Care must be taken, therefore, not to reify these frames or over-extend the metaphors that inform them.[2] These frames can, however, serve as useful heuristic devices for organizing certain forms of inquiry and guiding certain forms of practice – such as inquiry into the meaning of *human dignity* and the application of this concept in fields such as human rights and conflict resolution.

Before proceeding in this direction, it should also be noted that the frames outlined above sometimes co-exist in contradictory or fragmented ways. As Lakoff (2006b) explains, people employ interpretive frames in unconscious ways that are not always consistent or coherent, and that can change over time. In this regard, some people may employ the social contest frame in specific domains (such as governance, law, and the economy) while they employ the social body frame in other domains (such as family life or social affiliations). In addition, some people may unconsciously shift between these frames even when thinking about the same social domain. Interpretive frames can, therefore, be understood as patterned but shifting and sometimes fragmented tendencies that can nonetheless exert powerful influences on the ways people think, speak, and act in relation to various aspects of reality. With these insights in mind, we can examine the way each of the three deep frames outlined above encodes the concept of human dignity with different meanings.

Human Dignity within the Social Command Frame

Within the social command frame, the concept of dignity takes on its simplest, original meaning, as a signifier of status or rank. Dignity, as Rosen (2012)

---

[2]For an insightful discussion regarding the problems of reifying or over-extending the social body metaphor, refer to Levine (1995) or Elwick (2003).

explains, "originated as a concept that denoted high social status and the honors and respectful treatment that are due to someone who occupied that position" (p. 11). This hierarchical conception of dignity has been adapted in various ways. Beyond signifying people of high rank, the term has also been used to signify an elevated or refined manner or bearing, as well as elevated or weighty discourse.

What all these meanings share in common is the signification of relative worth or value. Dignity thus denotes the relative worth or value of people, or of their bearing and manner, or of their thoughts and speech. All these meanings denote social hierarchy in one form or another. In practice, such hierarchy has often been ascribed according to distinctions of class, race, creed, genealogy, and other socio-economic categories.

Human Dignity within the Social Contest Frame

Within the social contest frame, the concept of dignity takes on a more egalitarian meaning, often denoting a universal right to self-determination and autonomy. We are thus told that dignity "means no more than respect for persons or their autonomy" (Macklin, 2003, p. 1419). This usage reflects, in large part, the political philosophies that emerged in the European enlightenment, with their emphasis on liberty and equality. In also reflects the emergence of dignity as a legal concept in human rights discourse.

For instance, the Second World War and the Holocaust were widely (and rightly) interpreted as profound violations of human dignity. The Universal Declaration of human rights, written in the immediate aftermath of those experiences, thus asserts, in the first sentence of Article 1, that "All people are born free and equal in dignity and rights." Likewise, in direct response to the Holocaust, Article 1 of the post-war German constitution states that "Human dignity is inviolable. To respect it and protect it is the duty of all state power." Many other modern human rights documents echo this general usage.

In this context, one might ask what forms of dignity can be legally respected and protected by a state? In the context of Western-liberal political philosophy, the primary answer becomes the right to self-determination, autonomy, and agency – which is how human dignity is now frequently understood (Rosen, 2012). This focus on dignity-as-autonomy is consistent with the social contest frame. When human nature is conceived largely in terms of self-interested motives playing out within competitive social arenas, then the autonomy of individuals and groups to pursue their own interests, within a set of rules that apply equally to all, takes on paramount importance.

Human Dignity within the Social Body Frame

Within the social body frame, the concept of dignity assumes a more organic meaning. In this context, dignity can be understood in terms of the intrinsic value or worth of every human being as a member of an interdependent community – or social body.[3] The social body frame suggests that this intrinsic value is realized as individuals develop those latent capacities upon which the well-being of the entire body depends. These capacities include, for instance, the capacity for honesty and trustworthiness, for cooperation and reciprocity, for empathy and compassion, for fairness and justice, for altruism and selflessness, for discipline and moderation, for learning and the investigation of reality, for creativity and productivity. It is through the development of such capacities that an individual's latent potential is fully realized, and it is through the realization of this latent potential that the individual contributes to the well-being of the entire social body.

In this regard, the social body frame suggests a two-fold purpose that gives meaning to human existence. Our purpose is to (1) develop our latent individual potential so that we can (2) contribute to the development and progress of society. Furthermore, the social body frame reminds us that this purpose can only be realized within a social environment that fosters and protects these twin developmental processes. In this context, the responsibility of all social institutions – families, schools, media, corporations, the state – include fostering and protecting the development of human potential and channeling it toward the common good.

The social body frame thereby entails respect for individual agency and autonomy within the bounds of moderation. Respect for agency and autonomy is needed because the development of an individual's latent potential, and the direction of that potential toward the common good, cannot be imposed on an individual against their will. Rather, it can only emerge as an expression of free will that is informed by a consciousness of the essential unity and interdependence of humanity. Such a consciousness embodies agency even as it entails appropriate forms of self-restraint. Therein lies the key to human dignity within the social body frame: it is achieved through the voluntary subordination of self-centered instincts and appetites to the well-being of the entire social body – from which individual well-being ultimately derives.

A primary responsibility of the state, and all other social institutions, is to nurture and protect such processes. This implies more than merely guaranteeing individual liberty. It implies fostering the consciousness of the oneness of humanity and providing a framework for acting upon this consciousness in our private and public lives.

Such a social order, it should also be noted, would not be without hierarchy. Yet hierarchy, like dignity, takes on a new meaning within the social body frame. Hierarchy within an organic body is not a structure of dominance or an outcome of power-seeking behavior. Rather, organic bodies are characterized by internal hierarchies that empower rather than oppress the diverse members of the body. Differentiation of roles and functions is a natural expression of organic

---

[3]The conception of human dignity in terms of intrinsic value or worth has been articulated by a range of philosophers over the centuries, from Aquinas (in McInerny, 1998) to Kant (1785) to Kateb (2011). However, none of these philosophers have explicitly situated this intrinsic conception of human dignity within the logic of the social body frame, where it takes on a more organic, rather than atomistic, meaning.

interdependence. Organic hierarchy provides the organization, coordination, and efficiency by which the diverse potentialities of autonomous individuals can be realized and their energies can be applied in productive ways that promote the common good. Within such empowering hierarchies, human dignity can flourish.

Finally, the social body frame implies that justice must be the ruling principle of social organization. In its absence, the unity and hierarchy discussed above become oppressive and rob individuals of their dignity – as seen in the uncritical functionalist thinking of the early twentieth century. Yet *justice* also takes on a more mature meaning within the social body frame. In this context, justice can be understood as a latent capacity of discernment entailing fair-mindedness along with a recognition that the development and well-being of the individual are organically linked to the development and well-being of the community. This is a capacity that can be fostered and developed within every individual as they become conscious of the organic oneness of humanity. Similarly, at the collective level, justice can be understood as a capacity that is latent in all collective endeavors, entailing the conscious application of the principle of justice – understood in the organic sense alluded to above – as a guide to collective decision making and collective action. Only in such a context can human dignity be fully protected and promoted.

Practical Implications

The preceding analysis has practical implications. It suggests that human dignity cannot be achieved merely through legal enforcement – as important as that is. Ultimately, respect for human dignity, in its most mature form, arises from an emergent consciousness of the oneness of humanity. And the emergence of this consciousness depends on education in the broadest sense of the word – the ways we are nurtured, socialized, encouraged, trained, and empowered, within our families, our schools, our media environment, and the many other social institutions we participate in.

Consider, for instance, the problem of dignity violations. Such violations can be understood as a root cause of human suffering and conflict (Hicks, 2011). Moreover, such violations have a deep psychological component. Dignity, in this sense, can be understood not merely as a legal right, but also as an inner state of consciousness that, when violated, triggers powerful emotional responses. As Hicks (2011) explains, "our desire for dignity runs deep;" it is among "the most powerful forces motivating our behavior" and "in some cases... our desire for dignity is even stronger than our desire for survival" (p.14). Human dignity is thus not merely a philosophical abstraction or a legal construct. It is a phenomenological reality that has its basis in human consciousness.

Seeking to protect individuals and groups from gross violations of their dignity, through the construction of human rights frameworks and enforcement mechanisms, is clearly a laudable endeavor. But such efforts will always be limited in their scope and effect because the external regulation of human behavior is rarely effective unless it is reinforced by internal motivations and self-regulation. Hence enforcement efforts need to be coupled with the educational processes alluded to above. These educational processes, moreover, are not simply about reducing tendencies to violate the dignity of others. People also need to learn how to encounter indignities with dignity – or to preserve their inner state of dignity in the face of ostensible violations. In other words, education is not merely about learning to respect the dignity of others. It is also about learning how to preserve one's own dignity by responding to apparent dignity violations in thoughtful and mature ways that do not result in escalating cycles of indignity and conflict.

This is not an easy thing. On a psychological level, people are often inclined to respond to received dignity violations with retaliatory dignity violations, which can set in motion a vicious cycle (Hicks, 2011). This all-too-familiar dynamic plays out within homes, on the playground, in the workplace, in communities, and even in the theater of international relations. Breaking these cycles requires a remarkable degree of maturity. Among other things, it requires the capacity to recognize the nature of these vicious cycles, to subordinate emotional responses to a higher cause, to forgive the past, and to foster conditions in which all parties can move forward constructively. Such capacities are, in turn, fostered by a consciousness of the oneness of humanity, which brings into focus our underlying interdependence and the need to strive for more cooperative and reciprocal modes of interaction that promote the well-being of the entire social body.

The well-known example of Nelson Mandela is instructive in this regard. After growing up amidst the racial indignities of the apartheid regime in South Africa, and after suffering twenty-seven years of incarceration for his efforts to end the apartheid system, he helped negotiate an end to the regime, became president of a new South Africa, oversaw the drafting of its new constitution, and initiated a truth and reconciliation commission to help heal the nation and enable it to move forward constructively. In the process, he came to symbolize the maturity alluded to above, along with the capacities associated with it. Indeed, Mandela became an iconic symbol of human dignity in the twentieth century. Not surprisingly, his worldview was framed by a clear and conscious recognition of the oneness of humanity (Mandela, 2010, 2012).

Similar insights regarding the internal locus of human dignity, and its underlying source, can be gained from the case of the Bahá'ís in Iran. The Bahá'í community was founded upon an explicit commitment to the promotion of the oneness of humanity, which is understood by Bahá'ís as the imperative next step in humanity's collective social and spiritual evolution, without which humanity cannot adapt to conditions of ever-increasing global interdependence. As a result of this commitment, the Bahá'í community in Iran has, since its birth over a century and a half ago, been subject to recurrent waves of violent persecution that have claimed the lives of roughly 20,000 adherents in the most brutal and inhumane ways (Martin, 1984; Moomen, 1981). In the most recent wave of persecution, unleashed after the Iranian Revolution in1979, over two hundred Iranian Bahá'ís have been executed solely for their beliefs; thousands have been imprisoned and tortured in an effort to get them to recant their faith; tens of thousands have lost their homes, their property, their savings, their pensions, and their jobs; the entire community of several hundred thousand has been subjected to systematic vilification from the media and the pulpit; Bahá'í children and youth are systematically harassed at school and denied access to universities; Bahá'í gravesites are regularly desecrated; Bahá'í marriages are declared immoral; the activities of Bahá'í are widely monitored; and crimes are committed against Bahá'ís with legal impunity because the current Iranian constitution denies the Bahá'ís basic human and civil rights (Brookshaw & Fazel, 2007; IHRDC, 2006; Kazemzadeh, 2000).

Against this backdrop of repression and abuse the Bahá'í community has refused to relinquish its own dignity. It has remained a law-abiding community and refrained from any form of sectarian opposition or conflict. It has, instead, adopted a strategy of constructive resilience that has preserved its integrity and ensured its continued advancement (Karlberg, 2010). By these means, the Bahá'ís of Iran have never let their oppressors establish the terms of the encounter. They have refused to play the role of victim; refused to be dehumanized; refused to forfeit their sense of agency; refused to compromise their principles and commitments.

The resolve of the Bahá'í community, in this regard, has been motivated and sustained by an abiding consciousness of the oneness of humanity, which Bahá'ís are working to embody and promote. Bahá'ís see, in the actions of their oppressors, the machinations of immature and self-interested leaders who are desperately clinging to a corrupt and anachronistic social order that cannot be sustained indefinitely. Bahá'ís thus seek a higher meaning and purpose in their own suffering and sacrifice, as they labor side by side with all like-minded people who are working to construct a more just social order, founded on the consciousness of oneness which, they are confident, will ultimately prevail. In this consciousness, they have achieved a remarkable degree of psychological resilience (Davoudi, 2003; Ghadirian, 1998, 1994). They have also achieved a remarkable degree of efficacy. Indeed, though the Bahá'í movement began as an obscure movement with a handful of adherents in a remote region of nineteenth-century Iran, its adherents now come from every country on earth; number in the millions; are drawn from every ethnicity, class, and creed; and constitute the most diverse, widely distributed, democratically organized community on the planet (Hatcher & Martin, 1998; Smith, 1987; Weinberg, 2007). They are engaged, moreover, in collaborative efforts with growing numbers of like-minded people from all continents who are working to bring about a more just social order in which the dignity of all people is respected and promoted.

Conclusion

As the examples above illustrate, the maturation of practices leading to human dignity lies, ultimately, in the reframing of human consciousness. The work of reframing will have to occur, in part, at the level of discourse, because discourse is a primary medium through which the codes of human culture and consciousness evolve. At this critical juncture in history, this reframing has become an evolutionary imperative. Our reproductive and technological success as a species has transformed the conditions of our own existence. Over seven billion people now live on this planet and our technologies have amplified our impact a thousandfold. Inherited codes of culture and consciousness are proving maladaptive under these conditions.

In this context, reframing significant discourses according to the logic of organic interdependence is a vital adaptive strategy. Skeptics may dismiss this view as naïve and unrealistic. But is it realistic to assume that the prevailing culture of contest can be sustained indefinitely on a planet with over seven billion people wielding increasingly powerful and destructive technologies? Is it realistic to assume that narrowly self-interested motives can continue to drive human behavior in this context? Is it realistic to assume that the struggle for power and domination can continue to define our social existence indefinitely under such conditions? What is needed, in this regard, is a new realism – a new interpretive frame. The logic of the social body frame offers this. In the process, it provides a genuine foundation for human dignity.

References

Axelrod, R. (1984). *The evolution of cooperation.* New York, NY: Basic Books.

Bateson, G. (1954). A theory of play and fantasy. In G. Bateson (Ed.), *Steps to an ecology of mind* (pp. 177–193). New York, NY: Ballantine.

Becker, G. (1976). Altruism, Egoism, and Genetic Fitness: Economics and Sociobiology. *Journal of Economic Literature, 14*(3), 817–26.

Bowles, S., & Gintis, H. (2011). *A cooperative species: Human reciprocity and its evolution.* Princeton, NJ: Princeton University Press.

Brookshaw, D. P., & Fazel, S. (2007). *The Bahá'ís of Iran: Socio-historical studies.* Oxford: Routledge.

Davoudi, M. (2003). *Spiritual dimension of adaptation to persecution and torture among Iranian Bahá'í women.* Doctoral Dissertation, The Chicago School of Professional Psychology, Chicago.

De Waal, F. (2009). *The age of empathy: Nature's lessons for a kinder society.* New York, NY: Harmony Books.

Elwick, J. (2003). Herbert spencer and the disunity of the social organism. *History of Science, 41,* 35–72.

Fellman, G. (1998). *Rambo and the Dalai Lama: The compulsion to win and its threat to human survival.* Albany, NY: State University of New York Press.

Ghadirian, A. (1998). Intergenerational responses to the persecution of the Bahá'ís of Iran. In Y. Danieli (Ed.), *Intergenerational handbook of multigenerational legacies of trauma* (pp. 513–532). New York, NY: Plenum Press.

Ghadirian, A. (1994). Psychological and spiritual dimensions of persecution and suffering. *Journal of Bahá'í Studies, 6*(3), 1–26.

Gitlin, T. (1980). *The whole world is watching: Mass media in the making and unmaking of the new left.* Berkeley, CA: University of California Press.

Goffman, E. (1974). *Frame analysis: An essay on the organization of experience.* New York, NY: Harper & Row.

Hatcher, W., & Martin, D. (1998). *The Bahá'í Faith: The emerging global religion.* Wilmette, IL: Bahá'í Publishing Trust.

Henrich, J., Heine, S., & Norenzayan, A. (2010). The weirdest people in the world? *Behavioral and Brain Sciences* (33), 61–135.

Henrich, N., & Henrich, J. (2007). *Why humans cooperate: A cultural and evolutionary explanation.* Oxford: Oxford University Press.

Hicks, D. (2011). *Dignity: Its essential role in resolving conflict.* New Haven, CT: Yale University Press.

Howe, R. H. (1978). Max Weber's elective affinities: Sociology within the bounds of pure reason. *The American Journal of Sociology*, *84*(2), 366–385.

Iran Human Rights Documentation Center (IHRDC). (2006). *A faith denied: The persecution of the Bahá'ís of Iran*. New Haven, CT: IHRDC.

Karlberg, M. (2012). Reframing public discourses for peace and justice. In K. Korostelina (Ed.), *Forming a culture of peace: Reframing narratives of intergroup relations, equity, and justice* (pp. 15–42). New York, NY: Palgrave Macmillan.

Karlberg, M. (2010). Constructive resilience: The Baha'i response to oppression. *Peace & Change*, *35*(2), 222–257.

Karlberg, M. (2008). Discourse, identity, and global citizenship. *Peace Review*, *20*(3), 310–320.

Karlberg, M. (2004). *Beyond the culture of contest: From adversarialism to mutualism in an age of interdependence*. Oxford: George Ronald.

Kateb, G. (2011). *Human dignity*. Cambridge, MA: Harvard University Press.

Kant, I. (1785–1993). *Grounding for the metaphysics of morals*. In J. W. Ellington (Trans., 3rd ed.). Indianapolis, IN: Hackett Publishing Company.

Kazemzadeh, F. (2000). The Bahá'ís in Iran: Twenty years of oppression. *Social Research*, *67*(2), 537–558.

Keltner, D. (2009). *Born to be good: The science of a meaningful life*. New York, NY: W.W. Norton & Company.

Kohn, A. (1990). *The brighter side of human nature: Altruism and empathy in everyday life*. New York, NY: Basic Books.

Lakoff, G. (2006a). *Whose freedom? The battle over America's most important idea*. New York, NY: Farra, Straus & Giroux.

Lakoff, G. (2006b). *Thinking points: Communicating our American values and vision*. New York, NY: Farra, Straus & Giroux.

Leakey, R., & Lewin, R. (1977). *Origins: What New Discoveries Reveal About the Emergence of Our Species*. London: MacDonald & Jane's.

Levine, D. (1995). The organism metaphor in sociology. *Social Research*, *62*(2), 239–265.

Lewontin, R. (1991). *Biology as ideology: The doctrine of DNA*. New York, NY: Harpercollins.

Lunati, T. (1992). On altruism and co-operation. *Methodus*, *4*, 69–75.

Macklin, R. (2003). Dignity is a useless concept. *British Medical Journal*, *320*, 1419–1420.

Mandela, N. (2012). *Notes to the future*. Aukland, NZ: Atria Books.

Mandela, N. (2010). *Conversations with myself*. Aukland, NZ: PQ Blackwell Limited.

Margolis, H. (1982). *Selfishness, altruism, and rationality*. Cambridge: Cambridge University Press.

Margulis, L. (1988). *Symbiotic Planet: A New Look at Evolution*. New York, NY: Basic Books.

Martin, D. (1984). *The persecution of the Bahá'ís of Iran, 1844–1984*. Ottawa, Canada: Association for Bahá'í Studies.

McInerny, R. (Ed./Trans.). (1998). *Thomas Aquinas: Selected writings*. New York, NY: Penguin.

Mckinlay, A., & Mcvittie, C. (2008). *Social psychology and discourse*. Oxford: Wiley-Blackwell.

Monroe, K. (1996). *The heart of altruism: Perceptions of a common humanity*. Princeton, NJ: Princeton University Press.

Moomen, M. (Ed.). (1981). *The Bábí and Bahá'í religions, 1844–1944: Some contemporary Western accounts*. Oxford: George Ronald.

Phillips, N., & Hardy, C. (2002). *Discourse analysis: Investigating process of social construction*. Thousand Oaks, CA: Sage.

Rose, S., Lewontin, R., & Kamin, L. (1987). *Not in our genes: Biology, ideology, and human nature*. New York, NY: Penguin.

Rosen, M. (2012). *Dignity: Its history and meaning*. Cambridge, MA: Harvard University Press.

48   *Michael Karlberg*

Ryan, C., & Gamson, W. (2006). The art of reframing political debates. *Contexts, 5*(1), 13–18.

Schiffrin, D., Tannen, D., & Hamilton, H. (Eds.). (2001). *The handbook of discourse analysis*. Oxford: Blackwell.

Scott, N., & Seglow, J. (2007). *Altruism*. Berkshire: Open University Press.

Seville. (1987). Statement on violence, Seville, May 16, 1986. *Medicine and War, 3*, 191–93.

Smith, P. (1987). *The Bábí and Bahá'í religions: From messianic Shi'ism to a world religion*. Cambridge: Cambridge University Press.

Snow, D., & Benford, R. (1988). Ideology, frame resonance and participant mobilization. *International Social Movement Research, 1*, 197–219.

Sober, E., & Wilson, D. S. (1998). *Unto others: The evolution and psychology of unselfish behavior*. Cambridge: Harvard University Press.

Tannen, D. (Ed.). (1993). *Framing in discourse*. Oxford: Oxford University Press.

Tomasello, M. (2008). *Why we cooperate*. Cambridge, MA: MIT Press.

van Dijk, T. (2001). Critical discourse analysis. In D. Schiffrin, D. Tannen, & H. Hamilton (Eds.), *The handbook of discourse analysis* (pp. 352–371). Oxford: Blackwell.

Weber, M. (1949–1904). Objectivity in social science and social policy. In E. Shils & H. Finch (Eds./Trans.), *The methodology of the social sciences* (pp. 89–99, 110–112). New York, NY: Free Press.

Weinberg, R. (Ed.). (2007). *The Bahá'í world: 2005–2006* (p. 249). Haifa, Israel: World Center Publications.

Chapter 4

Promoting Human Rights and Human Dignity in an Axial Age

Michael L. Penn and Tri Nguyen

Introduction

In his book, *The Origin and Goal of History*, German philosopher Karl Jaspers (1953) described the period between 800 and 200 BCE, which he called the "Axial Age," in the following way:

> In this age were born the fundamental categories within which we still think today, and the beginnings of the world religions, by which human beings still live, were created. The step into univer-sality was taken in every sense. As a result of this process, hitherto unconsciously accepted ideas, customs and conditions were sub-jected to examination, questioned and liquidated. Everything was swept into the vortex. In so far as the traditional substance still possessed vitality and reality, its manifestations were clarified and thereby transmuted (p. 2).

During the Axial Age, there appeared, on the horizon of human conscious-ness a series of reverberations that were to shake, dismantle, and reconfigure the foundations of human thinking in various parts of the world.[1] This period of his-tory saw the appearance of such extraordinary figures as Confucius and Lao Tze in China; the Buddha in India; the prophets of Israel in Mesopotamia; Socrates, Plato, and Aristotle in Greece; and Zoroaster in Persia.

The Axial Age was remarkable because it was a time of great upheaval and suffering, a time of tremendous violence, instability, and social disruption. The violence was facilitated by new technologies of death associated with horseman-ship and the invention of the chariot. But, it was also a time when humanity, as a species, acquired the conceptual tools and the social pressures that would compel

---

[1]For a discussion of these themes, see Bellah and Joas (2012).

Interdisciplinary Perspectives on Human Dignity and Human Rights, 49–59
Copyright © 2020 by Emerald Publishing Limited
All rights of reproduction in any form reserved
doi:10.1108/978-1-78973-821-620191005

it to build a new mind. Since the mind is the reservoir from which civilization flows, the Axial Age gave birth to new forms of civilization.[2]

We invoke the memory of the Axial Age because it could be argued that for a little more than a century and a half, we have been living in another axial period in human history. As compared to earlier eras, the rate of growth and change, in

---

[2]It was during the Axial Age that small groups in the Middle East, India, China, and Greece began to reflect upon fundamental questions by thinking systematically about them. The human species began to subject its thinking to critical scrutiny and doubt. In this way, philosophy as a discipline was born. Superstitious thinking began to loosen some of its grip as philosophers, such as Thales, Anaximander, and Anaximenes, began to ask: What are the fundamental constituents of the world? Is it made of one kind of substance that appears in many forms (the one) or is it a composition of different kinds of elements (the many)? And they asked these questions as if the answers could be arrived at not by invoking an ancient myth, but by deep reflection and thoughtful discourse.

During this period Socrates, Plato, and Aristotle began to ask questions about the nature of human values: What is justice, what is love, how might these great forces be cultivated? What is the best system of governance? Who should govern and why? What is the basis of identity and what is the nature of a cause? To the east, Confucius in China began to speak about the goals that should animate human society and his ideas were extraordinary for their usefulness, their simple elegance and profundity.

In Persia, Zoroaster suggested that we live out our lives in a kind of moral ecology and that each person has moral responsibilities to himself and to others. He suggested that the quality of our existence depends upon the way that we discharge these moral responsibilities. Few had thought of humans as moral agents endowed with the capacity to choose a moral course and thereby to enrich their own lives and the lives of others. We tended to think of our destinies as shaped by forces that were largely beyond our control. Thus under the influence of the teachings of Zoroaster, new aspirations began to animate human life.

In India, the Buddha provided a tremendous reservoir of insight into what contributes to human suffering and how existential suffering could be overcome. He prescribed the cultivation of compassion, detachment, and wisdom as antidotes to many forms of suffering and suggested that right speech, right intention, right action, right effort, right mindfulness, right livelihood, and so forth, would serve as potent remedies to suffering. He suggested further that we would be happier if we avoided excesses of all kinds.

In Mesopotamia, there lived the prophets of Israel who began to speak about the responsibilities of kings and peoples to a higher justice. "Do what is just and right," said Jeremiah.

> Rescue from the hand of his oppressor the one who has been robbed.
> Do no wrong or violence to the alien, the fatherless or the widow, and
> do not shed innocent blood in this place.

The Jewish prophets were to provide the conceptual fodder for the assertion that Martin Luther King, Jr, would make 2,500 years later when he affirmed that although "the arc of the moral universe is long, it bends towards justice."

nearly every sphere of human engagement, has accelerated greatly. For example, alongside unprecedented degrees of suffering and exploitation, we have seen a flowering of human aspiration for freedom, for an end to conflict and violence, for greater sharing of the world's resources. We have seen an explosion of knowledge about the condition of the world and this expansion of awareness makes it possible for us to address problems the likes of which we never considered before. Nowhere is change greater than as relates to relations among and between peoples of different cultures, races, classes, and nations. The global scope and ethical core of the changes underway are captured succinctly in humanity's growing concern for human dignity, development, and human rights.

When we seek to protect human dignity, we are concerned with guarding the human race from that which would thwart or arrest the actualization of human potential. And while dignity, as the literature and discourse on human rights suggests, is the birthright of all human beings, as the horrific violence of the twentieth century has shown, human dignity is vulnerable to ideologies that justify the sacrifice of human security and development to private, cultural, or national interests. This chapter suggests that if the unique capacities and potentialities that define the human species and that provide a focus for human rights are to be safeguarded, the influence of the doctrine of materialism on the effort to advance human dignity will need to be addressed.

Our overall purpose is to demonstrate that modern conceptualizations of human rights and human dignity embody a universal notion of what it means to be human; that the emergence and global spread of such a notion is an essential element of the spirit of the age in which we live and serves as one of the most significant conceptual achievements of our times. We seek further to show that contemporary conceptualizations of human rights and human dignity are in tension with materialism because they are grounded in the recognition that the protection of civilization, in all of its forms, depends not merely on the machinery required for material development, but upon the protection and cultivation of the universal moral, intellectual, and spiritual capacities that are embodied in the notion of the "human spirit." Here we provide a rational account of the nature and needs of the human spirit and suggest that to the extent that development and human rights advocate neglect discussion of it, they surrender the civilizing process to the narrow range of accomplishments that may be brought within the scope of those materialistic philosophies that have dominated development discourse for a half century. We begin our exploration of these themes by reflecting on the great moral and conceptual achievement of the century just ended.

The Twentieth Century and the Dawn of the Consciousness of the Oneness of Humankind

The twentieth century was the most turbulent century in the history of the human race. As one assessment puts it:

> Let us acknowledge at the outset the magnitude of the ruin that
> the human race has brought upon itself during the period of

history under review. The loss of life alone has been beyond counting. The disintegration of basic institutions of social order, the
violation – indeed, the abandonment – of standards of decency,
the betrayal of the life of the mind through surrender to ideologies
as squalid as they have been empty, the invention and deployment
of monstrous weapons of mass annihilation, the bankrupting of
entire nations and the reduction of masses of human beings to
hopeless poverty, the reckless destruction of the environment of
the planet – such are only the more obvious in a catalogue of horrors unknown to even the darkest of ages past.[3,4]

Notwithstanding the devastation visited upon the human race during the
twentieth century, that century has also been referred to as a "century of light."
The "light" that marked the twentieth century as a turning point in the history
of humankind was the dawn of the consciousness of the oneness of humanity.

Nature published an edited volume containing twenty-one discoveries reported
in that journal during the twentieth century that "changed science and the world"
(Garwin, Lincoln, & Weinberg, 2003). The journal titled their volume, *A Century
of Nature*, and opened it with the 1925 paper reporting Raymond Dart's discovery of *Australopithecus africanus*. Dart's discovery in physical anthropology was
revolutionary because it was the first in a chain of discoveries that would provide
empirical evidence for the monogenesis of all peoples. Dart's work, which linked
all human beings to a single species whose biological heritage could be traced to a
common ancestor, would be followed by similar discoveries made by many others
over the course of the century.[5]

In the young science of psychology, the principle of the oneness of humankind
was to be demonstrated in the discovery of universal principles that govern the
nature and development of the human brain and mind, and that shape human
response to justice and love – as well as injustice, cruelty, trauma, and violence
(Schwartz & Bilsky, 1987). Notwithstanding appreciation for the vast range of
human diversity, today all of the sciences that take as their focus the human being
affirm the essential oneness of the human race.

In the realm of ideals and collective aspirations, the principle of the oneness
of humankind would incarnate itself in a practical way in 1945, with the establishment of the United Nations (Glendon, 2001). Following in December 1948,
ratification of the *Universal Declaration of Human Rights* provided the first glob-
ally agreed upon covenant that would enshrine international commitment to the
principle of the essential oneness of humankind (Danieli, Stamatopoulou, &

---

[3]*Century of Light* (2001, p. 1).
[4]According to reliable estimates, World War I alone left 8,528,831 soldiers dead,
21,189,154 wounded, and 7,750, 919 either as prisoners or missing. Another 150 million people would be lost to various ideologies before the century's end.
[5]See, for example, Henn et al. (2011), Stringer and McKie (1996), and Andrea Manica
et al. (2007).

Dias, 1999). At the heart of the document was the inspiring conviction that each human person is born into the world as a trust of the whole and that notwithstanding our diversity we constitute a single human family.

In addition to the birth and evolution of the human rights movement, as Frances Fukuyama (1992) has argued, the twentieth century also saw the victory of liberal democracy. And while many scholars dispute Fukuyama's conclusion that the collapse of the Soviet Union and the "triumph of democracy" signified "the end of history," it would be reasonable to argue that during the twentieth century, the liberal democratic movement won many friends. Indeed, democratization efforts continue to spread across the world today (Abramson & Inglehart, 1995; Mandelbaum, 2007). Underlying the growing popularity of this system of governance is the recognition that democratic rule is more in harmony with the protection of human rights than authoritarian, oligarchic, or monarchic regimes. Part of the appeal of democracy is that it shows respect for human dignity by empowering human beings to develop their innate capacities and affords opportunities for the use of those capacities in the governance of human affairs.

Protection of Human Dignity Requires Recognition of the Oneness of Humankind

We have argued elsewhere that the universal capacities that define and distinguish the human species are embodied in the notion of the *human spirit* (Penn & Malik, 2010). These capacities consist of the capacity to know, the capacity to love, and the capacity to will. When awakened and nurtured, the capacity to know stirs humanity in its ceaseless search for knowledge and wisdom; the capacity to will motivates us to pursue that which is thought to be good; and the capacity to love, animates our attraction to beauty and our longing for connection to nature, to one another, and to that which is sacred. Human development results, essentially, from the cultivation and refinement of these capacities. As these capacities unfold and express themselves in the life of the community, we see the emergence and efflorescence of the sciences, arts, and systems of ethics and jurisprudence upon which civilization depends. We also witness the incarnation in human action, and in the functioning of human institutions, of those virtues that redound to human honor and dignity, and which give order and harmony to the social world.

We have suggested that the health and prosperity of humankind depend upon the actualization of these capacities; that these capacities constitute humanity's intrinsic value; and that the protection and development of these capacities is the ultimate goal of all morally authentic relationships and all legitimate systems of community and governance. The development and protection of the human spirit thus serves as an appropriate focus for adjudicating the moral legitimacy of any human act, any social policy, or any cultural practice. For these reasons, it provides the essential focus for all human rights endeavors. In addition, over the course of the twentieth century, efforts to protect the human spirit have come to focus increasingly on the preservation of human dignity. One reason for this is a growing recognition that human dignity is tied inextricably to the capacities that animate the human spirit and its protection and development is the only sure way for advancing the prosperity of humankind in the fullest sense of the term (Nussbaum, 1998, 2000; Sen, 1999).

When we speak of human dignity, we are concerned with the dignity that goes hand in hand with being a human being. It was, of course, Immanuel Kant (1724–1804) who, in the eighteenth century, introduced in the clearest and most detailed terms the concept of intrinsic dignity. It would take more than two centuries, however, for this idea to find universal expression in humanity's political affairs. Prior to the twentieth century, the concept of dignity was largely tied to social address and was a matter of social permission. In the minds of the masses, human dignity was very much linked to hierarchy and was associated with ephemeral standards and socially constructed values – such as skin color, gender, degree of material culture, level of education, or religious affiliation.

At the end of the Second World War, as a consequence of the hubris and inhumanity of the Nazis, the concept of dignity began to center upon the inherent value of the human person – whatever his or her race, nationality, culture, creed, or station in life. Today, the "inherent worth of human beings" is the vocabulary that is customarily employed in human rights literature to capture the notion of human dignity. In other words, the notion of human dignity has become tied to the irreducible ontological status of each member of the human race. "All human beings are born free and equal in dignity and rights," affirms Article 1 of the *Universal Declaration of Human Rights*. "They are endowed with reason and conscience and should act towards one another in a spirit of brotherhood." *The International Covenant on Civil and Political Rights* requires that "all persons deprived of their liberty shall be treated with humanity and with respect for the inherent dignity of the human person" (Article 10); and the *International Covenant on Economic, Social, and Cultural Rights* prescribes that "education shall be directed to the full development of the human personality and the sense of its dignity" (Article 13). Further references, to the protection of human dignity, appear in a number of international covenants, transnational accords, and national constitutions.

References to Human Dignity Proliferate

Inasmuch as the preservation of human dignity is a prerequisite for safeguarding the healthy development of the human spirit, references to human dignity in official human rights documents have proliferated. A content analysis, undertaken by the current authors, of more than 100 human rights documents penned over the course of the last century, reveals more than a dozen ways that the concept of human dignity serves as a basis for advancing human rights claims. Protection of human dignity provides

(1) a standard for judging whether a practice (e.g., state-sponsored torture, capital punishment, and female genital mutilation) or a government policy (e.g., apartheid) ought to enjoy the support or incur the condemnation of the international community;

(2) a basis for condemning all forms of discrimination and a ground for state-sponsored responsibility to overcome the pernicious effects of particular doctrines (e.g., the doctrine of inherent racial, ethnic, or gender superiority);

(3) the logical foundation of equal treatment of all people – including equality of access to nutrition, health care, education, employment, self-determination, privacy, etc.;

(4) a basis for holding states responsible for the protection of cultural identity (e.g., the protection of a people's language and their right to use it);

(5) guiding principles for policies concerning the treatment of minorities, immigrants, and disadvantaged groups;

(6) a basis for regulation of the business sector against practices that assault the human spirit (e.g., human trafficking and sexual harassment);

(7) a rationale for special provisions for the protection of those whose circumstances may make it difficult for them to protect themselves (e.g., women and children in armed conflict, those held in detention, the mentally disabled, and the elderly);

(8) a rationale for defending standards for adjudicating the proper representation of groups in the media;

(9) a rationale for providing adequate health care to all persons – irrespective of their sexual orientation;

(10) justification for the condemnation of forced disappearance;

(11) a rationale for why prosecutors, law enforcement officials, and lawyers, as the essential agents of justice, must show respect for the human spirit;

(12) justification for the condemnation of humiliating and degrading treatment by agents acting on behalf of the state;

(13) the reason for having to give due consideration to the ethical legitimacy of biomedical procedures in the pursuit of scientific knowledge; and

(14) justification for honoring the right to privacy.

What is common to all of these usages is the recognition that human rights can be protected only when the moral conditions that are necessary for the development and expression of human capacities are preserved and the ethical standards that are required for the preservation of human dignity are respected.

An Overly Materialistic Focus in Human Rights and Development Discourse

Notwithstanding the recognition that the preservation of human dignity requires the protection of humanity's unique spiritual and intellectual capacities, as has been noted by Pargament (2002) and Pargament, Magyar-Russell, and Murray-Swank (2005), for most of the twentieth century academics, development workers, and human rights advocates have either ignored humanity's spiritual capacities and concerns, viewed them as pathological, or treated them as by-products of processes that can be reduced to more basic underlying psychological, social, and physiological functions. The Institute for Studies in Global Prosperity put the issue in the following way:

The assumptions directing most of current development planning are essentially materialistic. That is to say, the purpose of development is defined in terms of the successful cultivation in all societies of those means for the achievement of material prosperity that have, through trial and error, already come to characterize certain regions of the world. Modifications in development discourse do indeed occur, accommodating differences of culture and political system and responding to the alarming dangers posed by environmental degradation. Yet the underlying materialistic assumptions remain essentially unchallenged.

As the twentieth century draws to a close, it is no longer possible to maintain the belief that the approach to social and economic development to which the materialistic conception of life has given rise is capable of meeting humanity's needs. Optimistic forecasts about the changes it would generate have vanished into the ever-widening abyss that separates the living standards of a small and relatively diminishing minority of the world's inhabitants from the poverty experienced by the vast majority of the globe's population.

This unprecedented economic crisis, together with the social breakdown it has helped to engender, reflects a profound error of conception about human nature itself. For the levels of response elicited from human beings by the incentives of the prevailing order are not only inadequate, but seem almost irrelevant in the face of world events. We are being shown that, unless the development of society finds a purpose beyond the mere amelioration of material conditions, it will fail of attaining even these goals. (Bahá'í International Community Office of Public Information, 1995)

As has been noted by William Hatcher (1994), "to succeed, the human enterprise needs knowledge that is both true (accurate) and useful (for the satisfaction of human needs)." The twentieth century revealed an essential complementarity between the empirical and rational demands of science and the ethical conduct required of human beings if our relationships to one another and to nature are to secure life and promote development. At the heart of an approach that has begun to crystalize in the wake of the devastations of the last century is an ethical commitment to the oneness of the human race and the conviction that life and development are sustained by the creation and maintenance of unity within the context of diversity. In contrast to a wholly materialistic perspective, the emerging paradigm affords consideration of ethical and spiritual principles vital to any meaningful discourse on human needs and human rights. If they are to be comprehensive, if they are to escape the quagmire of superstition, and if they are to be universal in their appeal, these principles must be derived from an integration of knowledge obtained through empirical research, reasoned discourse, and the writings of the world's wisdom traditions – as they constitute the primary reservoir of humanity's ethico-spiritual heritage.

The tradition of human rights and development scholarship that is required for this new age must seek to harvest the greatest insights contained in all of the world's sacred, philosophical, and empirical traditions. Its epistemological outlook, its methodological openness, and its commitment to rendering scholarship a tool for the advancement of civilization are incompatible with parochial commitments to any particular ideological, methodological, or epistemological camp. We must be inspired by a vision of pragmatic scholarship and deep philosophical inquiry into the human condition that has begun to emerge in light of the pressing needs of the twenty-first century.

Human Dignity, The Human Spirit, and Human Rights

The protection of human dignity requires the recognition that each person possesses inherent value that is independent of any purpose that their labor, or their bodies, or even their minds may serve. Emmanuel Kant, David Velleman, and William Hatcher have each suggested that perception of another's intrinsic value, which is inherently linked to their dignity, is the basis for all genuine human relationships. In Velleman's view, a minimal perception of human dignity generates respect, while a maximal response to it evokes love. What respect and love have in common is that in both cases, the individual is seen as possessing inherent value and her goals and aspirations play important roles in determining the course of human affairs. In the realm of human rights law, such concern for another is embodied in the concern for justice.[6]

In his important essay, "Love and Barriers to Love," Raymond Bergner (2000) argues that the inability to perceive humans in all their uniqueness and dignity is the chief obstacle to love. In quoting Singer, Bergner writes that in true love, "The lover takes an interest in the beloved *as a person*, and not merely as a commodity." He goes further to note that "Love is a relationship in which, for the lover, the beloved is another person – is, in Martin Buber's terms, a "thou" and not an 'it.'" Loving involves what Martha Nussbaum calls *eudaimonistic* judgments: the judgment that something is valuable because it empowers a person to lead a good human life and the judgment that an individual is of intrinsic value. The claim is that another has value that does *not* depend on one's own personal goals and projects. In other words, another's value is not merely a matter of social utility. Nussbaum further claims that if it is to be ethical, an emotion that takes as its focus another human being must involve this dimension.

One may contrast this perspective with an appetite one might feel toward, say, food. Leaving aside consumption of animal products, for most of us, food does not have inherent value. Its only value is that it serves to keep us alive. My interest in food, for example, is only about *me*, nothing else. In Nussbaum's words,

---

[6]Justice regulates the expression of individual self-interests by requiring that the rights and needs of others be taken into consideration when determining a course of action. In this way, justice embodies the recognition of interdependence and makes community life possible. In the absence of justice, disunity, conflict and resentments are catalyzed and the social world becomes dangerous and unpredictable.

it is a *push*: there is something in *me* that requires fulfillment and food satisfies the criteria. There is a similarity here to Bergner's concept of the "imperialist role assigner" who "loves" others only insofar as they fulfill a personal need. No perception of intrinsic value exists, and this absence of real concern for the other insures a me-centered relationship. The global crisis in human trafficking, the exploitation of women and girls that is a common feature of the sex trade and pornographic industries, the high rates of violence perpetrated by governments in the pursuit of power, and the dehumanizing suffering that results from chronic poverty and unemployment in many parts of the world are among the social ills that reflect disregard for human dignity.

The significant development with respect to international human rights law is that the value of the human person can now be conceptualized in two different senses. First, human rights initiatives seek to protect the physical security and integrity of the human person by providing access to those political rights that would empower the community to protect itself from the tyranny of the state[7]; and second, thanks to second[8] and third[9] generations of human rights, as well as the pioneering work of Amartya Sen, Martha Nussbaum, Johannes Morsink, Jack Donnelly, and others, human rights aim, increasingly, to secure the identity of persons as persons.[10] Thus, we are coming to recognize that notwithstanding the power of international law to protect against assaults to the physical security and integrity of persons as members of specific groups, the dignity of humankind can be protected if, and only if, the cultivation of the capacities that distinguish and ennoble human life become the focus of our common striving as a species.

References

Prepared under the Auspices of the Universal House of Justice. (2001). *Century of light* (p. 1). Haifa, Isreal: Bahá'í World Centre.

Abramson, P., & Inglehart, R. F. (1995). *Value change in global perspective*. Ann Arbor, MI: University of Michigan.

Bahá'í International Community Office of Public Information. (1995). The prosperity of humankind. Retrieved from http://www.bahai.org/library/other-literature/official-statements-commentaries/prosperity-humankind/prosperity-humankind.pdf?7ae4cb9a

---

[7]Thus, human security, we argue, helps human beings realize human dignity.

[8]Speaking broadly, these rights seek to protect economic, social, and cultural rights.

[9]Broadly construed, third generation rights include rights to self-determination, the right to participate in one's culture, collective rights, communication rights, the right to a healthy environment, and so forth.

[10]At the same time, however, it is important to take note of the fact that within international law, the designation of what constitutes a people is inchoate. Except for the 1970 "Friendly Relations Declaration" legal definitions of peoples have been few and far between. This has created some conceptual issues in delineating collective standards for the protection of human dignity.

Bellah, R. N., & Joas, H. (Eds.). (2012). *The axial age and its consequences.* Cambridge, MA: Harvard University Press.

Bergner, R. (2000). Love and barriers to love. *American Journal of Psychotherapy, 54*(1, Winter), 1–17.

Danieli, Y., Stamatopoulou, E., & Dias, C. (Eds.). (1999). *The universal declaration of human rights: Fifty years and beyond.* New York, NY: Baywood.

Fukuyama, R. (1992). *The end of history and the last man.* New York, NY: Free Press.

Garwin, L., Lincoln, T., & Weinberg, S. (2003). *A century of nature: Twenty-one discoveries that changed science and the world.* Chicago, IL: University of Chicago.

Glendon, M. A. (2001). *A world made new: Eleanor Roosevelt and the universal declaration of human rights.* New York, NY: Random House.

Hatcher, W. S. (1994). *Minimalism: A bridge between classical philosophy and the Bahá'í revelation (p. 10).* London: Juxta.

Henn, B. M., et al. (2011). Hunter-gatherer genomic diversity suggests a southern African origin for modern humans. *Proceedings of the National Academy of Sciences of the United States of America, 10*(13), 5154–5162

Jaspers, K. (1953). *The origin and goal of history* (p. 2). New Haven, CT: Yale University Press.

Mandelbaum, M. (2007). Democracy without America: The spontaneous spread of freedom. *Foreign Affairs, 86*(5), 119–130.

Manica, A., Amos, B., Balloux, F., & Hanihara, T. (2007). The effect of ancient population bottlenecks on human phenotypic variation. *Nature, 448*(7151), 346–348.

Nussbaum, M. (1998). *Cultivating humanity: A classical defense of reform in liberal education.* Cambridge, MA: Harvard University Press.

Nussbaum, M. (2000). *Women and human development: The capabilities approach.* Cambridge: Cambridge University Press.

Pargament, K. (2002). Is religion nothing but …? Explaining religion versus explaining religion away. *Psychological Inquiry, 13*, 239–244.

Pargament, K., Magyar-Russell, G. M., & Murray-Swank, N. A. (2005). The sacred and the search for significance: Religion as a unique process. *Journal of Social Issues, 61*, 665–687.

Penn, M. L., & Malik, A. (2010). The protection and development of the human spirit: An expanded focus for human rights discourse. *Human Rights Quarterly, 32*, 665–388.

Schwartz, S. H., & Bilsky, W. (1987). Toward a universal psychological structure of human values. *Journal of Personality and Social Psychology, 53*(3), 550–562.

Sen, A. (1999). *Development as freedom.* Oxford: Oxford University Press.

Stringer, C., & McKie, R. (1996). *African exodus: The origins of modern humanity.* New York, NY: Henry Holt.

Chapter 5

How Does Dignity Ground Human Rights?

Jack Donnelly

Introduction

Human dignity is the foundational concept of the global human rights regime. As the *Universal Declaration of Human Rights* (1948) puts it,

> recognition of the inherent dignity and of the equal and in alien-
> able rights of all members of the human family is the foundation
> of freedom, justice and peace in the world.[1]

In addition, the 1966 *International Covenant on Civil and Political Rights* pro-
claims, "these rights derive from the inherent dignity of the human person."[2] The
Vienna Declaration of the 1993, World Human Rights Conference likewise affirms:
"all human rights derive from the dignity and worth inherent in the human
person."[3]

But "the framers of the international instruments did not define human dignity ... [n]or were they precise about the relationship between human rights and
human dignity" (Beyleveld & Brownsword, 2001; Henkin, 1992, Schachter, 1983).
This chapter argues that the absence of a definition of human dignity is largely
unproblematic given the nature of the linkage of human dignity and human
rights. This is explained in terms of John Rawls' notion of an overlapping consensus on a political conception of justice.

---

[1]First perambulatory paragraph. See also Articles 22 and 23.
[2]Second perambulatory paragraph. See also first perambulatory paragraph; *International Covenant on Economic and Social Rights*, Article 13 and *International Covenant
on Civil and Political Rights*, Article 10).
[3]Second perambulatory paragraph. See also paragraphs I.11.3, 18.2, 20, and 25. For
an overview of other international and regional legal instruments, see McCrudden
(2008).

Interdisciplinary Perspectives on Human Dignity and Human Rights, 61–67
Copyright © 2020 by Emerald Publishing Limited
All rights of reproduction in any form reserved
doi:10.1108/978-1-78973-821-620191006

Defining Human Dignity

The Webster's Dictionary (2005, 324) identifies six principal senses of the noun "dignity":

(1) The quality or condition of being esteemed, honored, or worthy.
(2) a. Self-esteem and poise b. Stately reserve in appearance and demeanor.
(3) The respect and honor associated with an important position.
(4) A high rank or office.[4]

Philosophical inquiries with an historical perspective typically produce similar lists. For example, Michael Rosen (2012) identifies three principal senses: "a valuable characteristic ... high social status ... [and] behavior with a respect-worthy character" (compare Meyer, 2002).

These senses suggest a core meaning of *worth that demands respect*. Different conceptions, accounts, or theories of dignity give a particular substance to the idea of worth that demands respect by, for example, specifying what counts as gravity or excellence, gives one worth, or is associated with high esteem.

A substantive conception of dignity must specify, at a minimum:

(a) the subjects of dignity (the types of entities that have worth that demands respect);
(b) the sources of dignity (what gives rise to that worth); and
(c) the form(s) of respect due to dignity.

Human dignity is the dignity that arises simply from being human – much as human rights are the rights one has simply because one is human. Nonhumans have dignity. And humans may have a dignity that is not rooted in their humanity. But human dignity, our topic here, is about the worth that humans have, as humans, and the respect due to that worth.

In contemporary understandings, the respect due to humans is largely specified in terms of human rights. In previous eras, other forms of respect, such as high status or rank, were seen as appropriate recognition of dignity. In fact, dignity originated as an attribute of an aristocratic elite. Today, however, all human beings (defined as members of the species *Homo sapiens*) are usually held to have. And all human beings usually are understood to be entitled to all human rights – which are somehow rooted in that dignity.

How, though, does human dignity thus understood give rise to human rights?

---

[4]The other four senses are astrological, canonical (and obsolete), algebraic (and obsolete), and an erroneous or fantastic rendering of the Greek *axioma*. *Dignité* in French has much the same senses. *"1. Valeur éminente, excellence qui doit commander le respect ... 2. Attitude de réserve et de fierté, inspirée par le respect de soi-même...Gravité noble qui inspire la considération, commande le respect, les égards ... 3. Fonction ou distinction qui confère un rang éminent dans la société"* (*Dictionaire de l'Académie Française*).

Linking Human Dignity and Human Rights

"Human dignity" is sometimes presented as a hopelessly vague notion that merely appears to provide a deeper foundation. "The concept of dignity is itself vacuous ... the term is so elusive as to be virtually meaningless" (Bagaric & James, 2006). "The concept of human dignity ... has different senses and often points us in opposite directions" (Davis, 2007). "Dignity is a fuzzy concept, and appeals to dignity are often used to substitute for empirical evidence that is lacking or sound arguments that cannot be mustered" (Chalmers & Ida, 2007; quoting Macklin, 2002). Some uses of human dignity do indeed lack clear substance. This, however, is accidental. We thus need to consider the two other conceptions that are prominent in the contemporary literature.

Human dignity is often presented as rooted in some particular characteristic. For example, Alan Gewirth (1992), argues that it is "constituted by certain intrinsically valuable aspects of being human." Reason and autonomy are frequently mentioned characteristics. Christians often root the dignity of humans in their creation in the image of God.

The leading alternative to this "essential attributes" approach sees as "foundational, declaratory, and undefined" (Beyleveld & Brownsword, 1998); and "a sort of axiom in the system or ... a familiar and accepted principle of shared morality" (Harris & Sulston, 2004); and "a bedrock concept that resists definition in terms of something else" (Weisstub, 2002). For example, Klaus Dicke (2002) presents human dignity in the *Universal Declaration* as "a formal, transcendental norm" or "a formal background value." Joel Feinberg (1973) suggests that attributing human dignity involves "expressing an attitude – the attitude of respect – toward the humanity in each man's person" (compare Parent, 1992).

This chapter argues, however, that human dignity is neither an unanalyzable "Ur-principle" (Witte, 2003) nor grounded in any particular set of attributes. Human dignity instead functions as an intermediate concept that links human rights to what John Rawls calls comprehensive doctrines through the mechanism of an overlapping consensus.

An Overlapping Consensus Approach

Rawls distinguishes between comprehensive doctrines – foundational moral or religious systems of thought or worldviews – and political conceptions of justice, or roughly "constitutional" principles of political legitimacy. He argues that in liberal democracies, people with very different, and even incompatible, foundational moral, or religious beliefs can and do support a single constitutional regime for more than instrumental reasons as a result of an overlapping consensus on that political conception of justice (Rawls, 1996).

Such a consensus is overlapping, rather than complete. It is consensus only on a *political* conception of justice, but it gives that political conception deep (multiple) moral or religious foundations. A political conception of justice thus justified is more than a *modus vivendi* or a merely instrumentally justified agreement to further the self-interest of the participants. It is a morally grounded conception of justice.

Elsewhere I have argued for extending this analysis to international human rights (Donnelly, 2013), understanding human rights as a political conception of justice around which an international overlapping consensus has formed over the past half century. Here, I want to extend the same analysis one level deeper. Human dignity is not truly foundational but more like a political conception of justice. Different comprehensive doctrines provide different accounts of human dignity that are sufficiently convergent to allow human dignity to serve as a shared quasi-foundation for human rights.[5]

This analysis supports Jeremy Waldron's (2012) strategy of starting to discuss human dignity with law rather than morality – *in a discussion focused on human rights*. Human rights, as I have argued elsewhere, are not foundational moral principles; they are a category of political and legal, not moral, theory (Donnelly, 2013, pp. 60–62). This, I am in effect suggesting, is how international human rights law treats human dignity: as a Rawlsian political conception of justice that points toward a *range* of underlying moral or religious conceptions.[6]

This two-step process limits the scope of acceptable "foundational" arguments. They must lead to human rights through the bridge of a universalistic and egalitarian conception of human dignity. But *any* comprehensive doctrine that works "up" to the rights of the *Universal Declaration* through universal human dignity is entitled to a full and equal "seat at the table" in international discussions of human rights. Some broadly defined but not empty conceptions of human dignity underlie, and thus help to shape, contemporary conceptions of human rights. In practice, pretty much any universalistic and egalitarian comprehensive doctrine can be made compatible with human rights – although such doctrines (e.g., Christianity) have often been understood and interpreted in ways fundamentally incompatible with human rights.

Internationally recognized human rights have no singular foundation; they have foundations. They thus are normatively, not just instrumentally, justified – but in multiple ways. And the web of multiple foundations is far stronger than any single foundation could be, given the extent of international disagreement over foundational doctrines (or the thinness of a lowest common denominator conception).

---

[5]Compare David Weisstub's suggestion that dignity "has emerged as a convergence point for what is perceived to be a non-ideological humanistic point of departure towards a social liberal ideal." (Dignity, however, can be a religious concept. An overlapping consensus account allows us to set aside the controversy between religious and secular/humanistic foundations because this disagreement doesn't matter for the purposes of agreement on human rights and human dignity.)

[6]Drawing a distinction between "thin" and "thick" conceptions of dignity points in much the same direction. Overlapping consensus, however, emphasizes the simultaneous presence of multiple converging thick accounts of the thinly specified notion of human dignity in international human rights law.

This account supports David Weisstub's (2002, p. 269) claim that "although ambiguous, dignity is a signaling term that goes to the heart of what constitutes the quality of humanness." That ambiguity, however, arises from neither lack of clarity nor the absence of deeper substantive foundations. Rather, it reflects the fact that for different individuals, traditions, and communities, human dignity points to different deeper foundations (which remove much of the ambiguity from the concept).

This, I believe, helps to explain the fact that "the dignity of the individual is a cliché, yet it retains surprising force" (Tinder, 2003; compare Witte, 2003, p. 121). Human dignity, however, is not *simply* a cliché, because of the deeper foundation in an overlapping consensus of comprehensive doctrines.

An overlapping consensus account also removes any element of irony or suggestion of insufficiently penetrating analysis in Jacques Maritain's often-quoted observation that, at the end of an extended cross-cultural exploration of the roots of human rights, "we agree about the rights, *but on condition that no one asks us why*" (UNESCO, 1948). The agreement is on the rights rather than their foundations. And certain kinds of disagreements on foundations are no serious impediment to agreement on human rights.

I thus concur with Jeff Malpas and Norelle Lickiss that "the breadth of the concept, its ubiquity ... and the difficulty of giving it a clear and unambiguous definition, all point towards its absolutely fundamental character." But fundamental, I have suggested, does not mean foundational in any strong sense of that term. I also agree with Malpas and Lickiss (2007) that "dignity connects up with too many other concepts, and in too many ways, for it to be amenable to any simple rendering." I further suggest, though, that this is because there are *multiple* renderings.

Four Concluding Observations

First, one of the great attractions of an overlapping consensus approach is that it emphasizes diversity and dialog among civilizations, cultures, religions, worldviews, and regions. It also provides an account of universality that is not merely compatible with but actively open to substantial localization in interpreting and implementing universal human rights.[7]

Second, the link between human dignity and human rights is increasingly normative. Human dignity is not logically connected to human rights. One *can* think of human dignity independently of human rights. In fact, the concept of human dignity originally emerged largely separate from the idea of human rights. (Kant, e.g., discusses the notion in the context of duties to oneself.) That, however, is becoming increasingly difficult and infrequent.

Third, the contemporary linkage between human dignity and human rights runs in both directions; human dignity and human rights have become mutually

---

[7]I develop such an understanding of the universality of internationally recognized human rights in (Donnelly, 2013, chapters 6 and 7).

co-constitutive. A list of human rights, rooted in the idea of human dignity, specifies particular minimum preconditions for a life of dignity in the contemporary world – and then these rights shape our understanding of human dignity. (A dignified life requires enjoyment of internationally recognized human rights, which in large measure specify the details of a life of dignity.)

Finally, human rights go beyond the *inherent* dignity of the human person to provide mechanisms for realizing a *life of dignity*. Human rights both specify forms of life that are worthy of beings with inherent moral worth and provide legal and political practices to realize a life that vindicates that worth. Individuals, groups, and societies across the globe today, drawing on a great variety of historical, cultural, and material resources, are grappling with the threats and opportunities provided by modern social life as they try, by claiming and practicing human rights, to make for themselves lives worthy of dignified human beings. And the linkage of universal human dignity to universal human rights is a powerful normative resource in these struggles.

References

Bagaric, M., & James, A. (2006). The vacuous concept of dignity. *Journal of Human Rights*, *5*(2), 257–270.

Beyleveld, D., & Brownsword, R. (1998). Human dignity, human rights, and human genetics. *Modern Law Review*, *61*(5), 663 and 797.

Beyleveld, D., & Brownsword, R. (2001). *Human dignity in bioethics and biolaw* (p. 11 and 21) Oxford: Oxford University Press.

Chalmers, D., & Ida, R. (2007). On the international legal aspects of human dignity. In J. Malpas & N. Lickiss (Eds.), *Perspectives on human dignity: A conversation* (p. 158). J. Dordrecht, The Netherlands: Springer.

Davis, J. (2007). Doing justice to dignity in the criminal law. In J. Malpas & N. Lickiss (Eds.), *Perspectives on human dignity: A conversation* (p. 177). Dordrecht, The Netherlands: Springer.

Dicke, K. (2002). The founding function of human dignity in the universal declaration of human rights. In D. Kretzmer & E. Klein (Eds.), *The concept of human dignity in human rights discourse* (p. 118 and 120). The Hague, The Netherlands: Kluwer Law International.

Donnelly, J. (2013). *Universal human rights in theory and practice* (3rd ed., pp. 57–60 and 69–71). Ithaca, NY: Cornell University Press.

Feinberg, J. (1973). *Social philosophy* (p. 94). Englewood Cliffs, NJ: Prentice-Hall.

Gewirth, A. (1992). Human dignity as the basis of rights. In M. J. Meyer & W. A. Parent (Eds.), *The constitution of rights: Human dignity and american values* (p. 12). Ithaca, NY: Cornell University Press.

Harris, J., & Sulston, J. (2004). Genetic equity. *Nature Reviews. Genetics*, *5*(10), 797.

Henkin, L. (1992). Human dignity and constitutional rights. In M. J. Meyer & W. A. Parent (Eds.), *The constitution of rights: Human dignity and American values* (p. 211). Ithaca, NY: Cornell University Press.

Macklin, R. (2002). Cloning and public policy. In J. Burley & J. Harris (Eds.), *A companion to genetics* (p. 212). Oxford: Blackwell.

Malpas, J., & Lickiss, N. (2007). Introduction to a conversation. In J. Malpas & N. Lickiss (Eds.), *Perspectives on human dignity: a conversation* (p. 1). Dordrecht, The Netherlands: Springer.

McCrudden, C. (2008). Human dignity and judicial interpretation of human rights. *European Journal of International Law*, *19*(4), 664–675.

Meyer, M. J. (2002). Dignity as a (modern) virtue. In D. Kretzmer & E. Klein (Eds.), *The concept of human dignity in human rights discourse* (pp. 196–197). The Hague, The Netherlands: Kluwer Law International.

Parent, W. A. (1992). Constitutional values and human dignity. In M. J. Meyer & W. A. Parent (Eds.), *The constitution of rights: human dignity and American values* (p. 64). Ithaca, NY: Cornell University Press.

Rawls, J. (1996). *Political liberalism* (pp. 11–15, 39, 75, and 144–154). New York, NY: Columbia University Press.

Rosen, M. (2012). *Dignity: Its history and meaning* (p. 16). Cambridge, MA: Harvard University Press.

Schachter, O. (1983). Human dignity as a normative concept. *American Journal of International Law*, *77*(4), 849.

Tinder, G. (2003). Facets of personal dignity. In R. P. Kraynak & G. Tinder (Eds.), *In defense of human dignity: Essays for our times* (p. 238). Notre Dame, France: University of Notre Dame Press.

UNESCO. (1948). *Human rights: Comments and interpretations, UNESCO PHS/3 (rev.)* (p. i). Paris: UNESCO.

Waldron, J., & Dan-Cohen, M. (Eds.), (2012). *Dignity, rank, and rights. The Berkeley Tanner lectures* (pp. 212–213 and 227–232). Oxford: Oxford University Press (Kindle locations).

Webster's II New College Dictionary. (3rd Edition). (2005). Boston, MA: Houghton Mifflin.

Weisstub, D. N. (2002). Honor, dignity, and the framing of multiculturalist values. In D. Kretzmer & E. Klein (Eds.), *The concept of human dignity in human rights discourse* (p. 2). The Hague, The Netherlands: Kluwer Law International.

Witte, J., Jr. (2003). Between sanctity and depravity: Human dignity in protestant perspective. In R. P. Kraynak & G. Tinder (Eds.). *In defense of human dignity: Essays for our times* (p. 119). Notre Dame, France: University of Notre Dame Press.

Section Two

Practice/Action

Chapter 6

Honor-based Violence in Pakistan and Its Eradication through the Development of Cultural and Jurisprudential Ethos of Human Dignity

Sania Anwar

Introduction

On average, one in every five homicides in Pakistan is an honor killing (T. Miller, 2009). Each day, at least two women are murdered by a member of their family in the name of honor. These murders are usually based on mere accusations.[1] The prevalence of the practice is deeply rooted in the cultural concept of "woman as a commodity," which rationalizes the killing of a female relative for marrying or wanting to marry a man of her choice, for refusing to marry a man of her family's choice, for seeking divorce, or for engaging in alleged illicit acts or relationships. In some cases, the conscious decision or subjective intent to engage in dishonorable behavior is not a prerequisite: women are sometimes killed after being raped since the rape constitutes pre-marital or extra-marital sex and, therefore, violates family honor (Nosheen & Schellman, 2011). Victims of honor killings are stoned, shot, burned, or buried alive, hacked to pieces with axes, or left to bleed out after brutal assault. In this chapter, the murdered or surviving victims are referred to as honor-transgressors.

In Pakistan, the concept of social honor is deeply rooted and upheld by two cultural processes: psycho-cultural forces – which include attitudes, beliefs, and values that provide the structures of consciousness that legitimize honor-related violence; and socio-structural forces – which include political, religious, and economic structures of authority that legitimize gender-based violence that has as its presumed purpose the preservation of family honor (Johnson & Karlberg, 2006;

---

[1]Human Rights Commission of Pakistan, State of Human Rights in 2015 (2016). Approximately 1,100 women were killed in Pakistan in 2015 by relatives on so-called honor grounds.

Interdisciplinary Perspectives on Human Dignity and Human Rights, 71–102
Copyright © 2020 by Emerald Publishing Limited
All rights of reproduction in any form reserved
doi:10.1108/978-1-78973-821-620191012

see also Ross, 2006, pp. 19–20). Internalization of gender-based oppression is thus best understood within a conceptual framework that explains how psycho-cultural and socio-structural forces are intertwined in the practice of honor killings. From such a perspective, an analysis of the "free will" of women (Higgins, 1996),[2] and perhaps even of many men, to engage in or legitimize honor killings becomes complex (Bertelsen, 2005, pp. 122–123).[3]

Through internalized oppression, many women in Pakistan not only endorse but also facilitate honor killings.[4] The deep cultural roots of the practice attract female support for it in the same way that the practice of female genital mutilation summons to its defense the voices of many powerful women (Benedek, Kisaakye, & Oberleitner, 2002, p. 271).[5] Those who resist condemnation of honor killing claim that it cannot be thought of as a violation of women's rights when it is supported and carried out by the members of the protected class itself. This chapter seeks to analyze the nature of the internalizing processes that sustain societal acceptance of honor as justification for violent acts against women.

We begin by describing the communitarian, collectivistic, and honor culture of Pakistan, which places a strong emphasis on the avoidance of shame. We then show that in such an environment, men defend honor through violence that is motivated largely by guilt, while women justify it as a defense against shame. Both men and women are thus trapped within a "shame culture" that conceals female sexuality by attempting to control or de-emphasize it. This analysis will focus largely on the psycho-social forces that discourage women from taking a stand against honor-based violence. The discussion illustrates how emotional and psycho-social responses that justify honor killings are reinforced by a number of

---

[2]"The question still remains as to how feminists can reconcile the possibility of internalized oppression, or false consciousness, with the anti-essentialist rejection of any core of womanhood, or true consciousness."

[3]"For the behaviour of a subject to be considered the product of free will, therefore, it is sufficient, according to soft determinism, that the subject's entire functional apparatus, including the psyche, has not been thwarted by any external or internal forces in performing its function: namely, to behave in the way that is optimal for that subject in a given situation."

[4]A high profile incident that highlighted internalized oppression in honor killings was the murder of Samia Sarwar. On April 6, 1999, 29-year old Samia, a law student and mother of two, was shot to death in her lawyer's office in Lahore for seeking a divorce from her abusive husband. Samia's mother was a doctor and her father was the president of the Chamber of Commerce in North-West Frontier Province in Pakistan. During a meeting between Samia and her lawyer, her mother barged in the office accompanied by a contract killer who pulled out a gun and shot Samia in the head (see Ali, 2001).

[5]"Traditionally the FGM procedure was performed by women, a role either inherited or learned from a relative. In the Gambia, the procedure is performed by a woman, the N'gasimba, who is highly respected and believed to possess supernatural powers. In some communities, performing this role brings respect to women who originate from poor families and ethnic groups that are otherwise regarded as inferior."

political, legal, and religious factors at play in Pakistani society, including procedural injustices inherent in Pakistan's Sharia law, public shame sanctions, and the increasing anti-Western social and political fervor.

Based on the analysis of social, psychological, religious, political, and legal factors that come together to produce a culture that justifies honor killings, we outline recommendations for addressing these dynamics. The argument here is that Pakistan's women's rights movement must undergo significant reconceptualization if it is to combat societal internalization of destructive gender norms. This process of reconstruction must have two objectives: to build an effective autochthonous movement by advocating for change from within existing institutional frameworks and to enhance the representation of women leaders within the country.

Finally, we close by outlining the most effective means to minimize internalization of social honor and the consequential gender-based violence – the development of a counter-culture of human dignity, which is neither an attribute of one's social rank nor an attribute of one's conformity to the societal honor code, but is grounded in the equal and inherent worth of all human beings. This chapter advocates the idea that human dignity, wherever it may be found, has, at its core, universalistic "minimum content" based on the intrinsic value of all human beings. However, despite the pluralistic "minimum content" of human dignity, the vehicles for developing human dignity as a value require customized frames for different cultures. Postulating a workable definition of human dignity for Pakistan requires that it be anchored in established Islamic sources that safeguard personal integrity and freedom from coercion. The key in renovating Sharia law in Pakistan would be to develop the least restrictive legal procedures and principles that promote human dignity without imposing intolerant majoritarian norms. A successful outcome of such a model can establish the potential for a pragmatic evolutionary trend in Sharia law as a microprocessor for transnational discourse on human dignity.

Factual basis of Honor Killings

Common justifications for the practice of honor killings include a range of acts or omissions by women that can be perceived as infringement on a man's or a family's honor. Such acts include defiance of social and sexual norms, pursuing a marriage or relationship of choice, seeking a divorce, or suffering a rape. To a large extent, the factual basis for an honor killing is largely socially irrelevant, as the killing is simply legitimized by a declaration of an honor violation by any male relative. Dishonor resulting from mere assertion of defiance of social norms, regardless of its validity, is sufficient. The alleged nonconformity with social norms can be based on superficial and frivolous grounds (Amnesty International, 2002).[6] Inflicting death as punishment for a dishonorable action is not an exclusive prerogative

---

[6]A man killed his wife alleging she took too long to serve him a meal and another man murdered his wife after he had a dream that she had been unfaithful.

of the honor-transgressor's husband or father, but rather is transferable to any male in the family.

A woman's identity is tied, by law, to her relationship with a male family member.[7] As a result, a woman's behavior must always conform to an established code of conduct, and actual or perceived failure to do so results in forfeiture of her right to protection within the family.

Another force driving the growth of honor killings in Pakistan is referred to as the "Honor Killing Industry" (Amnesty International, 1999). In situations involving honor violations, if only the *kari* ("blackened woman," this term refers to the woman who has brought dishonor) is killed and the *karo* ("blackened man," which refers to the man who may be involved in the dishonorable act) escapes, as is often the case, if his life is to be spared, the *karo* has to compensate those whose honor has been stained, which is usually the *kari's* husband, brother, or father (Amnesty International, 1999). This arrangement creates perverse financial incentives to assert false allegations of dishonor (Ali, 2001, pp. 12–13)[8] as many men are willing to fabricate dishonor in order to secure compensation. At times, the compensation may also be in the form of a new wife, provided by and from within the *karo's* family, especially when his family lacks monetary resources (Amnesty International, 1999).[9]

In this regard, it should be noted from the outset that the current discussion deals with the "genuine" perceptions of honor and shame when they are applied to justify honor crimes. Therefore, it addresses the emotions and beliefs that are active when social actors subjectively believe that honor or shame justifies the violence. These emotions are arguably absent in the context of the honor killing industry, which fabricates honor infringements by women for monetary gains.

The Pakistani Culture

Culture can be defined as "the shared assumptions, values, and beliefs of a group of people which result in characteristic behaviors" (Storti, 1998, p. 5). The study of value patterns within a culture asserts that while everyone within a

---

[7]See "National Identity Card for Overseas Pakistanis, Consulate General of Pakistan, New York. Retrieved from http://pakistanconsulateny.org/index.php?section=Nadra_nicop_dob.html. Accessed on August 24, 2012. Requirements include name of the "head of the family" on the National Identity Card, a mandatory identification card for all Pakistanis, and defining "head of the family" as "the father if applicant is unmarried and the husband i[f] applicant is married."

[8]Citing the example of the murder of a seventy-nine-year old woman in Ghauspur: one of her relatives owed seventy-five thousand rupees to another man. The relative simply shot her dead and accused the debtor of being her lover. The debt was settled almost immediately after the murder.

[9]"[A] man reportedly vouched for his wife's innocence after she had been attacked by his brother who alleged that she was guilty of an illicit relationship. The husband took her . . . for treatment but when told that she would be permanently paralyzed from the waist down, he reneged, declared her a kari and took a woman in compensation from the karo's family."

particular group will not share the same values, a majority of individuals within that group will conform to similar values, thereby creating the "dominant culture" (Gold, 2005; citing Bennett, 1998, pp. 157–158).

It is especially challenging to describe Pakistani culture because a variety of conflicting political, provincial, tribal, social, and religious identities coexist (Castetter, 2003).[10] There are numerous sub-cultures within Pakistani society that conceptualize honor in different ways. Honor killings are committed in urban, tribal, and rural communities. This chapter acknowledges the diverse social conditions under which honor killings occur in Pakistan but will be focused on the dynamics of the rural communities because of their pronounced societal role in perpetuation of patriarchy in Pakistani culture. Rural Pakistan also shares its dominating collectivistic/communitarian- and honor/shame-based values with most of Pakistani sub-cultures, such as in the urban, tribal, and the *Pashtun*-majority areas.[11] In addition, the analysis of cultural and emotional conditioning of rural men and women presented in this chapter can be applied to most of the sub-cultures.

Compared to most urbanites, people in rural areas have less access to education and the roles of men and women are more rigidly drawn. A kind of feudal culture predominates, and although it lacks tribal *jirgahs,* or assemblies of tribal elders exercising judicial functions, feudal lords, referred to as *waderos,* may perform functions similar to the *jirgahs.* Some women work with the men in the fields but are otherwise confined to their domestic roles and boundaries. Religion plays a prominent role and local *imams,* or religious clerics, enjoy a high status and influence within the community.[12]

Individualistic or collectivist dimensions of cultural value patterns describe the relationship between the individual and larger society (Gold, 2005, p. 296). In an individualistic culture, the needs of the individual come before those of the group,

---

[10]"The notion of national identity or loyalty has little value to the Pakistani citizens. Ethnic, regional, caste, and family loyalties factor more in society than the national loyalty .... [S]ociety has disintegrated into a collection of individual and tribes where the lawlessness further reinforces the tribal loyalties."

[11]Pashtun are an ethno-linguistic group primarily in Afghanistan and northwestern parts of Pakistan. See "Pashtun," Countries and Their Cultures. Retrieved from http://www.everyculture.com/wc/Afghanistan-to-Bosnia-Herzegovina/Pashtun.html. Accessed on August 24, 2012. This website describes Pashtuns as traditionally pastoral nomads or herders with a strong tribal organization.

[12]"Imam," Looklex encyclopedia. Retrieved from http://lexicorient.com/e.o/imam.htm. Accessed on September 3, 2012.

> The congregational prayer performed in the mosque is supposed to have a leader, and this person is called "imam" .... In [theory] it is the most learned and most respected person in the assembly who is offered the honour of being imam. However, in modern times, many mosques have made their imam into something more: an employed leader of the congregation, a counterpart of a priest, nothing less.

These Imams often have little familiarity with Islamic scholarship or established sources of religious authority.

individual identity is more important than group identity, individual rights are more important than group rights, and important values include self-sufficiency, autonomy, and personal freedom (Gold, 2005). In a collectivist culture, by contrast, identity is tied to a primary group, usually the family, and the overarching belief is that the survival of the group will ensure each member's survival because the success of the group benefits the individual. Therefore, interactions within a collectivist culture are based on promoting the significance of "ingroups," with prominent perception of a common fate and a shared emphasis on loyalty within the group. Those who are not part of "ingroups" are perceived as unequal, distant, or even threatening (Gold, 2005). The social response to deviants from societal norms differs in individualist versus collectivist cultures. Individualistic cultures tend to focus on guilt, which is a moral emotion centered in the individual, while shame is paramount in collectivist societies because moral violations reflect on the status of the larger group (Gold, 2005, p. 297).

Pakistani culture embodies the values of collectivism and communitarianism. In such cultures, an individual's identity is derived from the community itself and is dependent on the community's evaluation and perceptions. In communitarian societies, the ideal way of life and the roles associated with it are already given; the task of the individual is to live up to them and the guiding moral principle is to achieve excellence in discharging the roles for which one is responsible (Slaughter, 1993). The reward is the honor and respect of others, and moral identity is grounded in this reward (Slaughter, 1993). The philosophical principles that animate the communitarian idea may be traced to the German philosopher, Hegel, who argued that the self can gain its own identity only through recognition of another, and that by recognizing itself in another, the self recognizes itself as an "I" (Slaughter, 1993).[13] Charles Cooley's concept of "the looking glass self" developed this Hegelian insight and held that identity is dependent on reputation or image in the eyes of the community, and thus, within a communitarian system, the self is driven between honor and shame (Slaughter, 1993).[14]

In Pakistan's collectivist/communitarian culture, non-conformist acts threaten the harmony of the group and are viewed as disrespectful (Elmer, 2002, p. 136).[15] Each individual is expected to act in accordance with the expectations of the group, and his or her own desires are subordinated to the groups (Elmer, 2002). This position is based on a communitarian vision of the person in which

---

[13]"The other is literally constitutive of self. Sittlichkeit, or community nomos, provides the conditions for personhood: the ideal life is one in which communal norms and ends are the ones by which individuals define themselves. For Hegel, the community and the self are reconciled in the "I" that is "We" and "We" that is "I.""

[14]"Because people are necessarily motivated to maintain close social bonds with each other, they continually monitor how they are perceived and regarded by others. They see their own self-image as if through a looking glass and imagine how that image is perceived by others. This process is continuous and evaluative, and indicates whether social bonds are forged or broken."

[15]"Because each person belongs to the community, the community values and traditions must be lived out in each member."

"religion, tradition, and culture – particularly the culture of honor – is constitutive of personal identity" (Slaughter, 1993, p. 185). Therefore, for Pakistani men and women, honor and shame are fundamental to social existence and to lose one's honor is to lose one's personhood (Slaughter, 1993, p. 191). Reputation as honor defines the

> social images associated with a hierarchical status society … the very existence of the self is in the hands (or eyes) of the community, and hence the only possible social life is one that is dependent on good name and repute. (Slaughter, 1993)

The bond between self-identification and the community shows that the stronger the communitarian orientation, the more reputation is integral to identity, and the greater the damage when reputation is injured (Slaughter, 1993, p. 192). Therefore, due to the incontrovertibly strong communitarian orientation in the Pakistani culture, honor must be protected and, when lost, must be repaired at all costs (Slaughter, 1993, p. 193).

A Culture of Interdependence

Scholars have distinguished between two broad sets of tendencies people have in social life: independence and interdependence. "Independence" refers to a set of tasks or psychological tendencies to separate the self from the social context; it encompasses goals of agency, autonomy, and disengagement from others (Tangney & Fischer, 1995, p. 443). "Interdependence," on the other hand, "refers to a set of tasks or psychological tendencies to connect the self with others …" (Tangney & Fischer, 1995) Pakistan's communitarian and honor-based society expects and enforces strict conformity to community norms. Therefore, interdependence, rather than independence, is characteristic of this culture (Elmer, 2002, p. 136). Psychologists and cultural anthropologists who study cultures and societies similar to Pakistan's have determined that the "major normative task of the self [in such cultures] is to maintain the sense of interdependence among individuals – or, more specifically, to adjust to and fit into important relationships, to occupy one's proper place," and to engage in appropriate actions (Tangney & Fischer, 1995, p. 443) Within an interdependent view of self, individuals strive to meet duties, obligations, and social responsibilities (Tangney & Fischer, 1995). Pakistani men and women are thus acutely cognizant of their pre-determined and intractable societal duties and obligations, which are rigidly drawn in order to maintain the predictability and stability of social relationships.

In describing the dynamics at play in interdependent cultures, psychologists compare the manifestation of "self-esteem" as it may exist in these cultures, to its significant and prominent role in independence-preferring cultures. According to one theory, just as "self-esteem" is central to the affirmation of identity of the self as independent, "'esteem' or satisfaction with one's social relationships may be pivotal to the affirmation of the identity of the self as interdependent" (Tangney & Fischer, 1995, p. 454). Thus, among interdependent cultures, self-esteem may be less central in constructing the self: the interdependent selves are more likely to use interpretation of expectations held by relevant others in evaluating their own performance or behavior and, consequently, their success or failure (Tangney & Fischer, 1995, pp. 454–455).

This framework for understanding the role of self-esteem and social esteem can be applied to the psychological dilemma faced by Pakistani women. Not only do they find themselves constrained and inhibited by pre-prescribed cultural, religious, political, and social limitations, but, as interdependent actors, their "esteem" also lies in binding themselves faithfully to these same limitations. This predicament creates a double barrier in women's quest to block or challenge society's concepts of honor and its punishments for honor-transgressors. The distinction between "esteem" and "self-esteem" should be a relevant consideration in designing recommendations to suppress internalization of oppressive honor-based norms. An approach that focuses solely on the development of "self-esteem" may not be well received by most Pakistani women if the message of self-esteem comes at the price of their social esteem. Therefore, for a women's rights movement to have apparent legitimacy, it must acknowledge both self-esteem and social esteem as concurrent and simultaneous requirements of a fulfilling life.

An Honor/Shame-based Culture

From a psychological perspective,

> honor is above all the keen sensitivity to the experience of humiliation and shame, a sensitivity manifested by the desire to be envied by others and the propensity to envy the successes of others. (W. I. Miller, 1993, p. 84)

Honor is considered the disposition that makes a person act to shame or humiliate others who have been a source of shame or humiliation (W. I. Miller, 1993). One relevant definition recognizes that references to honor tend to signal to others that you were not to be "trodden upon" (W. I. Miller, 1993).

Despite similar social tendencies within honor and collectivist cultures, honor cultures cannot be squarely equated with collectivist cultures because honor cultures emphasize a particular set of values centered on the maintenance of honor and the avoidance of dishonor pursuant to the honor code (W. I. Miller, 1993, p. 195). Psychological and philosophical discussions of honor cultures recognize that honor serves as the bridge between self and society and that this value relates the self to the community's most fundamental norms, its way of life, and its traditions (W. I. Miller, 1993).

In honor cultures, social interactions are centered upon the avoidance of dishonor (Tiedens & Leach, 2004, p. 194). Avoiding dishonor, and thereby shame, can be achieved by strict adherence to the honor code, which involves a "set of values that define normative standards for what is considered honorable and dishonorable, disgraceful behavior" (Tiedens & Leach, 2004). The core values of the honor code are constituents of one's identity (Slaughter, 1993, p. 193)[16] but are "internalized to different degrees at the individual level, leading to individual differences in the extent to which an individual is attached to the honor code" (Slaughter, 1993).

The values embedded in the honor code can be divided into four major domains on the basis of the common theme each group of values shares: family honor, social interdependence (as discussed above), feminine honor, and masculine honor (Slaughter, 1993, p. 194).

In honor cultures, the family is conceptualized as a "social unit that shares a common identity," and this identity is expressed in the notion of family honor (i.e., the value and status of the family in the eyes of others) (Slaughter, 1993, p. 195). Family honor, therefore, requires concern about social evaluations of one's family, the impact of an individual's action(s) on family honor, and protection of family reputation (Slaughter, 1993).[17] Feelings of self-worth in honor cultures are, therefore, strongly dependent on the actions of one's relatives, their evaluations by society, and "the capacity of the self not to dishonor the family's collective reputation" (Slaughter, 1993). The central idea in the female honor code is sexual shame or chastity. In contrast, masculine honor centers on notions of virility.

The values at play in the context of honor killings include family/group honor (honor of the family or the tribe) and masculine honor (honor of the men in the family or the tribe). Although it can be argued that in the context of an honor killing, the honor-transgressor's actions undermine her own individual honor in society, female honor (honor of the women in the family or the tribe) in Pakistani culture is largely a factor of group or masculine honor. A group or man's honor is measured by, among other variables such as wealth and power, the rule-abiding behaviors of women in the group or those related to the man, and the effectiveness of the punishment meted out to honor-transgressors.

In honor cultures, "honor arises from a view of the self as socially contextualized, where the self is defined by its roles and the obligations inhering in them" (Slaughter, 1993, p. 194). The self is merely an "outline waiting to be filled in" (Slaughter, 1993; citing Geertz, 1983, p. 55 and 67). Identity is founded in social relations, and outrage against or violation of honor amounts to "pollution and sacrilege" (Slaughter, 1993, p. 196). This is especially applicable in Pakistan's prevailing honor culture where the fault line between honorable and dishonorable is often expressed by what is religiously permissible and what is prohibited or *h'aram* (Slaughter, 1993, p. 197). The consequences of dishonor in these cultures are dire because "loss of honor is loss of social existence and shame is almost literally experienced as annihilation" (Slaughter, 1993, p. 195).

---

[16]"[The honor code] is a system of values one has internalized and made part of one's identity, not simply a set of external rules of coercion that are necessary for the survival of the group."

[17]"Honor is thus both a personal attribute and an attribute shared with one's own family, which implies a strong interdependence between personal and family honor."

Honor goes hand in hand with shame (S. Miller, 1993, p. 117). Honor-based cultures can also be defined as shame cultures because of the pervasive threat of dishonor or shame. Shame is, therefore, in one sense, nothing more than the loss of honor (S. Miller, 1993). In Pakistan's culture of honor, one can be shamed only if one has honor. Pressures to conform to the norms of the society are explicit, while in guilt cultures there is an internalized sense of "wrong" so that one who feels guilty punishes himself (Elmer, 2002, p. 172; citing Condon & Yousef, 1975).

Who Are the Actors and Whose Perceptions Matter?

Violence is "perspectival" (S. Miller, 1993, p. 55) As is the case with any act of violence, there can be three actors involved: the victim, the victimizer, and the audience (S. Miller, 1993). The boundaries between the three are often not clearly demarcated, and an actor can play more than one role at any given time. In the case of honor-based violence, the role that arguably remains static is that of the women subjected to the violence or the threat of violence. However, studies show that victims often do not perceive their own victimization, or they engage in blaming themselves for the harms they suffer (S. Miller, 1993, p. 57). Theorists generally identify the observer to be in an arbitral position, empowered to define the nature of the event at stake (S. Miller, 1993, p. 59). Although both the victim and victimizer may not see themselves as they really are, the observer imagines himself or herself as one or the other or as both (S. Miller, 1993, pp. 59–60).

Acquiescence of a female observer to an honor-based crime may be explained by various factors, such as social intimidation, fear of being deemed an honor-transgressor herself, or actual or perceived futility. However, many women also act as active or passive accomplices in the violence, and their support requires a more nuanced understanding of the psychological and social factors of internalized oppression.

In Pakistan, sexually chaste women represent the epitome of honor (Nesheiwat, 2004) and a man's responsibility is to safeguard the chastity of the women in his family. An honor violation reflects a man's failure to carry out his responsibility, and thus, swift and brutal measures are commonly required to restore his honor and redeem his masculinity following a perceived loss of honor.

Shame Versus Guilt

Shame and guilt are both moral and social emotions. To say that they are social emotions is to affirm that they are socially constructed and that they arise out of social interactions that have implications for the moral worth of the self and others (Tangney & Fischer, 1995, p. 25). The distinction between shame and guilt takes numerous forms. The traditional approach distinguishes the two emotions along the public–private dimension: "shame is a developmental precursor to guilt – an emotion that exists before one has internalized standards of good and bad behavior" (Tangney & Fischer, 1995, p. 27). From this perspective, shame is thought to be the bad feeling that arises from misdeeds when one has been caught or observed by another; guilt, on the other hand, is viewed as the tendency to feel bad about misdeeds because they violate one's own internalized standards Tangney & Fischer, 1995). Therefore, a child experiences shame when caught in wrongdoing, but an adult that has internalized standards of good and bad may experience guilt at his misdeed, regardless of its private or public nature.

Another distinction between guilt and shame establishes shame as a sense that the entire self is bad, while guilt involves a focus on particular misdeeds (Tangney & Fischer, 1995). Shame and guilt also differ in the following ways:

(1) shame concerns moral transgressions *or* defeats, whereas guilt only concerns moral transgressions;
(2) shame involves focus on the *self's* deficiencies, whereas guilt involves focus on the negative *event* for which one is responsible; and
(3) shame involves a passive or "helpless" self, whereas guilt involves an active self (Tangney & Fischer, 1995, p. 28).

Arguably, in the context of honor killings, women who are involved or are affiliated with the alleged transgression may feel shame as manifestation of innate weaknesses, while men are influenced more by guilt in failing to restrain behaviors of those under their charge, female family members.

While there are many variables that distinguish between guilt and shame – including "stability of the cause, controllability of the outcome, public loss of respect versus private pangs of conscience, moral responsibility for harm doing versus incompetence or weakness, and the behavioral tendencies that stem from each emotion" (Branscombe & Doosje, 2004) – the most critical factor in our analysis is the perceived "controllability of the outcome" (Branscombe & Doosje, 2004). People feel guilty primarily for actions or inactions that they control and accept accountability for but feel shame for outcomes that they could not control or were not in control of but that portray them as weak or inferior (Branscombe & Doosje, 2004, p. 29). Because the social responsibility of "controlling" female sexuality in Pakistani culture is granted to male relatives, women's sexual infractions are perceived as a failure on the part of the men in the family to keep their behaviors in check. Furthermore, in Pakistani culture, which is collectivistic in its conceptualization of the relationship between the individual and others, men are invested with the power to exercise control in the protection of family honor by enforcing strict compliance with gender norms within their families (Branscombe & Doosje, 2004).

Thus, Pakistani men regard themselves and are regarded by others as the guardians of the women within the familial domain. The women who fall within a man's guardianship include his mother, sisters, daughters, cousins, and wives (Nesheiwat, 2004, p. 440). The numerous cases of honor killings undertaken by victims' distant male relatives illustrate the wide radius of the role of men as women's guardians. Insofar as the role of guardian is an essential part of male social identity, men defend honor crimes as legitimate because they would be made to suffer tremendous guilt in the wake of an honor violation if they failed to address this breach in the discharge of their responsibility: "[a male relative] is made to feel that he is 'unmanly' if he does not wash the family honor with blood ..." (Accad, 1978, p. 23). The man's guilt in failing to guard or discipline the honor-transgressor provides a measure of moral justification for the violence meted out in order to restore his family's honor.

Women's Sexuality and Shame

"Oppressed groups are all too familiar with shame ... it has been their lifetime companion" (Randall, 2004, p. 107) The state of feeling inferior is often called shame and shame has been defined as

> a painful emotion arising from the consciousness of something dishonoring ... or indecorous in one's conduct or circumstances (or in others whose honor or disgrace one regard's as one's own) or of being in a situation that offends one's modesty or decency .... (Eurich-Rascoe & Vande Kemp, 1997, p. 86; citing Merriam-Webster's Collegiate Dictionary, 1993)

The "other" is always present in shame, as there can be no sense of dishonor or disgrace without some interpersonal referent (Lewis, Haviland-Jones, & Barrett, 2000, p. 629). Within Pakistan's patriarchal social structure, any perceived threat of shame coerces women's compliance to a powerful other's prescription for social behavior and the concept of shame relevant here goes hand in hand with female sexuality.

According to traditional ethnographic accounts, in patriarchal cultures similar to rural Pakistan's, shame is female sexuality itself – literally her sexual organs. In such societies, roles of men and women are rigidly defined in order to preserve the family unit (Zafar, 1991, pp. 298–302). Mothers are regarded as the "vehicles of reproduction" and the initial "instructors" of future generations (Zafar, 1991). As such, women are seen as integral to the perpetuation of legal, moral, and social codes.

In Pakistan, women's sexuality is dealt with in relation to its effect on men (Howland, 2001, p. 204). When men are involved in unsanctioned relationships with women they are often seen as victims of female sexuality (El-Azhary Sonbol, 2003, p. 207). While men's pursuit of women is mostly accepted as a natural instinct, women's sexuality is considered an impulse that one must suppress. The responsibility to counter temptations is thus delegated to women (El-Azhary Sonbol, 2003).

Collective Shame and Collective Responsibility

Insofar as members of a group share a sense of collective identity, they may feel that a group member's shame-inducing behavior reveals a group flaw. Pakistani women may feel a sense of individual and collective shame for the blameworthy actions of their female relatives (Branscombe & Doosje, 2004). If women view infringements of honor as a reflection of inherent feminine inferiority, they may reduce their own shame by condoning the violence directed at an honor-transgressor. For example, a mother refused to help the police in removing the mutilated body of her dead daughter, who had been killed as a *kari* in front of her (Amnesty International, 1999, p. 3). Arguably this could have been an attempt to dissociate herself from her dishonorable daughter, even after her death. One of the ways a woman can signal distancing or dissociation from the honor-transgressor in the family is by actively or passively partaking in the killing of the honor-transgressor. A 1998 documented case of an honor killing, depicted the reaction of the victim's mother shortly after her three sons killed her daughter and her daughter's alleged paramour. According to the mother, "there is no grief in *ghairat* [honor], it was right to kill them ... they saw them together and they killed them" (Amnesty International, 1999). In a similar honor killing, a victim's mother-in-law stated, "*I* have been violated. This was a *zulm* [oppression/injustice] against *me*. So we axed her" (Amnesty International, 1999).

Women may be driven to sanction honor killings because men often blame women who are related to or associated with the honor-transgressor for either supporting the honor-transgressor or for permitting, explicitly or impliedly, her actions. In 2001, a man who suspected his 11-year-old daughter of having an illicit affair axed her to death. When her mother and sister tried to protect her, he killed them too. He then gave himself up to the police, stating that he had no regrets, as "it was a question of honor" (Amnesty International, 2006). In attempting to protect the original honor-transgressor, the mother and sister had become unwitting passive participants in the dishonor.

Judgments of Deserving: Political, Legal, and Religious Factors

Pakistani women's acceptance of honor violation punishments as deserving may result from processes of self-blame. If women recognize Pakistani social codes, laws, or law enforcement processes as unfair, they will likely feel that their treatment is undeserved (Tiedens & Leach, 2004, p. 282). However, isolated and often uneducated rural or tribal women are mostly unaware of the principles that animate their social system and legal processes and, therefore, have no basis to judge them to be fair or unfair. Further, a woman who accepts the notion that women's sexuality serves to tempt men is also apt to view punishments meted out for sexual transgressions as deserving. For her, violent punishment is a warranted consequence of not only failing to keep female sexuality in check but also inflicting harm on the seduced man.

Along with the various psychological phenomenon discussed above, political, legal, and religious factors also play a substantial role in promoting the acceptance of honor as the rightful basis for violent crimes against women. Prominent among these factors is the inherent procedural inequality of the Pakistani legal system. It not only enforces patently discriminatory and oppressive laws related to social norms and behavior but also fails to implement or enforce punishments for honor killings. This systemic failure to establish effective means of redress for victimized or threatened women reinforces the notion of violence as a "deserved" outcome for honor-transgressors.

The two main statutory sources of state-sponsored gender-based victimization are (1) the *Hudood* (*Ḥudood* in Arabic is the plural of *ḥadd*, meaning limit or boundary) ordinances of 1979 – prescribing punishments for unlawful sexual intercourse, including lashes for pre-marital sex and death by stoning for extra-marital sex and (2) the provisions of the Penal Code relating to *Qisas* – the doctrine of equal retaliation based on the principle of an eye for an eye, and *Diyat* – blood money.[18]

When Pakistani law criminalizes personal and private behavior and relationships in the name of religion and prescribes corporeal punishments for the offenders in a public forum, it has profound and perilous implications for public perceptions and societal development. When shame sanctions are applied to sex and commerce, the public assumes the role of the government. The victim becomes a "plaything of the populace" (Whitman, 1998). This "lynch justice" and "mob mentality," engendered by Pakistan's shame sanctions toward women and their sexuality legitimizes privately undertaken honor killings.

Shame sanctions are an especially disturbing species of lynch justice (Whitman, 1998, p. 1055). In shaming, the state does not simply mete out punishment through its own established institutions – it invites the public to punish the offender. This is not only an unreliable way to punish but also one that is intrinsically problematic. It invites the "mob" to act as a tyrant over weaker or unpopular members of the community (Nussbaum, 2004, p. 234). Although some authors have identified the deterrent value of "shame sanctions"[19] by the resultant

---

[18]The *Qisas* and *Diyat* ordinances marked a profound shift from then applicable British common law and divested the state from enforcing and controlling punishments for crimes. These ordinances allowed the victim or the victim's heirs to forgive the perpetrator of the crime and drop charges at any point of a prosecution in return for "blood money" from the criminal. See Gottesman (1992). At the time of their adoption, *Qisas* and *Diyat* ordinances were referred to as having the most shocking impact on Pakistani legal culture. See Smith (2003). Forgiveness from the victim's family is hardly an obstacle when the family itself sanctioned, if not initiated, the honor-transgressor's murder. Since the research and draft of this chapter, Pakistan enacted an Anti-Honor Killing Law in 2016. The legislation followed the Academy Award winning documentary film on honor killings by a Pakistani filmmaker and the murder of Qandeel Baloch, a young social media star who was strangled by her own brother. According to this law, honor killings can now be classified 'fasad fil ardh,' 'corruption on earth' - a crime against the State and one carrying a sentence of a minimum of 25 years to life imprisonment. The provisions allowing relatives to forgive offenders will no longer apply to cases of honor killings. However, whether a murder can be defined as a crime of honor is left to the judge's discretion. That means culprits simply claim another motive and are pardoned under Pakistan's Qisas (blood money) and Diyat (retribution) law. Therefore, despite the recent law, human rights organizations and activists report continued increase in honor based violence.

[19]See, for example, Kahan (1996). He argues that shaming sanctions help shape and reinforce public norms that condemn criminality. See also Massaro (1991) and Morton (2001).

> [A]lthough societal conditions in modern America do significantly
> differ from those in colonial times, the deprivation of privacy deserves

deprivation of the offenders' privacy, these punishments thwart social development. Shame sanctions are wrong because they represent an unacceptable style
of governance through their play on public psychology (Whitman, 1998, p. 1059).

On a psychological level, punishments meted out for sex-related behavior
under Sharia law serve to intensify women's internalization of shame and turn
that shame into a powerful tool of social control. On a spiritual level, some men
and women believe that earthly violence against violators of religious and social
norms prevents or mitigates their punishments in the afterlife. Such thinking
tends to provide justification for murder, death, and suicide in pursuit of religious
goals (Selengut, 2003, p. 184). Indeed, throughout religious history, women have
been encouraged to endure suffering as a sign of religious devotion, and this has
included toleration of abuse (Selengut, 2003, p. 216). Due to these internalized
concepts of religious absolution, honor killing is sometimes viewed as the exclusive atonement of the honor-transgressor's sins.

Another factor that promotes honor-related violence is the increasing political
and social rhetoric that casts western liberal countries as enemies of Islam. Two
prominent human rights attorneys, Hina Jilani and her sister Asma Jahangir, were
accused by elected officials of "misleading women in Pakistan and contributing
to the country's bad image abroad" (Hussain, 2006). Some religious organizations
publicly stated that honor crimes were condoned by religious and tribal traditions
and issued *fatwas* against the two attorneys, declaring them *kafirs,* nonbelievers,
and calling upon all Muslims to kill the two women (Hussain, 2006). A Pakistani
Senator, Ilyas Bilour, issued the following statement regarding Jilani and Jahangir:
"we have fought for human rights and civil liberties all our lives but wonder what
sort of rights are being claimed by *these girls in jeans*" (Hussain, 2006, p. 243).

Although accessibility of information through new age and social media creates greater international scrutiny for local human rights abuses, it has also allowed
for wide dissemination of conspiracy theories regarding victims and human rights
activists. These false characterizations often portray them as traitors manipulating
western liberal sympathies for personal gain. This process ensures that activists'
voices are ignored and they are labeled as "outsiders." In determining the appropriate approach to combat internalization of honor crimes as legitimate practices, this
increasing cultural trend must be considered.

Reconstructing the Movement Against Honor Violence in Pakistan

Pakistan's movement against honor-based violence will need to be capable of
addressing the range of psychological, cultural, and political forces arrayed

---

recognition as a powerful deterrent and rehabilitative mechanism attendant in these sentences .... Because privacy has become so essential in
the collective mind of society today, scarlet letter sentencing can successfully rehabilitate and deter some offenders and would-be criminals.
For more, see, Schwarcz (2003). "Shaming can be a cheaper and more effective
punishment than imprisonment for low-level offenders."

against it. The challenge lies in defining a movement that can bring about radical social and political change without the deployment of a radical narrative that will alienate Pakistani women or mobilize cultural forces that resist western hegemony.

In order to overcome the resistance that accompanies advocacy for women's rights, the movement should be derived from the culture's own ideals and values. For example, arguments for an increase in women's access to education and economic resources can be articulated as factors that enhance their ability to carry forward their established, yet vital, social roles, such as advocating education for mothers to enhance the physical and spiritual health of their children and the rest of the family; these arguments will be more persuasive and socially endorsed than those which seek to enhance individualistic interests.[20]

An approach that is perceived as or is vulnerable to characterization as a threat to the moral code of society will be derailed without allowing for effective advocacy for other important but more socially palatable rights such as of women's economic independence, political empowerment, and education. The strong correlation between the emotion of shame and sexuality further emphasizes the need to initially focus primarily on rights for women that are not associated with cultural shame. Political and economic empowerment may be the most effective means of reducing women's susceptibility to psycho-social forces governing gender roles.

De-Politicizing the Movement's Narrative

In June 2002, a young woman, Mai, was sentenced to a gang rape by an unofficial *jirgah*, tribal jury, in order to restore the honor of another woman from a higher tribe, with whom Mai's brother was alleged to have had an affair (Castetter, 2003, pp. 544–545)."

Although Mai's ordeal caused widespread public outrage and outcry within Pakistan the international rhetoric surrounding the incident was subsequently used to deflect the focus from the need for internal change to a concern for outside interference. In a statement that sparked outrage and protests by women's groups, the then Pakistan's President, Pervez Musharraf noted,

> This has become a money-making concern. A lot of people say
> if you want to go abroad and get a visa for Canada or citizen-
> ship and be a millionaire, get yourself raped. (Hussain, 2006,
> pp. 245–246)

Thus rather than a much needed public dialog about the values and processes that could be mobilized in support of basic rights for both men and women, the discourse was transformed into a discussion of the political motives of anti-Pakistan "outsiders." This misappropriation of the movement's narrative can be

---

[20]See generally Choudhury (2007). It discusses the Afghan women's rights activists' lobbying of provisions in the newly drafted constitution related to protections for women as mothers as a means of improving women's position.

checked through rhetorical strategies aimed at challenging the status quo from "within."

Creating A "Change from Within": Using Islam to Deconstruct Religious Legitimacy of Gender-based Violence

Women's rights movements everywhere have had to make room in the power strata of society for a group which has traditionally and systematically been disenfranchised from civic order (Stevens & Malesh, 2009, pp. 71–72). "Women must first invent a way to speak in the context of being silenced and rendered invisible as persons" (Ritchie & Ronald, 2001). In Pakistan, this often requires that women begin by acquainting themselves with the administration's espoused principles and then holding this language of cultural values up to the mirror of cultural practice in the demand for greater compliance and authenticity (Stevens & Malesh, 2009, p. 82). This strategy of using "the master's tools to dismantle the master's house" offers a nuanced and novel approach to creating and rationalizing women's rights from the ideals and values that are already at play in Pakistani society. (Stevens & Malesh, 2009, p. 84)[21] One element of such a strategy would be to build a Muslim feminist jurisprudential basis which redefines the movement as restoration of the rights of women as originally intended in Islam where, "for better or worse, Islam and Islamic law are a part of democratic governance and legal structure" Choudhury (2007, p. 166).[22]

The transformative potential of a women's rights movement in Pakistan can be realized not only by challenging the legal and extra-legal gender barriers but also by reshaping the movement in conformity with major aspects of Pakistan's prevailing socio-religious context. Most Pakistani men and women are devout adherents of Islam and for them, their faith is "the guarantor par excellence of women's rights."[23] The cultural manifestations of Islamic religious values are thus integral to their self-definition. These values must be mobilized more effectively in the struggle for women's rights. At present, Islamic values and teachings are marshaled largely in the defense of women's oppression and subjugation. In addition, recent increases in anti-western rhetoric in mainstream Pakistan has greatly weakened the efficacy of any activism or argument based on secular notions, which are easily discounted as western liberal constructions (Choudhury, 2007, p. 161).

---

[21]They note that "[i]n the transition between ideological spaces, the tool itself is no longer the location of all agency; instead, agency is taken on by the one who wields it."
[22]She discusses similar religious connotations in Afghani politics and notes that during the constitution-making process, advocates were sensitive to the need to ensure that women's rights claims were "not … perceived as imposed by foreign interests."
[23]See Warren (2008); see also Choudhury, supra note 110, at 163 (discussing Afghani activists' work of framing secular demands in the language and idioms of Islam).

Religious Interpretative Tools for a Feminist Movement

Women often challenge the misogyny within the social order by using imbedded values of the androcentric community against the oppressive use of these values (Stevens & Malesh, 2009, p. 70). As discussed above, it can be an effective strategy to argue that Islam, when first introduced (Warren, 2008, p. 42),[24] guaranteed women's rights by making it a component of both divine law and the Prophet's *Sunnah,* which refers to the Prophet's normative practice. Islamic jurisprudence thus provides activists the tools necessary to lobby for progressive legislation within the socio-religious framework that is a part of Pakistan's self-professed value system.

Sharia allows new interpretations of existing precedent in at least three situations: (1) in cases of "necessity or public interest"; (2) when there is a "change in the facts which gave rise to the original law"; and (3) when there is a "change in the custom or usage on which a particular law was based" (Warren, 2008, p. 50) This sanctioned flexibility in Islamic Jurisprudence can be employed to further feminist interests. Arguments based on modern times or changing circumstances,[25] although reasonable and valid, will likely lack the necessary social potency in light of the current political rhetoric of Pakistan, which often casts modernism or progressive arguments as western liberal propaganda. However, a cogent public movement which highlights the adulteration of Islamic doctrine pursuant to the *Hudood* ordinance – its misconstruction and the abuse in its application – necessarily calls for modification of the law as a "necessity or in public interest." An argument based on the public's interest and the well-being of society can be legitimately advocated on religious grounds pursuant to the Islamic purpose of human existence, which is "to do the will of God and create a social order that reflects the equality and dignity of all human beings" (Sonn, 2001, p. 74).

Most Islamic scholars agree that pursuant to various established Islamic principles of equity and fairness (Warren, 2008, p. 51),[26] "if a practice results in suffering or oppression, it cannot be considered to be in accordance with Islamic principles." Applying this reasoning, the practice of honor killings and other acts of violence against women, along with the state-sanctioned violence pursuant to

---

[24]She notes that "Islam was the first religion in the world to honor women and outline legislation stipulating that women should be treated as independent human beings."

[25]One argument, based on the "theory of gradualism," provides that the Qu'ran allows evolution of laws for conformity with changing needs and times. See Warren(2008, p. 55). She discusses the gradual emergence of the prohibition against drinking alcohol as example of the theory of gradualism.

[26]"Principles of usul al-*fiqh* include a number of ameliorating doctrines that are designed to ensure fairness and conscience in the application of the law. Istihsan, like its approximate common law counterpart, equity, is inspired by principles of fairness and conscience. If strict enforcement of a law would lead to a hardship or an unfair result, istihsan permits that the rule be abandoned. Istislah, also known as maslahah mursala, requires consideration of public interest ... (internal citations and quotations omitted)."

the implementation of *Hudood* laws, should be recognized as incompatible with Islamic religious principles.

Promoting Women's Participation and Representation

The discriminatory and oppressive laws in Pakistan, as drafted and applied, and the resulting perpetuation of patriarchal norms can only be reversed through the participation of women themselves, both as active advocates and as passive supporters. This goal addresses two major issues impeding progress "from within": (1) the marginalization of Pakistani women from Islamic legal discourse, scholarship, and leadership and (2) the widespread misinformation in Pakistan and other similar Muslim countries regarding the rights of women and their role in society as provided by those Islamic religious principles that are largely undisputed.[27]

Prominent female Islamic scholars in other countries have achieved substantial success in rebuilding societal constructs of women's role and rights using an Islamic framework. Their work provides the movement with an international platform for Islamic reform (Warren, 2008, pp. 56–58).[28] However, true reform, especially one that targets various socio-political factors regulating gender norms endemic to Pakistan, can only be achieved by direct participation of Pakistani women in light of the following relevant considerations. There are a few factors that seem especially relevant to achieving success.

First, it is likely that male reformists will have to work alongside their female collaborators; otherwise male leadership in this area is apt to perpetuate patriarchal values that are indeed at the root of the problem.

Second, a significant increase in the number and prominence of female advocates of Islamic jurisprudence is necessary – not only to check patriarchal interpretations of law at the state level, but also to lend the movement's leadership more representational credence at a societal level. The critical mass necessary for the movement to gain any momentum can only be achieved when the movement's

---

[27]See generally Choudhury (2007, p. 165). She discusses similar issues facing women's rights activists in Afghanistan and notes that although Afghan women feel strongly that Islam, more than any other religion, guarantees equal rights to men and women, a Max Planck Institute report found that 70% of men and 80–85% of women interviewed in field research in Afghanistan were unaware of the rights afforded to women in Islam.

[28]She recognizes the work of women Islamic scholars including Asifa Quraishi, Azizah al-Hibri, and Madhavi Sunder, and of organizations such as Sisters in Islam, in Malaysia, the League of Demanders of Women's Right to Drive Cars, in Saudi Arabia, and the Women's Aid Collective and BAOBAB in Nigeria); *see also* Coleman (2006). Coleman discusses relevant work done in Indonesia by a group called Fatayat, the women's wing of the country's largest grass-roots organization (known as Nahdlatul Ulama), by training its members in Islamic *fiqh* (jurisprudence) so that they can hold their own in religious debates, and in Algeria by Women Living Under Muslim Laws (wluml), by giving information on progressive Islamic systems around the world to local activists, who use the information to fight for greater freedoms.

intended beneficiaries view the leaders as "one of their own."[29] The potent influences of the internalizing processes make it challenging for women to remove themselves from the comfort of solidarity they may find with other female proponents of the honor killing practice. However, when similarly situated women who oppose honor killings are given a voice, even those women who have tended to support the practice may find it easier to align their loyalties with more progressive forces.

Third, the movement should seek to increase its educational reach toward women, as increasing women's literacy and powers of critical consciousness are essential for sustained progress. For example, most women are unaware of the religious rights that Islam grants to them, including the right of divorce and inheritance. Indeed, as one scholar noted,

> it is not Islam itself, but the fact that most Muslim women do not know what Islam is, or what the rights of women within it are, that has created the best opportunity for men to abuse this situation and enforce male-oriented traditions, or whatever suits them to oppress women. (Choudhury, 2007, p. 165)

Framing human rights demands in religious language and idioms (Choudhury, 2007, p. 163) is not only a strategic tool for political legitimacy; it is necessary to build support from that significant majority of women that are attached to the values and principles that animate Islam.

Increasing Women's Literacy and Scholarship

The current dismal state of adult literacy for women in Pakistan[30] remains a significant barrier to the movement to eradicate honor killings. Without basic literacy, women remain dependent on men within the confines of a domestic role. Lack of access to education required for entering into professions deprives women of the opportunity to participate in shaping the future of Pakistani society. Furthermore, marginalization from religious scholarship and teaching prevents women from entering the strictly guarded domain of religious interpretation and

---

[29]See, for example, Choudhury (2007, pp. 167–168). She discusses the strategies of female drafters of the Afghani Constitution who identified themselves in the opening line of the document as "We, the Afghan Muslim …" and therefore by

> framing their demands within the Western template of a bill of rights, these women established from the very beginning that they are not Western interlopers, but indigenous Afghans and sincere adherents of Islam who are legitimate and adequate representatives of the women of Afghanistan.

[30]"Pakistan: Statistics" UNICEF, last updated December 27, 2013. Retrieved from http://www.unicef.org/infobycountry/pakistan_pakistan_statistics.html. This shows that women's adult literacy rates are at 58.7% that of men in adult literacy rate (as a percentage of males: females as a percentage of males, based on data from 2005 to 2010).

theological reasoning about the meaning of Islamic law. Female activists must acquire the

> ability to engage with Islamic sources, to articulate their interpre-
> tations in the common language of Islamic discourse, and to per-
> suade others, particularly male leaders, including family members,
> mullahs (religious clerics), tribal leaders, judges, and legislators
> (Choudhury, 2007, p. 195).

Making Room for Male Advocacy

As a corollary to increased participation by educated female representatives, it is imperative that the movement also attracts support from men. The movement must mobilize male advocates to preempt a certain degree of male backlash from the perceived increase in power and influence of women leaders. A transforma-tion of gender norms in Pakistan will be met with much resistance. For this rea-son, the movement should not only remain inclusive of both men and women but should also allow male advocates to play a prominent and strategic role in the movement's leadership from the earliest stages of its redefinition.

Application of International Law and Notions

The role of international law in Muslim countries like Pakistan as an external catalyst for reform is a matter of controversy (Warren, 2008, p. 60). A growing trend in scholarship argues that encouraging liberalized interpretations of texts and laws by Islamic scholars themselves, rather than dictating from outside a list of universal standards, presents a more promising avenue for social reform and women's advancement (Warren, 2008, p. 61). However, a social movement seek-ing reform "from within" does not foreclose the role of the international com-munity, especially when that role emphasizes leadership support, skill-building, and educational resources for the local women leaders, instead of international publicized endorsement. Along with offering resources for advocacy and edu-cation for all activists, international support must also be made available to progressive religious scholars working to advance the role of women through established religious channels either pursuant to subjective belief in the reli-gious guarantees of rights for women or as strategic use of available means of social change (Coleman, 2006, p. 25).

Developing a Cultural Ethos of Human Dignity

As has been noted by others in this volume and elsewhere, historically, the con-cept of human dignity had been linked primarily to one's social rank or status. Over the course of time, however, and especially following the atrocities commit-ted against humanity in Nazi Germany, theological, philosophical, and political discourses led to the development of a different notion of human dignity. Rather than deriving human dignity from one's social standing, human dignity was seen increasingly as deriving from one's inherent worth as a human being.

Honor, as a powerful cultural force in Pakistan, is akin to the form of dignity that predates the twentieth century. This more traditional conceptualization of honor and dignity is not inherent to one's nature, but can be lost and restored as a function of one's actions as perceived through the lens of an ancient and socially constructed honor code. As noted earlier, dishonor pursuant to this understanding of dignity often results in gross violations of the values and principles that animate contemporary conceptualizations of human dignity.

Here, we explore the concept of developing a foundation of human dignity in Pakistan through its consolidation in jurisprudential values and principles. Renovating Sharia law, which enshrines the overarching moral code and values that animate life in Pakistan, with principles of human dignity that are counterparts to its contemporary understandings, is, perhaps, critical.

Defining Human Dignity and Its "Minimum Content"

The concept of human dignity has deep theological and philosophical roots. Immanuel Kant's deontological philosophy of dignity situated it in a communitarian setting and defined it within a paradigm of absolutists. He conceptualized dignity as involving "an innate capacity of each person, which imposes obligations on us as members of an organized society" (Carmi, 2008; Wells, 1997)[31] The English-speaking philosophers, such as Locke, Hobbes, Berlin, and Nozick, viewed human dignity more from a teleological perspective addressing natural rights, liberalism, free speech, and nonintervention by the state (Carmi, 2008, p. 280; citing Berlin, 2002, p. 170). Human dignity as a constitutional term and right is a relatively modern concept for human rights discourse and it has emerged as a pivotal value for an increasing number of Western democracies. It is at the very center of the constitutional systems of Germany and South Africa, which view this commitment both as a source of and constraint on certain rights and liberties (Carmi, 2008, p. 285; Kretzmer & Klein, 2002, p. 52).[32]

It is often suggested that identifying a transnational concept of human dignity would be a formidable task given the varied cultural, theological, and sociopolitical circumstances and histories of people around the world. The proposal explored in this chapter advocates the idea that human dignity, wherever it may be found, has, at its core, universalistic "minimum content" (Barroso, 2012). However, despite the pluralistic "minimum content" of human dignity, the channels

---

[31]Compare with Isaiah Berlin (2002, p. 198). He notes that Kant's earlier works were based upon more individualistic notions and that his change of mind was led by "peculiar evolution."

[32]"Basic Law for the Federal Republic of German," article 1. Retrieved from https://www.gesetz-im-internet.de/englisch_gg/; "The Constitution of the Republic of South African," articles 1 and 10. For example, constraints on free speech in Germany and prohibition on prostitution in South Africa are justified through human dignity rationales despite the resultant restriction on personal autonomy and free speech.

or instrumentalities for developing human dignity as a value require customized frames for different cultures.

The "minimum content" for human dignity is the intrinsic value of all human beings, the ontological element of human dignity linked to the very nature of the human being (Barroso, 2012, p. 362). This intrinsic value is sometimes defined as the condition that provides human being a special status in the world, distinct from other species (Barroso, 2012). However, another approach views mankind's intrinsic worth, not in terms of a domineering comparison with other species, but simply as a virtue of human potential, which demands certain guarantees for every individual, including the autonomy of every individual or the right to be free from state intrusion without just cause and due process. Minimum standards also require freedom for self-actualization, the right to justice or equal protection, and the right to integrity (Barroso, 2012, pp. 364–365),[33] both mental and physical. This understanding of human dignity encapsulates two basic postulates (1) anti-utilitarian concerns, consisting of formulations of Kant's categorical imperative that every individual is an end in him or herself, and not a means for collective goals or the purposes of others and (2) anti-authoritarian concerns, based on the idea that the state exists for the individual, not the other way around (Barroso, 2012, p. 363).

Acknowledgment of the minimum content of human dignity has little societal value without means to disseminate the package through persuasive and culturally appropriate means. The identification of the most effective frame for a given society is critical for enhancing social and institutional commitment to all basic human rights.

Theological Concepts of Human Dignity and Renovating Sharia

Theological concepts of human dignity share a long and influential philosophical history. The Judaeo-Christian notion of the dignity of humanity had roots in stoic ideas found in the work of Cicero, Seneca, and others (Waldron, 2011). Religious grounding of many theories of natural rights produced rights based on the idea of a duty or responsibility to God. This thesis was crucial to John Locke's idea of limited government:

> [A] man, not having the power of his own life, cannot by compact or his own consent enslave himself to any one, nor put himself under the absolute, arbitrary power of another to take away his life when he pleases. Nobody can give more power than he has himself, and he that cannot take away his own life cannot give another power over it. (Waldron, 2011, p. 1129; citing Locke, 1988)

---

[33]"The right to physical integrity includes the prohibition of torture, slave labor, and degrading treatment or punishment … [and] the right to mental integrity, which in Europe and many civil law countries comprises the right to personal honor and image, [and] includes the right to privacy."

A substantial scholarship on human dignity addresses the risk in grounding inherent human dignity in metaphysical authorities by turning the discourse into one about moral standing or how one ought to act rather than about rights of human beings in treatments, actions, and laws applicable to them. Secular notions of human dignity represent an effort to free it from any particular religious or political doctrine and seek to justify it by the power of *public reason* as articulated by theorists like John Rawls (Barroso, 2012, p. 360; citing Rawls, 1999, pp. 547–583). These notions, which have their origins in the abstract processes of human reasoning, often overlook the developmental reality of social convictions. They disregard the fact that societies engage in an ongoing reflective process, sometimes modifying the sources of foundational commitments to fit evolving social judgments and values. However, if moral commitments to foundational principles such as the notion of inherent dignity are to find practical expression, they must be grounded in and carried through means that appear to a particular culture as credible. In Pakistan, a country where religious values are at the foundation of society, one of the most significant instruments for developing a consciousness of human dignity may be found in Sharia jurisprudence.

The key in renovating Sharia law in Pakistan would be to develop least restrictive procedures and principles that promote human dignity without imposing intolerant majoritarian norms. Notwithstanding the abuses to which it has been put, Islamic law offers a unique opportunity to develop notions of human dignity that would comport well with the deeply held values of the people of Pakistan. Advocating public morality through compulsion or state intrusion in private behavior runs afoul of human dignity. For example, contained in Sharia law, and echoed throughout Islamic jurisprudence is an anti-coercion principle that recognizes the inherent human dignity and one's right to integrity.

And while a route to the development of a concept of human dignity that would have currency in Pakistan is not theologically neutral, if it is widely embraced it could provide necessary procedural safeguards for personal autonomy. For example, while offenses against God (which include victimless crimes such as fornication) may still be widely viewed in society as immoral, recognition of the theological procedural protections that effectively insulate private behavior from state intrusion and prosecution can create the motivation for jurisprudential acknowledgment of personal autonomy and individual liberties. It is hoped that, in due course, these collateral protections for individual liberty will gain adequate mainstream social significance to transform them into freestanding foundational commitments, with their associated imperative of tolerance.

Building a human dignity foundation by seeking to derive it from a libertarian philosophy of individual autonomy or unrestricted free speech will be culturally and socially incongruous to prevailing norms in Pakistan. In the case of societies with strong communitarian values, the focus is not on an individual's right or autonomy to engage in prohibitive conduct, but on the limitations on the state and the public, which are essentially prevented from compelling the individual to stand in judgment before a court of law or before other individuals for private conduct. It is this constraint on state intrusion into the private affairs of individuals that cultivates social acceptance for some degree of personal autonomy. As stated in the Qur'an:

> Now, indeed, We have conferred dignity on the children of Adam and carried them on the land and sea and provided for them of the good things and preferred them over much of what We have created, with [definite] preference. (Surah 17: Al-Isra':70)

Postulating a workable definition of human dignity for Pakistan requires its ontological value to be anchored in established Islamic sources that safeguard individual integrity and freedom from coercion. This aspect of law that protects human dignity must be tailored for all aspects of Sharia jurisprudence. A successful outcome of such a model can establish the potential for a pragmatic evolution toward the protection of human dignity and individual integrity through Sharia jurisprudence.

Sharia law, as currently developed and carried out in Pakistan, has encouraged the brutalization of society and contributed to the social acceptance of the idea that private conduct is not only subject to public censure but also demands punishment in the form of lynch justice as supported by the law's "shame sanctions." There is a critical need for renovating Sharia jurisprudence using its own inherent legal norms. Individual liberty stands at odds within the prevailing rubric of Sharia jurisprudence as developed and implemented in Pakistan. At the same time, advocacy paradigms based on notions of equality have gained little traction in challenging laws that are, for the most part, on the face of them neutral, but are atrociously discriminatory and oppressive as applied and enforced. One such ordinance, the *Hudood* Ordinance,[34] prescribes severe and degrading punishments for victimless "crimes against God," including acts constituting *zina*, that is, fornication or adultery.

Muslim scholars have rejected imposition of these punishments on the ground that application of the *Hudood* punishments must be limited to societies which have provided for the welfare of all its inhabitants (Saifee, 2003).[35] This principle is supported by the precedent established by Caliph Umar ibn al-Khattab, who suspended punishment for theft during a time of famine (Saifee, 2003, p. 156). Thus despite the seemingly inelastic nature of Sharia, it is infused with various principles of interpretation that can be used as authority to protect the intrinsic value of the human person. Although beyond the scope of this paper, it is

---

[34]The Hudood ordinances of 1979 were adopted pursuant to Pakistan's Sharia law and enforced severe punishments for various acts and personal behaviors including pre-marital or extra-marital sex. The punishment for extra-marital sex is death by stoning. See Pakistan Penal Code (Act XLV of 1860).

[35]She cites Peters (2002). He suggests the argument that Sharia penalties may not be applied until just Islamic society has been set up.

important to note that human dignity constructs grounded in concepts endorsing personal liberty and freedom from coercion and fear can be applied to support other vulnerable, and often targeted, groups in Pakistan, including sexual and religious minorities.

Identifying a Workable Model for "Dignity Jurisprudence"

> O you who have believed, be persistently standing firm in justice, witnesses for Allah, even if it be against yourselves or parents and relatives. Whether one is rich or poor, Allah is more worthy of both. So follow not [personal] inclination, lest you not be just. And if you distort [your testimony] or refuse [to give it], then indeed Allah is ever, with what you do, Acquainted.[36]

Human dignity concerns often surface, when private behavior clashes with public morality or reputational issues. Sharia laws, as currently applied in Pakistan, enhance the reputational concerns in society while infringing on safeguards against intrusion, state or public, in private behavior. It thereby encourages victimization of women for the sake of preservation of dignity or honor. However, until *Hudood* punishments can be modified or eliminated altogether, proper application and enforcement of the same laws can provide the necessary platform for building "human dignity jurisprudence."

This model of "dignity jurisprudence," established through Islamic theological support for deference to human dignity,[37] rests upon the evidentiary requirements and procedures prescribed in Islamic law regarding consensual sexual behavior, adultery, and fornication, including the strict penal consequences of violating these requirements. The model seeks to immunize private sexual behavior – behavior that is often cited as justification for honor-based violence – from state and public intrusion and judgment.[38] The *Hudood* Ordinance sets out severe and demeaning punishments for private consensual[39] behavior: public lashings for fornication and

---

[36]Qur'an, Verse 135 of Surah Al Nisa (The Women).

[37]This should be distinguished to some extent from concepts of divine mercy, which imply forgiveness or a write-off of an offense. This deference implies the "willingness to look the other way." This "divine" disinclination to demean and indignify needs to find its jurisprudential reflection through legal protection of human dignity.

[38] See Quraishi (1997, 296–299) (discussing Qur'anic prohibition on speculating about sexual improprieties of women.)

[39]The crime of rape, as addressed by Pakistani Sharia Court, is a different matter. Classification of rape as a subset of *zina* according to Pakistan's Sharia law allows for grotesque application of *zina*'s procedural requirements. A woman who alleges rape, must produce four male witnesses to the crime – an impossible task considering any eyewitnesses would likely be co-conspirators in the crimes – and if the victim is unable to meet this absurd evidentiary burden, her allegation is deemed a confession of fornication, thereby charging rape victims with the crime of *zina*. This is where Pakistan's

stoning to death for adultery.[40] However, contrary to popular understanding of Islamic law and the frequent misapplication of the *Hudood* law by an unqualified and biased judiciary, scholars of Islamic law have argued that individuals who privately engage in such acts are answerable only to God, and not the state or the public.[41] This is because the law provides strict evidentiary requirements and

---

Sharia law completely falls apart, both in letter of the law and in its application. A movement for "change from within" as discussed earlier in this paper, can advocate to not merely eliminate the provision, but to modify it for conformity with established Islamic law on the following basis (1) Islamic jurisprudence specifies duress as a negation of intent for *zina*; (2) an individual who has been raped cannot be punished with the *Hadd* penalty for *zina* because the act of *zina* requires an element of free will; (3) early Islamic teachings and rulings prohibited punishing a rape victim for *zina*; and finally; (4) *zina* is a crime of public indecency whereas rape is a crime of violence. Therefore, scholars have classified rape under the category of *hiraba*, a crime of forcible assault, under which four eyewitnesses to the act of penetration is not required to establish proof. Under all Sunni schools of thought, a woman who alleges rape is free and not held liable for *zina*. See Saifee (2003, pp. 432–433).

[40]The Qur'an makes no mention of death by stoning for adultery; the legitimacy of the punishment is based on *fiqh*, Islamic jurisprudential interpretations, and not on the Qur'an.

[41]An individual may be subject to state's prosecution in the case of a confession which meets the Islamic legal standard for voluntariness: the confession must be a product of one's own free will and must be made with complete knowledge and understanding of the potential punishments. According to a hadith, the Prophet was once approached by a man who confessed that he had committed *zina*. The Prophet sent him away, telling him only to turn to God for repentance. The man returned and again confessed his act, asking for his punishment. The Prophet once again sent him away. This occurred two more times and on the fourth confession, the Prophet considered his case by asking him specific questions to ensure actual penetration. See Saifee (2003, p. 419; citing Sidahmad, 1995, p. 163) and Joseph Schacht, (1982, p. 177; noting that in all crimes of *Hudood* except for *Qadhf*, it is even recommended that the judge suggest retraction to the confessor); see also Saifee (2003, pp. 420–422).

Some jurists hold that the Qur'an requires repetition of the *zina* confession four times, corresponding to the quadruple witness requirement. Additionally, if criminal penalty is based solely on confession of the accused, withdrawal of confession at any time before or after sentencing, or during execution of the sentence, prevents *Hadd* punishment, except in the case of *Qadhf*, where confession cannot be retracted. An overarching principle, governing Islamic criminal law in general and the crime of *zina* in particular, is the doctrine that doubt invalidates application of the *Hudood*. This jurisprudential principle acts as a recurring theme in the context of *zina* confessions, as evidenced from the juristic determinations that (1) *zina* must be described in detail, leaving no room for doubt; (2) one co-conspirator's denial of *zina* casts doubt on the truth of the other party's confession; and (3) withdrawal of *zina* confession at any time nullifies the *Hadd* punishment.

procedures that effectively negate a prima facie case for adultery or fornication. These requirements include concurrent quadruple eyewitness testimony regarding a private act (the eyewitness testimony must relate to the observance of the actual act of sexual penetration), respect for the right to privacy in one's dwelling, application of judicial ameliorative principles, and the right to fairness and justice. Presenting false or uncorroborated testimony (e.g., three eyewitnesses instead of the required four) is, in itself, a crime of *Qadhf*, and carries the same punishment as that for adultery or fornication. Judgment by other members of society – which often results in "lynch justice" – is especially abhorrent in the light of the *Qadhf* provision,[42] which provides criminal liability for slander or uncorroborated accusations. These theological legal safeguards for private behavior can be cited as a "divine acknowledgement" of the need to protect human dignity by protection of privacy and personal autonomy.[43]

---

[42] *Qadf*, which criminalizes speech, can be perceived as a threat to human dignity and its associated autonomy guarantees. However, most western liberal democracies have developed legal concepts balancing human dignity and free-speech rights and values. See, for example, Carmi (2008, p. 286).

> The balancing formulas among most western democracies lead to similar outcomes to the German-Kantian approach to human dignity, even in the absence of an absolute approach to human dignity. Once human dignity considerations are "balanced vis-a-vis freedom of expression concerns, it almost automatically leads to speech-restrictive results."

Furthermore, a commitment to dignity foundation can potentially lead to revision or even abolishment of the blasphemy laws, which criminalize speech deemed disrespectful of Islam, in Pakistan because of the "zone of privacy" for conduct and speech considered as crimes against God. Blasphemy laws punish individuals for offense against God, not individuals. *Qadf*, on the other hand, promotes human dignity principles by criminalizing slander and libel and false or uncorroborated testimony regarding private behavior – all offenses against the individual. The challenge lies in the hands of the jurists who must promote *Qadf* not as the indicator that one's reputation is the all-important societal value, thereby further promoting the idea of dignity as honor, but as a reflection of the impermeability surrounding an individual's zone of privacy.

[43] Privacy rights, although inherent in Islamic jurisprudence, are too often buried underneath patriarchal biases and traditions. By renovating Sharia jurisprudence with infusion of human dignity principles based on privacy rights, Sharia law can offer an effective platform for developing a culturally appropriate human dignity frame in Pakistan. As discussed herein, the following two aspects of Sharia law create a clear zone of privacy (i) prosecutions for acts constituting *zina* are virtually impossible, given the strict standard of proof, the consequences of failure to meet evidentiary requirements, and the Islamic guarantees against scrutiny of behavior conducted in a dwelling and (ii) such acts are protected from public morality judgments or societal denigration by the mandatory criminal liability, through *Qadhf*, for slander regarding *zina* and for failure to meet the evidentiary requirement for *zina* accusations. Although these protections may not be referred to collectively as an enumerated right to privacy, such right is certainly derived from the enumerated rights to be free from

Conclusion

As has been suggested dignity, as a community value, often inspired by paternalistic or moralistic motivations, underlies judicial decision making in Pakistan. A Sharia legal principle that can effectively enhance personal freedoms must resist ideological polarization in an acutely radicalized political culture; must circumvent self-perpetuating societal moralism and paternalism, and must overcome deeply entrenched misogynistic attitudes, especially as applied to human sexuality and private sexual conduct. We also recognize that the development of "dignity jurisprudence" requires that we ascribe a value to human dignity which does not feed into its socially derived dignity counterpart and thus further enhances the validity and internalization of honor as justification for violence, discrimination, and oppression of women.

In the Pakistani context, this would require the development of a discourse on human dignity that is anchored primarily in the emancipatory potential of human dignity as provided in Islamic discourse, values, and juridical principles. We thus advocate the cultivation of a Muslim feminist jurisprudence that seeks restoration of the rights of women as the original intention of Sharia law. In this way, the movement to eradicate honor violence acquires legitimacy, resonance, and credibility "from within." A successful outcome of such an approach can establish the potential for the pragmatic evolution in Sharia jurisprudence as a microprocessor for transnational discourse on human dignity.

References

Accad, E. (1978). *Veil of shame: The role of women in the contemporary fiction of North Africa and the Arab World (p. 23)*. Sherbrooke, Canada: Naaman.

Ali, R. (2001). *The dark side of honour: Women victims in Pakistan* (pp. 12–13). London: International Solidarity Network.

Amnesty International. (1999). *Pakistan: Violence against Women in the name of honour*. New York, NY: Amnesty International.

Amnesty International. (2002). *Pakistan: Insufficient protection of women*. Amnesty International. (Index No. ASA 33/006/2002). Retrieved from https://www.amnesty.org/download/Documents/116000/asa330062002en.pdf.

Amnesty International. (2006, October 16). *Annual report 2001: Pakistan*. Retrieved from https://www.amnesty.org/download/Documents/132000/pol100062001en.pdf

---

state or public intrusion and judgment for private conduct. Compare with Saifee, (2003, p. 370) (discussing that the real right of privacy resides in Islamic jurisprudence). This right to privacy does not require balancing of public morality or community values and individual interests because these procedural protections for private conduct can neither be waived nor compromised in the interest of majoritarian concerns. See, for example, Saifee, (2003), where she cites Chaudhry (1997), noting that during time of Prophet Muhammad, woman who openly practiced prostitution was not punished because there was no proof of *zina*.

Barroso, L. R. (2012). Here, there, and everywhere: Human dignity in contemporary law and in the transnational discourse. *Boston College International & Comparative Law Review, 35*, 353.

Benedek, W., Kisaakye, E. M., & Oberleitner, G. (Eds.). (2002). *Human rights of women: International instruments and African experiences* (p. 271). London: Zed Books.

Bennett, M. J. (Ed.). (1998). *Intercultural communication: A current perspective, basic concepts of intercultural communication* (pp. 157–158). Boston, MA: Intercultural Press.

Berlin, I. (2002). Two concepts of liberty. In I. Berlin & H. Hardy (Eds.), *Liberty: Incorporating four essay on liberty* (p. 198). Oxford: Oxford University Press.

Bertelsen, P. (2005). *Free will consciousness and self: Anthropological perspectives on general psychology* (pp. 122–123). New York, NY: Berghahn Books.

Branscombe, N. R., & Doosje, B. (Eds.). (2004). *Collective guilt: International perspectives.* Cambridge: Cambridge University Press.

Carmi, G. E. (2008). Dignity versus liberty: The two western cultures of free speech. *Boston University International Law Journal, 26*, 285.

Castetter, M. D. (2003). Taking law into their own hands: Unofficial and illegal sanctions by the Pakistani Tribal Councils. *Indiana International & Comparative Law Review, 13*(543), 552–553.

Chaudhry, M. S. (1997). *Code of Islamic Laws, 1*, 83.

Choudhury, N. (2007). Constrained spaces for Islamic feminism: Women's rights and the 2004 constitution of Afghanistan. *Yale Journal of Law & Feminism, 19*, 174.

Coleman, I. (2006). Women, Islam, and the new Iraq. *Foreign Affairs, 85*(1), 32.

Condon, J. C., & Yousef, F. S. (1975). *An introduction to intercultural communication.* Upper Saddle River, NJ: Prentice Hall.

El-Azhary Sonbol, A. (2003). *Women of Jordan: Islam, labor, and the law* (p. 207). Syracuse, NY: Syracuse University Press.

Elmer, D. (2002). *Cross-cultural connections: Stepping out and fitting in around the world* (p. 136). Downers Grove, IL: IVP Press.

Eurich-Rascoe, B. L., & Vande Kemp, H. (1997). *Femininity and shame: Women, men, and giving voice to the feminine* (p. 86). Lanham, MD: Rowman & Littlefield.

Geertz, C. (1983). From the native's point of view: On the nature of anthropological under-standing, in local knowledge. In C. Geertz (Ed.), *Local knowledge: Further essays in interpretive anthropology* (p. 55 and 67). New York, NY: Basic Books.

Gold, J. A. (2005). ADR through a cultural lens: How cultural values shape our disputing processes. *Journal of Dispute Resolution, 2005*(2), 289 and 295.

Gottesman, E. (1992). The reemergence of Qisas and Diyat in Pakistan. *Columbia Human Rights Law Review, 23*(11), 436.

Higgins, T. E. (1996). Anti-essentialism, relativism, and human rights. *Harvard Women's Law Journal, 19*(89), 92.

Howland, C. W. (Ed.). (2001). *Religious fundamentalisms and the human rights of women* (p. 204). New York, NY: Palgrave Macmillan.

Hussain, M. (2006). Take my riches, give me justice: A contextual analysis of Pakistan's honor crimes legislation. *Harvard Journal of Law & Gender, 29*, 242.

Johnson, K., & Karlberg, M. (2006). Rethinking power and caste in rural India. *The International Scope Review, 7*(12), 1–15. Retrieved from http://faculty.wwu.edu/karlberg/articles/Power&Caste.pdf

Kahan, D. M. (1996). What do alternative sanctions mean? *University of Chicago Law Review, 63*, 630–653.

Kretzmer, D., & Klein, E. (2002). Foreword. In D. Kretzmer & E. Klein (Eds.), *The concept of human dignity in human rights discourse* (p. 50). Amsterdam, The Netherlands: Springer.

Lewis, M., Haviland-Jones, J. M., & Barrett, L. F. (Eds.). (2000). *Handbook of emotions* (2nd ed., p. 629). New York, NY: Guilford Press.

Locke, J. (1988). In P. Laslett (Ed.), *Two treatises of government, bk. II, § 22*. Cambridge: Cambridge University Press.

Massaro, T. M. (1991). Shame, culture, and American criminal law. *Michigan Law Review, 89*, 1884.

Merriam-Webster's Collegiate Dictionary (10th ed.). (1993). p. 1126. Springfield, MA: Merriam-Webster Incorporated.

Miller, S. (1993). *The shame experience* (p. 117). New York, NY: Routledge.

Miller, T. (2009). *Study finds honor killings a major portion of Pakistan's homicides*. PBS *NewsHour*, April 6. Retrieved from http://www.pbs.org/newshour/updates/health-jan-june09-pakistan_0406/

Miller, W. I. (1993). *Humiliation: And other essays on honor, social discomfort, and violence* (p. 84). Ithaca, NY: Cornell University Press.

Morton, B. C. (2001). Bringing skeletons out of the closet and into the light – 'Scarlet letter' sentencing can meet the goals of probation in modern America because it deprives offenders of privacy. *Suffolk University Law Review, 35*, 100–101.

Nesheiwat, F. K. (2004). Honor crimes in Jordan: Their treatment under Islamic and Jordanian criminal laws. *Penn State International Law Review, 23*, 259.

Nosheen, H., & Schellman, H. (2011). Refusing to kill daughter, Pakistani family defies tradition, draws anger. *The Atlantic*, September 28. Retrieved from http://www.theatlantic.com/international/archive/2011/09/refusing-to-kill-daughter-pakistani-family-defies-tradition-draws-anger/245691/

Nussbaum, M. C. (2004). *Hiding from humanity: Disgust, shame, and the law* (p. 234). Princeton, NJ: Princeton University Press.

Peters, R. (2002). Islamic law in Nigeria. *New York University: The Law School Magazine, 12*(Autumn), 85.

Quraishi, A. (1997). Her honor: An Islamic critique of the rape laws of Pakistan from a woman-sensitive perspective. *Michigan Journal of International Law, 18*, 296–299.

Randall, M. (2004). *Narrative of power: Essays for an endangered century* (p. 107). Monroe, ME: Common Courage Press.

Rawls, J. (1999). In S. Freeman (Ed.), *Collected papers* (pp. 547–583). Cambridge, MA: Harvard University Press.

Ritchie, J., & Ronald, K. (Eds.). (2001). *Available means: An anthology of women's rhetoric(s)* (p. xvii). Pittsburgh, PA: University of Pittsburgh Press.

Ross, M. H. (1995). *The management of conflict: Interpretations and interests in comparative perspective* (pp. 19–20). New Haven, CT: Yale University Press.

Saifee, S. (2003). Penumbras, privacy, and the death of morals-based legislation: Comparing U.S. constitutional law with the inherent right of privacy in Islamic jurisprudence. *Fordham International Law Journal, 27*, 427–428.

Schacht, J. (1982). *An introduction to Islamic law* (p. 177). Oxford: Oxford University Press.

Schwarcz, D. (2003). Shame, stigma, and crime: Evaluating the efficacy of shaming sanctions in criminal law. *Harvard Law Review, 116*, 2207.

Selengut, C. (2003). *Sacred fury: Understanding religious violence* (p. 184). Lanham, MD: Rowman & Littlfield.

Sidahmad, M. A. A. (1995). *The Hudood: The Hudood are the seven specific crimes in Islamic criminal law and their mandatory punishments* (p. 163). Muhammad Ata al Sid Sid Ahmad Boulder, CO: Al Basheer Publications.

Slaughter, M. M. (1993). The Salman Rushdie affair: Apostasy, honor, and freedom of speech. *Virginia Law Review, 79*(1), 153 and 190.

Smith, P. S. (2003). Silent witness: Discrimination against women in the Pakistani law of evidence. *Tulane Journal of International Law & Comparative Law, 11*, 49.

Sonn, T. (2001). Conventional Expectation Versus This Religious Tradition: What Do Husbands and Wives Owe One Another? In J. Neusner (Ed.), *Ethics of Family Life* (pp. 67-84). Belmont, CA: Wadsworth.

Stevens, S. M., & Malesh, P. M. (Eds.). (2009). *Active voices: Composing a rhetoric for social movements* (pp. 71–72). Albany, NY: State University of New York (Kindle edition, internal citations omitted).

Storti, C. (1998). *Figuring foreigners out: A practical guide* (p. 5). Boston, MA: Intercultural Press.

Tangney, J. P., & Fischer, K. W. (Eds.). (1995). *Self-conscious emotions: The psychology of shame, guilt, embarrassment, and pride.* New York, NY: Guilford Press.

Tiedens, L. Z., & Leach, C. W. (Eds.). (2004). *The social life of emotions* (p. 194). Cambridge: Cambridge University Press.

Waldron, J. (2011). Third annual Edward J. Shoen leading scholars symposium: Dignity, rights, and responsibilities. *Arizona State Law Journal, 43,* 1119.

Warren, C. S. (2008). Lifting the veil: Women and Islamic law. *Cardozo Journal of Law & Gender, 15,* 56.

Wells, C. E. (1997). Reinvigorating autonomy: Freedom and responsibility in the Supreme Court's first amendment jurisprudence. *Harvard Civil Rights – Civil Liberties Law Review, 32,* 165.

Whitman, J. Q. (1998). What is wrong with inflicting shame sanctions? *Yale Law Journal, 107,* 1076.

Zafar, F. (Ed.). (1991). *Finding our way: Readings on women in Pakistan* (pp. 298–302). Lahore, Pakistan: ASR Publications.

Chapter 7

(In)Dignity via (Mis)Representation: Politics, Power, and Documentary Film

Justin de Leon

Introduction

> The existence of Third World women's narratives in itself is not
> evidence of decentering hegemonic histories and subjectivities. It
> is the way in which we are read, understood, and located insti-
> tutionally that is of paramount importance. After all, the point
> is not just to record one's history of struggle, or consciousness,
> but how they are recorded; the way we read, receive, and dissemi-
> nate such imaginative records is immensely significant.Chandra
> Mohanty (2003, pp. 77–78)

The title *(In)dignity via (Mis)representation: Politics, Power, and Documentary Film* gets at core of the contribution of this chapter: how individuals and
groups are represented can either dignify or dehumanize.[1] Documentary (or
non-fiction) film is one such site of representation where interactions between
"distant peoples" takes sensory/corporal form (Shohat, 2006). Documentary
film, however, is not void of the political, there are choices constantly being
made and remade. These choices can both recreate and reinforce or challenge
these relationships of unequal power.[2] Critical reflexive practices act as an
important mechanism for ameliorating the pernicious effects of representational cinematographic choices.

---

[1]I am appreciative to the efforts of the editors Michael L. Penn and Hoda Mahmoudi,
as well as Kate Seaman in compiling this special volume. I also want to recognize
Margaret Stetz whose conversations with and continued mentorship have led to the
construction of this piece.
[2]This work avoids reifying any particular definition of configuration of dignity and
representation; rather, it calls for greater attention to reflexive practice. The use of
parenthesis in the title is to motion to the dynamic and relational nature of both
concepts.

Interdisciplinary Perspectives on Human Dignity and Human Rights, 103–130
Copyright © 2020 by Emerald Publishing Limited
All rights of reproduction in any form reserved
doi:10.1108/978-1-78973-821-620191013

Film can be an expression and celebration of both human dignity or indignity, presenting dignifying or dehumanizing acts. Suheil Bushrui suggests that the opposite of human dignity is humiliation (see Bushrui's contribution in this volume). Closely tied to humiliation are dehumanizing acts, or acts that strip agency and reinforce difference and over-simplification.

Feminist scholar Jacqui Alexander (2005) reminds us the importance of academic theory, "Scholarship isn't just about books. Scholarship is about how to create the tools that will free us from oppression" (p. 178). Critical reflexive practice is one such tool that can disrupt oppression and is readily accessible to academics and practitioners. This essay explores the relationship between (mis) representation and (in)dignity through analyzing three documentary films: *Kony 2012* (2012), *Half the Sky* (2012), and *Give to Live* (2015).

Documentary film is an important medium of analysis for many reasons, two of which are its wide distribution and global reach as a result of technological advances and increased accessibility and its ability to bring people into contact with each other, thus informing conceptions of how others live, organize their lives, and their cultural values. More profoundly, aside from introducing us to others, film also has the power to introduce ourselves *to ourselves*.[3] That is, how we encounter difference tells us equally about ourselves than those who we come across. (Mis)representations are political acts imbued with enactments of power (easily translated into violence) that can simultaneously strip and endow subjects with agency and value.[4] Documentary films can reinforce global power inequalities and oppressive relationships, while, conversely, act as sites of resistance and celebrations of human experiences in its multiplicity of forms.[5] They can encourage and animate thinking of new arrangements of justice and understanding. They are a critical site for the operations and enactments of power. Documentary film can redefine the bounds of possibility.

The following explores the relationship between (in)dignity and (mis)representation through the medium of documentary film – as a political act – to suggest that the practice of documentary film can benefit from (renewed) attention to reflexive practices. Reflexivity is a deliberative, self-aware process – understood as a "sociology-of-knowing approach" – that provides a source of insight and allows researchers to examine critically, reflect upon, and analytically explore the research and production process (Fonow & Cook, 1991). It calls for critical reflection upon how inquiry is conducted and has its roots in sociology, critical/

---

[3]This notion was introduced to me by the respected Iranian filmmaker Mohsen Makhmalbaf during a 2016 film training through the Institute for the Studies of Global Prosperity.

[4]The study of power and representation has a long historical trajectory that includes postcolonial scholarship such as Said (1978), Spivak (1988), and Escobar (1995) and critical feminist scholarship such as Mohanty (1991), Rabinowitz (1994), Chowdhry and Nair (2002), Shohat (2006), and Silvey (2010).

[5]Tuck (2009) presents the notion of "complex personhood" as a referendum on what she refers to as "damage-based" research.

hermeneutic traditions, and feminist theory.[6] At its core, it is about conscious-raising – consciousness of how one's actions (or inactions) contribute to oppression and (mis)representation. Critical reflexivity can lead to insights about contradictions and intersections of injustice of society.

This chapter locates itself at the juncture of theory and practice, or praxis, by assessing three documentary films and how filmmaker choices of representation have a dignifying or dehumanizing effect for historically marginalized peoples.[7] It aims at showing how critical reflexivity, or the lack thereof, impacts representation and calls for critical reflexive practices to move academics and practitioners to be cognizant of production-oriented representational choices. Documentary film possesses unique and powerful characteristics that have real-world implications on how distant peoples are conceived. It begins with a brief introduction, setting up the chapter's argument. It is then divided into three sections and proceeds as follows. First, it examines the unique attributes of the medium of documentary, such as the ability to (mis)represent distant peoples through the operations of the visual gaze, the sensuous nature of the medium, and its close tie to science and so-called objectivity. It explores the relationships of power (and violence) nested within the practice of documentary film, illustrating documentary film as a political act that favors and reinforces specific power relationships over others. Second, it focuses on documentary film praxis by comparing and contrasting various aspects of three documentary films.[8] It concludes with reflections on the impact of filmmaking choices of representation and human dignity. This chapter calls for critical reflexivity as a means to

---

[6]In my research I use gender in multiple ways: as a noun, verb, and logic of difference. Gender as a noun is simply counting sex (i.e., counting male or female legislators in a governing body), gender as a verb represents the formation of subjects based on relations of domination or subordination (i.e., the use techniques of emasculation during war), and gender as a logic of difference is based on the notion that relations between sexes is *the* foundational dyad of difference within any social or communal context – thereby providing a productive space and framework in which to analyze other relationships of dominance and difference. I visualize this as different layers of an onion, where each layer is a different context and sphere of treatment of difference, where the center of these concentric circles is the relationship/treatment/behavior between a society's or community's socially constructed meanings around sex. I take inspiration from Shepherd (2008) who, aside from gender as a noun and verb, sees gender as a productive logic – both a product and producing – of performances of violence.

[7]Swarr and Nagar (2012) give an example of focusing on praxis (the juncture of theory and practice) in relationship to activism and social change. They do this by employing a lens that locates power through representation, while being attentive to postcolonial feminist convictions.

[8]My conceptualization of praxis is based on Freire (1970/2005) who states,

To no longer be prey to [oppression] […] one must emerge from it and turn upon it. This can be done only by means of the praxis: reflection and action upon the world in order to transform it. (p. 51)

achieve a more critical, thoughtful, and dignifying practice of documentary film and draws from my examples of my experiences with my first feature-length documentary film *Give to Live*.

Power Through Discourse

Discourses are defined as the "social processes and the systems of knowledge through which meaning is produced, fixed, lived, experienced, and transformed" (Barnett & Duvall, 2005, p. 55). The study of international politics is closely tied to the study of power and violence. Why is it important to talk about power and violence when it comes to documentary filmmaking? Documentary filmmaking is an act of engaging and creating discourse, thus, is not value-free; rather, it is a political act conceptualized, created, and received within the context of specific power relationships. Though subtler and often less direct, discursive power is no less pernicious than direct coercion. The following is a brief overview of conceptualizations of power within the study of international politics.

The dominating understanding of power in the field of international relations is compulsory power, as defined as direct control of one actor over the actions and conditions of existence of another. Interactions between people or other actors shape circumstances and the possibilities of action. The very definition of a state has been intimately connected to power and violence. Political theorist Max Weber (1918) defines the state as "A human community that (successfully) claims the monopoly of the legitimate use of physical force within a given territory" (p. 1). A second understanding of power is power as structural. "Co-constitutive, internal relations of structural positions" determine how various actors socialize and interact (Barnett & Duvall 2005, p. 53). Interests, subjectivities, and social capacities are shaped by social, political, or cultural position held. Similarly, a third understanding of power as institutional, suggests that actors are constrained and shaped by rules, norms, and procedures.

A fourth conceptualization of power, one that presents an entry point for productive discussions about documentary film and creativity, is productive power. Productive power operates through diffuse constitutive relations in ways that produce actors' social and political capacities. This understanding moves away from structures and institutions to systems of meaning and social forces. Productive power differs from structural and institutional power by focusing on more diffuse and generalized social processes. Productive power is the "constitution of all social subjects with various social powers through systems of knowledge and discursive practices of broad and general social scope" (Barnett & Duvall, 2005, p. 55).

French critical theorist Michel Foucault (1977) posits an understanding of productive power that is attentive to the "capillary character" of the operations and relations of power, or what he calls the "microphysics of power" (p. 26). A Foucauldian approach to power accounts for a wider conceptualization of power – deviating from power-as-a-singular-form. Power is not a commodity that can be possessed but rather as a regime of domination within unequal power relations; rather, it circulates in networks and constitutes individual identities and subjectivities. Productive power allows for focus on discursive practices through instruments of power, or how practices and mechanisms are "formed into ideologies and knowledges" (Neal, 2009, p. 168). Discourse is one such mechanism and practice in which power operates, referring not only to communication between actors (see the Habermasian concept of communicative action), but also the everyday practices that define what is natural, normal, possible, and/or problematic. This later approach calls for the analysis of the maneuvers of power, existing at the same time concentrated and direct, as well as diffuse and indirect. It involves looking at how discourse produces and constitutes the social world. Documentary film is a site of representation and, therefore, a site of transformation. As such, documentary film is a political act and an expression of power – one that hails into place the subjectivities of peoples in ways that celebrate and express human (in)dignity. How discourse is articulated and created requires an understanding of how people, concepts, and cultures are portrayed and represented.

Significance of Selected Documentary Films

Documentary film acts as a form of productive power through communication that produces meaning, shapes identities, and forms attitudes. How the political is structured requires looking at language and representation – both through claims and its silences. One such discourse that impacts how the other is viewed and how difference is conceptualized is documentary film. The timely significance of the medium cannot be understated. Of the top 20 grossing documentary films of all-time, 18 of them come from after 2000.[9] Documentary film takes on heightened importance in light of the global impact of Internet-accessible documentaries. In 2012, the Youtube-released documentary *Kony 2012*, about the rebel group Lord's Resistance Army (LRA) in northern Uganda, saw over 100 million views in six days (Wasserman, 2012). *Half the Sky*, a Public Broadcasting Service (PBS) prime-time documentary film, that at the time of this writing was available on Netflix, starring New York Times reporter Nicholas Kristof was said to redefine the documentary genre by its strategic "transmedia" nature (or that it has multiple entry points in which the audience can engage) and which garnered such star power as Desmond Tutu and George Clooney.[10]

---

[9]Taken from BoxOfficeMojo.com – http://www.boxofficemojo.com/genres/chart/?id=documentary.htm.

[10]Another documentary phenomenon was *Class Dismissed* (2009), a short documentary by *New York Times* reporter Adam Ellick featured Malala Yousafzai and her father as they struggled against Taliban bans against the education of girls. After their failed assassination of Malala (which left her in the hospital with massive head trauma for months), the Taliban issued a press release branding her as spy that was spreading propaganda and was in collusion with the American military. On the press release was a still image from the documentary showing Malala meeting a US official which was to serve as visual "proof" (Mackey, 2012). Though this film was released in 2009, it resurfaced in relevance in 2012 because of the Taliban attack on Malala.

These two documentary films will be looked at in more detail, along with a third film *Give to Live,* my first feature-length film that I directed in 2015 with a collaborative team of filmmakers. All three films confront global injustice, poverty, and human compassion – *Kony 2012* focuses on bringing the rebel leader Joseph Kony (who's responsible for the killing and displacement of thousands) to justice, *Half the Sky* on injustice faced by girls around the world can be mitigated through an increased focus on education, and *Give to Live* the impact of foreign aid and charitable giving in Africa (East Africa in particular). Rather than comparing these three films, they are being used to highlight choices of representation that have an impact on the (mis)representation of people and/ or issues. I share experiences with the production of *Give to Live* to bring into analysis experiences of production and process, not to suggest that the film is of the same level of production or distribution reach as the previous two.[11] My understanding of the importance of representation and production is greatly shaped by my first act of making a feature-length film – my practice informed my theory.

Kony 2012

Kony 2012 is a short film created by the organization Invisible Children. In particular, it appeals to young people in the US to come out and stand against the atrocities of Kony and his LRA. It builds off of an earlier produced film *Invisible Children* (2006) by Jason Russell and a few of his college friends who witnessed the impact of the atrocities on young boys and girls in northern Uganda. This earlier film showed how these young children sought refuge at night in the center of nearby towns so to escape the LRA rebel forces. These rebels were kidnapping the young boys and girls and conscribing into the rebel army. Revisiting parts of this film, *Kony 2012* is a call to action premised on the technological advances – Facebook, Skype, and YouTube are all prominently featured within the narrative. Invisible Children, the non-profit organization, is an organization that creates films to highlight the atrocities of the LRA and to encourage global action. It was an organization founded in 2004 on film and storytelling. Its website reads, "Each film aims to introduce the audience to the complexities of the LRA conflict, highlight the human resilience that transcends borders, and inspire immediate action" (Invisible Children website, 2013).

This film flows from a personal narrative of Russell and starts with home footage of the birth of his son Gavin. Throughout the 30-minute film, featured are

---

[11]*Give to Live* is not an example of correct practice, necessarily, as so much as it is a sharing of first-hand experiences to help illuminate salient points. My second feature-length documentary is a collaboration entitled *More Than a Word* (Directors Kenn and John Little, Media Education Foundation 2017) about the problematic use of Native mascots in professional sports. *More Than a Word* has screened at over 250 Universities in North America and nominated *Best Documentary* at the 2018 San Francisco American Indian Film Festival.

the atrocities of the LRA and how individuals here in the US can get involved to bring Kony to justice. The film asserts,

> Arresting Joseph Kony will prove that the world we live in has new rules, that the technology that has brought our planet together is allowing us to respond to the problems of our friends.

Kony 2012 was hugely successful in terms of YouTube and sparked rallies and showings on college campuses around the US.

Half the Sky

The 2012 **PBS** documentary *Half the Sky* is inspired by the book of the same name written by Nicholas Kristof and Sheryl WuDunn (2010). It highlights the oppressive circumstances faced by women and girls around the world, including sex trafficking, rape, and prostitution as well as the broader themes of poverty, gender-based violence, and lack of opportunity. The documentary is also led by *New York Times* journalist Kristof and features both US government officials and Hollywood celebrities such as George Clooney, Meg Ryan, Eva Mendes, Gabrielle Union, Olivia Wilde, Diane Lane, America Ferrera, Madeleine Albright, Desmond Tutu, Gloria Steinem, and Hillary Clinton. It has been heralded by its creators and by the press alike as redefining the medium of documentary film – creating a new type of film categorized as transmedia. It is claimed that it has the potential to more fully engage the audience because of its "multiple entry points and interactive experiences" (Astle, 2012). The four-hour **PBS** film was put forward by its creators as a "landmark" film which they aired as a prime-time broadcast event for US and international audiences.

Its multiple entry points for audience engagement include a Facebook-hosted social action game, multiple websites, mobile internet device apps and mobile games, educational videos with accompanying texts, an impact assessment plan, and a comprehensive social media campaign with over 30 partner non-governmental organizations (NGOs). *Half the Sky* was a large-scale production with large funders such as the Bill & Melinda Gates Foundation, Ford Foundation, Goldman Sachs Foundation, Rockefeller Foundation, Nike Foundation, United States Agency for International Development (USAID), and Coca-Cola. It was filmed in 10 different countries and follows Kristof and various female American celebrities. The film follows several stories of individuals who are experiencing forms of gender-based violence and individuals who are working to transform those situations and work against gender-based injustices. On its website, the creators of *Half the Sky* hold:

> Across the globe oppression is being confronted, and real meaningful solutions are being fashioned through health care, education, and economic empowerment for women and girls. The linked problems of sex trafficking and forced prostitution, gender-based violence, and maternal mortality – which needlessly claim one

woman every 90 seconds – present to us the single most vital opportunity of our time: the opportunity to make a change. All over the world women are seizing this opportunity.

Half the Sky is a **PBS** documentary film that explores gender-based violence. It is the centerpiece of a larger **PBS** transmedia project. It aims to confront the global oppression of women and sparked renewed debate about American's role in global justice and gender equity.

Give to Live

Give to Live is a documentary film project that explores charitable giving and foreign aid in East Africa. It assesses the economic impact of charitable giving and foreign aid, the psychology behind giving and receiving, and the ripple effects of human compassion. The film addresses misconceptions around giving and the development field to provide viewers with a critical perspective, inspiration, and incentive to address these important global issues in ways that are more effective and sustainable. Since its completion in 2015, the film has shown at multiple film festivals around the country, winning multiple awards.

Similar to *Half the Sky*, it follows the stories of both individuals who have experienced injustice and hardship, as well as those who are working on their behalf. Featured are East African- and American-based NGOs, including: Kenyan Community Development Foundation, Nyakach Community Development Association, Medecins Sans Frontiers (Doctors Without Borders), Heifer International Kenya, Water is Life Kenya, and Janada L. Batchelor Foundation for Children, as well as academics such as Vandana Shiva, Frances Moore Lappe, Dacher Keltner, Peter Singer, Charles Ngugi, and Richard Mshomba. It highlights the gendered nature of injustice and inequality throughout the world. The film team consisted of six members: a director (myself), two producers, director of photography, creative consultant, and editor. It is a five-year project that was filmed throughout the US and parts of East Africa and was funded by dozens of private funders.

The film attempts to leave the audience with more questions than answers, adopting a critical and questioning stance about development. It asks the audience to think about these issues in various ways and through multiple vantage points.

Section 1: Documentary Film and Representation

How people are able to interact with each other around the globe has taken on new forms through technological advances of just the last decade. Photographs and moving images portray the customs and values of a physically distant other. Advances in technology allow us to bring the world into our homes at the click of a button. Documentary film and non-fiction film has also seen many advances because of increased accessibility of cameras and editing programs, as well as a slew of distribution options through social media that were not even conceivable just a few decades ago. It is now easier for anyone to make a film, a fact that is both good and bad, especially knowing the unique qualities of non-fiction film. Three unique elements to documentary film that make it able to (mis)represent other cultures are the power of the camera and the visual gaze, the visual being linked to the sensual, and its relationship to scientific objectivity.

Camera and the Visual Gaze

Images through the media shape how we see ourselves and others. "The contemporary media shape identity; indeed, many argue that they now exist close to the very core of identity production," asserts Ella Shohat (2006), continuing, "By facilitating a mediated engagement with 'distant' peoples, the media 'deterritorialize' the process of imagining communities" (p. 325). Media has the power to objectify and disembody distant peoples –separating them from context and history, while producing consumable spectacles and exhibits. This is particularly the case when it comes to marginalized populations (see Smith, 2012). Modernity and its attendant technologies have, in many communities of color, introduced an "objectifying regime of visuality," or scopic regime, that dictates how the so-called other is conceived or, as often is the case, misunderstood and misconceived (Escobar, 1995, p. 155).

Early documentary film was closely tied to imperial projects of the late nineteenth and early twentieth centuries. American and continued European colonial expansion fueled the searching out for new territories and "pure" civilizations (Juhasz, 1999). Documenting this impulse through film and photography allowed for the visual transmission of distant peoples, allowing for a unique colonial combination of objectifying gaze and voyeurism. This has been referred to as the colonial or post-colonial gaze (Said, 1978). The very beginnings of cinema "coincided with the imperialist moment," where the apparatuses of social control moved from the metropole to the periphery (Shohat, 2006, p. 24). This visual engagement through the colonial gaze turned peasants, farmers, women, and the environment into foreign spectacles and objects to be controlled and consumed. This visuality and voyeurism were made possible through non-fiction, documentary film.

This colonial, visual gaze evoked a distance and separation. It developed pity and a sense of superiority, rather than empathy for others – empathy has been found to be a critical aspect in compelling an audience to develop a sense of mutuality (Dolby, 2012). This visual gaze, and its subsequent objectification, is as powerful today as it was then. For example, the rise in so-called slum tourism challenges the premise that mere visual exposure to poverty necessarily equates to a rise in empathy and action. Observing poverty is not enough. In actually, many of the world's most impoverished settlements are often in plain visual sight of, or right next to, more affluent areas and homes. Slum tourism, which involves the taking of film and "photos of people's private lives without consent, without thought, and certainly without empathy," can be likened to the effects of the visuality of documentary film (Dolby, 2012, pp. 104–105).

Bringing audiences to impoverished and exotic locations, if not done carefully and thoughtfully, can reinscribe difference and pity, evoking a desire to comfort rather than relationships of mutuality. Relations based on pity are largely framed in a lack-need or "damage-based" perspectives (Tuck, 2009). In contrast, empathy allows the construction of a whole person, one that requires empathy and the ability to see a "full, complex, intelligent human being, not simply an object of pity" (Dolby, 2012, p. 93). The objectification and commodification of distant peoples through the operations of the colonial visual gaze robs people of their agency and dignity and has serious implications.

> If you have little respect for the dignity of individuals you are trying to help, you are not going to give THEM much say in what THEY want and need, and how you can help THEM help themselves? (Dolby, 2012, pp. 95–96)

Sensuous

Documentary film deals with bodily senses, or the sensual. Documentary highlights stories of individuals in ways that bring to life sounds, textures, and smells of faraway environments. Though it may deal with travel and nature, it ultimately captures dimensions of human experiences and emotions. Jane Gaines (1999) refers to documentary's ability to engage bodily senses as "political mimesis." Audiences physically experience the same injustices and physical challenges as the subjects in the film. Bodily engagement "lead[s] the spectator" in ways that are not "exclusively a matter of the head but can also be a matter of the heart" (Gaines, 1999, p. 87). This is where documentary shows great potential for social change and action.[12] Being present in one's life and death struggles – complete with sweat, tears, and blood – can compel audiences in significantly different ways than of written texts. No other medium captures the corporality and physicality of experience and struggles quite the same way as a documentary film.

Science and Objectivity

The unique nature of documentary film goes beyond the visual gaze and its ability to engage the sensual, but it also acts as a means for social production. Non-fiction film was created out of an impulse to see and verify, the same impulses that have motivated scientific inquiry. Science itself was born out of the intersection of words and things, "enabling one to see and to say" (Foucault, 1975, p. xii). The century-old idiom "seeing is believing" attests to the power of visual proof as the most primary form of evidence-collecting. Seeing not only verifies but also

---

[12]Much has been written about documentary film's ability to act as a means of social change, a piece that summarizes many of its unique characteristics and potentialities is Walker (2018).

provides a mandate to believe – to see is to believe and to believe is to see. For instance, the beginnings of modern medicine coincide with physician's ability to operate on a corpse. The physician was able to look inside to see and therefore understand the inner workings of the human body.

With its origins in anthropology, the documentary film acted as a means of collecting evidence to inform and justify theory (Renov, 1999). In this manner, non-fiction film has taken on an anthropological and historiographical role in writing identities of others, allowing it to "resuscitate forgotten and distant civilizations" (Juhasz, 1999, p. 112). Science's first interactions with peoples outside of America and Western Europe were through the anthropological project of "discovery": the explorer sees for his own eyes (they were exclusively male), collecting and taking back "authoritative" accounts of life and cultures in distant lands.

A desire to find "uncontaminated" civilizations motivated these anthropological efforts. This, in turn, was connected to the project of science and objectivity. Objectivity, however, was a premised upon white, male European normativity. Objectivity and science lead to the measurements of human skulls in an attempt to justify European and American superiority and domination of people of color (Smith, 2012). It is no mystery, then, how the killing, enslavement, and genocide of these "distant peoples" was carried out in the name of civilization-building, science, and objectivity. The claim of objectivity and science has not been a historically value-free practice. Representation, through the visual gaze, engaging the sensual, and its relationship to science and objectivity, has serious implications on how perceptions of individuals and cultures are understood and fixed (whether dignifying or dehumanizing). Representation through documentary film, therefore, acts as a discursive power no less pernicious than that of direct power or violence.

Representation and Filming

Every time a camera is turned on and pointed at a scene, particular aspects are framed and captured while others are left out. Decisions of what to include and how to include are constantly being made. At every step, questions have to be answered. Who, what, and how do you film? Where to film it? Do you ask questions or just observe, and if you do ask, what and how do you ask? And these are only a few of the pre-production questions needing to be answered.[13] Hundreds of other questions are considered before a film can be ready for audience-viewing. For instance, how does the film team gain access to the communities you wish to film? How do you present (or do you present) specialized, insider knowledge? How do you edit the filmed sequences? The following is just a short list of questions and decisions that must be considered in the three stages of filmmaking (pre-production, production, and post-production):

---

[13]There are three stages to a documentary film – pre-production, production, and post-production – roughly divided into the planning and storyboarding, filming, and editing stages respectively.

Pre-production

- Funding sources (Are there conditions regarding distribution and/or content?)
- Level of budget (Who is the audience? What is the purpose?)
- Subject matter (What and how to explore? Why do you want to tell the story?)
- Storyline (Are you the best person to tell the story? Who is?)
- Narration (Should you use captured dialog? Testimony or interview? Voiceover narration?)
- Point of view (Who's writing the script? Who's telling the story?)
- Level of analysis (What are you going to be exploring? Institutions, structures, communities, or individuals?)
- Production time (Is the topic time-sensitive?)
- Aesthetic principles of captured images (What are the length of takes? What are the envisioned scenes? How to capture storyline best with the technical settings of the camera?)
- Personnel involved (What is the optimal size of the team? What are the needs of the team?)
- Length of the film (closely tied to desired audience – roughly 3 minutes for internet viewing, 10 minutes for a short documentary film festival entry, 26 or 56 for television broadcast, or over 65 for a feature-length film)
- Camera operation (Is it going to be self-filmed? Do you need a Director of Photography or team of camera operators?)

Production

- Film team interaction with subjects/subject matter (How do you interact with the space you are filming? Are you insiders or members of the community? Do you portray yourselves as academics, filmmakers, artists, students, or professionals?)
- Technical camera(s) usage (Are you making sure you have matching footage? Are you set up for multiple angles or special shots like time-lapse or slow motion? What type of image are you going for, smooth, still, shoulder-mounted reporter style, or mobile handheld?)
- Filming equipment (Do you want a film-like or digital video look? Are you going to use drones, cranes, tripods, or jibs? use of external lighting, natural lighting, or a mix; types of microphones; or use of cranes, tripods, dollies, and jibs verses relying predominantly on handheld)
- Lighting (Are you going to use external lighting or natural lighting? How will lighting help you tell the story better?)
- Audio (What type of audio do you wish to capture? Wild or natural sounds, ambient sounds, and/or interviews? What types of microphones to use?)
- Size of team (What is the most effective size in regard to the story you're wanting to tell?)
- Legal documentation and releases (Do you have writer's agreements in place? Will you use and how will you prepare your media release forms? Are there certain cultural contexts that you need to be aware of while drafting legal documentation?)

Post-production

- Editors (Who is editing? How involved are is the Director or Producer? Are there multiple editors involved?)
- Paper edit (To what extent does your Editor bring to life the story? Do you create a paper edit using scene cards for your Editor to follow?)
- Storytelling (How do you communicate with the Editor the desired pacing and cadence?)
- Footage review (Which members of your team are going to be responsible for reviewing the hours of footage? How do you organize the footage and information?)
- Title cards and subtitles (Do you use any? How are individuals are introduced and when to use subtitles or voiceovers?)
- Editorial decision-making (What is the collaborative creative process going to look like? What are the defined roles of creative collaboration?)
- Music (Will it be endogenous to the footage or external? How will it help with the storytelling?)
- Finalizing and mastering (Will you master the sound and color? How will you uniform the look and sound of the finalized piece? Can you afford a professional mastering or do you have to do it in-house?)
- Distribution (How will your film reach its intended audience? How do you connect with distributors to reach those audiences? Are their film festival and/or distributor agreements and constrictions on where and how you can show the film? Are there royalties involved? Do you have to make up for any initial costs invested by distributors?)

These questions are not a "how to" list and it is certainly not comprehensive in any way. Instead, I offer these considerations to provide a cursory view of what goes into the making of a documentary film and the multitude of choices and options that need to be considered. Films do not just happen, they are not just stumbled upon by happenstance; rather, they are the result of many paths chosen over others, regardless of whether paths are intentional. How each of these questions is treated has real-world consequences on viewers' knowledge and impression of the subject matter and, ultimately, the representation of individuals and cultures.

The act of pushing the record button is fraught with decisions, decisions that impact how subjects, themes, and culture are portrayed and (mis)represented, or, as filmmaker and scholar Susan Sontag (2003) suggests, "To photograph is to frame, and to frame is to exclude" (p. 47).

Central to the visual power of documentary film is to understand its origins in the colonial gaze, its engagement of the sensual, and its tie to the project of science and objectivity. Documentary acts as a site of interaction, representation, and definition for distant peoples to be experienced, named, and produced. How choices are made through the filmmaking process can have profound adverse effects on individuals and communities. Alternatively, documentary can fashion new ways of connectivity and community. The next section explores various practices of representation within the practice of documentary film.

Section 2: Documentary Film Praxis

To illustrate how documentary film's productive powers of representation become operationalized through filmmaker choices, the following assesses three major concepts that illustrate certain representational film practices. They are (1) the location of expert knowledge, (2) the over-simplification of complex issues, and (3) the appropriation of others' stories. Each represents a productive site where filmmaker choices impact how distant peoples are (mis)represented. These concepts can constitute a framework in which to assess the significant relationship between (mis)representation and (in)dignity.

Expert Knowledge

In most films there is a voice, or multiple voices, of authority and insight, sources that lead the viewer to new ways of thinking and understanding. Why should it matter where knowledge is coming from within a film? How a film locates specialized knowledge is significant because who is portrayed as knowledgeable, or as "expert," motions to the audience who has the intellectual authority (and, implicitly, who does not have the authority) to understand the complexity and contours of the subject matter. Making a choice to rely exclusively on outside expertise can subconsciously reinforce bias and externally prescribed histories for distant peoples, especially those without the resources to create their own films (Waldman & Walker, 1999). These choices locate knowledge. Historically, expert knowledge has been confined to the Western academy and, more specifically, from white, male academics. Women, Indigenous communities, and people of color have largely been left out of this space.

To reinforce the importance of differing perspectives and voices, Faye Ginsburg's (1999) looks to the scientific concept of parallax, or the parallactic angle. That is, by offering a slightly different angle and new position, the observer (or audience) gains the ability to challenge the otherwise fixed cinematic representations of their position. This concept is adopted from the field of astronomy and refers to the act of looking at an object in space from a different position, resulting in a new perspective and insight. In doing so, the contours and detail of the subject matter is better understood than would have originally been achieved if seen from single fixed points. Spatial distance is significant. Parallax is not just about seeing through different lens; rather, it prioritizes the changing of the physical distance of the observer to gain deeper insight into subject matter. Within the context of film, physical differences and separation nurtures creativity and possibility. Difference provides a space and freedom to imagine new collective and interdependent ways of being (Lorde, 1984). Locating expert knowledge outside of the hegemonic white, male academic, challenges audiences to recognize distance and difference, providing an opportunity to rethink preconceived notions and relationships with distant peoples.

In *Half the Sky*, specialized knowledge comes from *New York Times* reporter Nicholas Kristof himself. The contextual information about the situations of each country comes from conversations between Kristof and particular American celebrities assigned to each injustice and location. These conversations take place in the documentary at the beginning of each country-specific segment. Each starts with a car ride where Kristof provides the celebrity (and viewer) with history and an overview of the major issues going to be explored in that location. In between each story segment, interviews with Western academics further contextualizes the plight of those in the featured stories. Throughout the film, there was not one featured academic indigenous to the country of filming. Moreover, during the car rides with Kristof, the viewer saw shots of passing neighborhoods featuring poverty and squalor interspersed with Kristof's contextual history. The perspective of looking out from the car window (as the car was quickly moving in and out of neighborhoods) implies a separation from the dirty and unsafe outside environment and the safety of the modern car.

Kony 2012 also followed *Half the Sky* by placing specialized knowledge within the film through their use of outside experts. In this case, all contextual information came from the filmmaker Jason Russell, the main subject and star of the film. Russell provides the background information for the issues described in the film, including the involvement of child soldiers, the evolution of the LRA, and the hunt for its leader Joseph Kony. No specialists from Uganda were involved in providing the context of the story and background.

Throughout production of *Give to Live*, there was an intentional effort to ensure specialized knowledge and context were coming from both Western and African scholars and specialists. The reliance on filming location-based experts required much more coordinating efforts to identify and connect with the appropriate people. It did, however, lead to a more balanced representation of where and how specialized knowledge was located throughout the film. Much of the film, and specifically the country-based explorations, came from specialists (not all academics) who were located within those very communities and countries.

Over-simplification

The commodification, possession, and "thingification" (Cesaire, 1972) of peoples, cultures, and ways of life have been driving forces in the dispossession, dehumanization, and colonization of much of the world's peoples.[14] A dominant culture of oblivion brings about the belief that it is acceptable to appropriate, consume, and destroy other cultures to suit current fancies (Juhasz, 1999). In doing so, racialized subjects become frozen in time as depoliticized and ahistorical entities.

An outcome of the culture of oblivion, commodification, and possession is a popular over-simplification of otherwise complex peoples and issues of, more often than not, racialized distant peoples. Documentary film can produce feelings of both pity and empathy, the former leading to simplification and the later to

---

[14]See Smith (2012) on the compartmentalization and commodification of Indigenous peoples, Moreton-Robinson (2015) on white possession, and Cesaire (1972) on thingification.

complexity and solidarity. Pity, or sympathy, motivates individuals to console and comfort. Though these feelings are not bad in themselves, they often occur from simplified understandings of a person's situation, hardship, or injustice. It occurs when subjects are void of complexity and agency. Over-simplification does not require an intelligent and thoughtful protagonist, one that is constantly adapting and persevering in ways that, at times, may be contradictory.

For example, if Person A is facing injustice through Hardship B, then Person A is subject to the effects of Hardship B and simply needs to remove themselves from that relationship. This simplified relationship of hardship reinforces essentialist understandings of both person and hardship – person A is fixed and bound to a single identity of victimhood (Ginsburg, 1999). There is no choice or complexity for Person A in regard to Hardship B.

By contrast, if Person A is being affected by Hardship B, C, and D and Person A resists through Actions X, Y, and Z, then the complexity of Person A, as well as the impact of Hardship B, are portrayed in a more true-to-life, complex fashion. Likewise, moving away from simplistic cinematographic representations that evoke pity to more nuanced and complexed representations. Simply, "conferring the respect on others that comes from presuming that life and people's lives are simultaneously straightforward and full of enormously subtle meaning" (Gordon, 1997, p. 5).[15]

Half the Sky tackles the theme of global education in a simplified manner. It provides a simple solution to a complex problem, the need for female education that will lead to the ending of the oppression of women. There is no question that emphasis on education is laudable and much needed, though throughout the film it is portrayed as a panacea – not all education and education systems are the same, content and approach can vastly differ. In the film, celebrity Gabrielle Union rides a bike with a young Vietnamese girl. In a voice over, you hear Union state, "If you want something bad enough nothing will stand in your way," continuing, "These girls are only limited by their desire and their passion for education and it seems limitless." The structures and complexities of Vietnamese education are not explored with great detail. In the film's final scene, Kristof is standing in a doorway with a young Somali girl of about ten years old. He asks, "Do you think Somali girls should go to school?" "Yes," the girl answers. "I agree with you," says Kristof. As the scene patiently holds, the actor George Clooney is heard in a voiceover asserting, "Maybe if we just kept that one school open, what would happen?" Throughout the film, education is promoted as being a solution to a very complex problem, yet the complex problem is never fully examined in each of the particular contexts it was being examined.

Kony 2012 also falls prey to a tendency to over-simplify. The film received much public criticism in large part due to its shallow treatment of the complexities of the 26-year-long conflict. To begin with, the film gave the impression that Kony is still terrorizing the northern part of the country and that violence is still ever-present. This was not fully true at the time of the film in 2012. The

---

[15]Found in Tuck (2009, p. 420).

last LRA attack in Uganda came in 2006 (Matsiko, 2011). It also does not challenge or scrutinize the role of the Ugandan government and its President Yoweri Museveni. Museveni has long received criticism for his role in initiating and prolonging the conflict. From 1986 to 2006, Museveni led decentralization programs that created an environment of violence, as localization of governing power led to opportunities for in-group vying for leadership (Green, 2008). Additionally, government forces were found complicit in the brutalization of the northern ethnic Acholi people. The National Resistance Movement (the party of Museveni), which became the Uganda People's Defense Force in 1995, created so-called protected Internally Displace Peoples camps that were likened to concentration camps. Soldiers carried out murders, rapes, and beatings all while supposedly protecting the people from Kony's terror (Behrend, 1998). All of this was omitted from *Kony 2012*, opting instead for a simplified story of the conflict and those caught in the crossfire.

Appropriation of Story

A necessary question when watching a documentary film is whose story is being told and who is telling that story? A majority of stories are told by outsiders, rather than the individuals or communities themselves. This is not to say that the telling of others' stories is not important, as other people's stories are central in crafting our own identity and sense of self. There is, however, an interesting paradox that occurs when one attempts to tell the story of another: by putting one's self in someone else's shoes, they automatically erase the "uniqueness and specificity of the other's experience" (Dolby, 2012, p. 102). This is what Nadine Dolby (2012) refers to as the "paradox of appropriation". This paradox motions to the idea that even though one can understand and take on the pain of another, they still keep a distinct sense of self and separation from the experience. As a result, appropriating the pain and suffering of others detracts from the experiences of those whom you work on behalf. Consequently, working beside those who are experiencing hardships allows subjects to "talk back" on their own terms (Ginsburg, 1999).[16]

In one scene in *Half the Sky*, Kristof is accompanied by John Wood, a former Microsoft Director and founder of the NGO *Room to Read*, as they visit a Thai family. This segment in Thailand was unique because there was a strong male father figure present in the story, something that the other segments lacked. The scene takes place over lunch at the family's home. Kristof and Wood are sitting on one side of the table and the father Hiep Van Dao and his daughter Phung Ngoc Dao on the other. The translator sits unseen near the camera at the end of the table and Kristof proceeds to compliment the single father of the

---

[16]This is a complex theme. In principle it is desirable to work with, rather than in front of those you are trying to assist. This relationship, however, is fraught with imbalanced power relationships that can are better recognized than reconciled. See Payne (2017) on participatory action research and White (2003) on participatory video.

fourteen-year-old girl for working multiple jobs to support their family. The scene unfolds as such:

KRISTOF (TO DAUGHTER PHUNG):	When you are alone here, when your father is away [working], what time do you wake in the morning?
PHUNG:	I wake at 3 a.m.
HIEP:	Sometimes when I'm away at work I can't sleep at night, thinking about how hard it is for the kids without their mother.
KRISTOF (TO FATHER HIEP):	Do you ever think of asking Phung to leave school and raise money for the younger children?
HIEP:	I told my children I don't have land to give them when they grow up, the only thing I can give them is education, so I don't want my children to drop out from school. When [Phung] has parent-teacher meetings, I take a day off of work so I can monitor which subjects my daughter could improve.
WOOD (TO TRANSLATOR):	So when there are parent meetings he will stop working, pay the motorcycle taxi, the commuting fees and come back for the parent meetings?
HIEP:	Yes
WOOD:	I am sorry, can you just tell him how much I admire him, that he is making these difficult decisions, but that these children are so lucky to have him as a father.

The segment continues by showing the family eating while the audience cuts away to a separate interview with first Wood and then Kristof.

WOOD:	I was thinking, if he takes one day off, he's losing about two to two and a half days wages and he's already living on the margins, so for me it was just so emotional. He said, if I take one day off, I may be slightly more poor, but if my children don't get educated, they will always be poor [the audience sees and hears the family in the background] [...]
KRISTOF:	I think John Wood should be incredibly proud of what he has done for families like Phung's [audience sees Wood with family at table] and girls like Phung are hugely empowering for John. [...] He spends much of his time out fundraising, trying to get people to give money, dealing with headaches, and there he is face-to-face with a family he is transforming for generations to come [audience sees Hiep and Phung eating with each other].

The powerful segment starts with Hiep and his desire for a better life for his daughter and his unwavering support of her education. His story is then subsumed by the story of Wood, an American who makes great sacrifices to transform this Thai family. Emphasized is Wood's sacrifice of giving up a high-powered job and traveling around the world raising funds, while those sacrifices of Hiep (working non-stop and devoting all of the money earned to the education of Phung) are deemphasized. Kristof makes multiple statements which moves attention away from Hiep and Phung and toward Wood. This is achieved through Kristof's comments, such as "Wood should be incredibly proud of what he has done for families like Phung" and "There he [Wood] is face-to-face with a family he is transforming." Phung is said to "empower" the American donor and, throughout the scene, Wood's emotional experiences take precedence over the family's experiences. Hardship, perseverance, and agency are taken from Hiep and Phung and granted to Wood. The American is the one portrayed as making sacrifices for Phung (and her family), rather than Hiep's efforts for his own family.

In the second portion of the dialog detailed above, we see Wood speaking over the family while the audience continues to see and hear them in the background. This creates a sidebar conversation where privileged information and analysis is being shared, information and analysis that comes from Kristof and Wood and not members of the Thai family.

There are other appropriative aspects involved in this scene. Immediately before we meet Hiep and Phung, we learn about Wood's story in a dedicated segment of who he is and what he has done. Kristof narrates as the audience sees images of Wood walking in a contemplative manner from village to village:

> John is a former Microsoft Marketing Director who was running around the world in the technology sector working way too hard and then he ended up in Nepal in 1998 trekking, trying to get away from it all and chanced upon a school that had a library for 450 kids and virtually no books. John decided he would get them a few books, he glided over the problem that it was a two-day hike from the nearest road and that actually getting those books by donkey-train to that school. He realized that addressing global illiteracy is much more rewarding than peddling Windows software for Microsoft.

The story of the American former Microsoft Director takes the role as the primary story, through which the audience learns about Phung and Hiep, as if they were a sub-story of the larger Wood story. Even though Hiep and his family are very strong individuals with a compelling family story, their story was not allowed to stand alone, nor was it any more than a surface-level exploration of their plight. Hiep and Phung's story was portrayed as embedded within the larger story of an American businessman. The segment started with Wood's personal story and ended with his final reflections, undermining, and subsuming the agency of the male father figure. The lunch-table scene ends with Wood's reflections,

With Phung, we see a girl who has told me today that she wants to go on to University to receive a degree in accounting [...] and that makes me an optimist because you're seeing, in one generation, everything changing.

In *Kony 2012*, the story is told through the story of the director Jason Russell. The stories of the Ugandan children and the main Ugandan character (Jacob) are made known through Russell and his young son Gavin. For example, when the stories of the young boys who flee LRA attacks by sleeping in the local town, we hear and see it through Russell and his white, American college friends. In fact, the main narrative structure is set up through the relationship between father (Russell) and his newly born son (Gavin). The first scene is taken from home videos Gavin's birth and the dubbed-over dialog indicates the father's desire to make the world a better place for his son. It is through Russell's experience and through his reflections that we come to know the experiences of the boys in Uganda. The opening sequence is set up through the eyes of Russell and his son Gavin:

Every single person in the world started this way [audience sees Russell's wife giving birth to Gavin]. He didn't choose where or when he was born, but because he's here, he matters [in the home video the wife says, "we were waiting for you, you made it"]. My name is Jason Russell and this is my son, Gavin. He loves jumping on trampoline, being a ninja, and dancing and just like his dad, he likes being in movies and making movies; but he was born into a pretty complicated world and, as a dad, I want him to grow up in a better world than I did. And because of the events in my life, I see a way to get there. It has become my job [audience sees Russell speaking to a group of high schoolers asking, "Who are you to end a war? I am here to tell you, who are you not to?"]. Years before Gavin was born, the course of my life was changed entirely, by another boy, Jacob [showing of a Facebook timeline zooming back to years before when Russell first met Jacob]. It has been almost ten years since Jacob and I became friends, but when my friends and I first met him, it was in very different circumstances. He was running for his life.

The audience hears a story from the point-of-view of a father's desire for his son, centering focus on Russell and Gavin rather than Jacob or the child soldiers in Uganda. Every aspect of Jacob's story is told through Russell and his experiences.

Both *Kony 2012* and *Half the Sky* have multiple instances where members of the film are analyzing, consoling, taking on, or making sense of the pain and hardship of those they are filming. In *Half the Sky,* there are scenes of Western celebrities consoling and caring for the young girls facing hardship. Phrases like "you're so brave" are accompanied by hugs and questionable (in terms of genuineness) scenes of emotional connection. On multiple occasions, after the audience hears about the plight of the girls, they are transported into the celebrity's private hotel room for a personal video diary. During these sessions, the audience hears about the emotional impact and toll these experiences are having on the celebrities. They speak about reevaluating their lives and purpose, how the hardships in the US pale in comparison to what these girls face, and how they have been inspired by the girls' drive and desire. The stories of the strong girls featured throughout the film are not permitted to stand on their own; rather, they are mediated and appropriated through multiple Western celebrity figures. These celebrities are somehow better situated to make sense and contextualize the plight and hardships of those who are experiencing them. Seemingly acting as surrogates, these celebrities symbolically give birth to other peoples' stories, reinforcing the well-worn trope of being a voice for the so-called voiceless. This is problematic since everyone already has a voice. The platform in which that voice is amplified or muffled, however, differs significantly.

The examples above illustrate how the personal experiences and stories of those who are inspired and empowered (in this case the Western celebrities and activists) can act as means for appropriation, an appropriation that takes away the agency and power of the subjects (the girls and families persevering through these hardships). In doing this, it freezes the subjects into the role of the victim being enacted upon by the hardship. They are locked into an imbalanced power relationship that can only be understood and mediated upon by outside western analysis and intervention. This is an outcome that any conscientious filmmakers would wish not to achieve.

Section 3: Concluding Thoughts

Power operates at many different levels, from state expressions of violence, structural and institutional constraints which shape the actions of others, to how reality and difference is articulated through discourse. Documentary film is a unique form of discursive power that is linked to the visual gaze, engages the bodily senses, and is associated with science and objectivity. Calling for increased awareness of cinematographic representations within documentary filmmaking practice, this section turns its attention to the practice of reflexivity by exploring examples of such practices in the process of making the film *Give to Live*.

Critical Reflexivity

Reflexivity can be understood in multiple ways. Within documentary film tradition, it has been seen as a filmmaking technique that makes clear to the audience the process of the film being made. "The film tells a story about itself, about the activities of the cameraman instead of a central narrative character" (Chapman, 2009, p. 122). Filmmakers allow the audience to see how they came to their conclusions and how they found what they found. This can take on the form of a filmmaker showing the process of decision-making or steps taken to investigate certain subject matter or issues. For example, in Michael Moore's *Roger and Me* (1989), much of the film consists of the research process (phone calls, planning, negotiations, etc.) of the filmmakers, elements traditionally associated with the pre-production planning of making a film. This aspect of reflexivity is also seen (though, in a different way) in the 2010 Oscar-nominated documentary *Wasteland* where the filmmakers intentionally show the planning and consultative process of the featured artists in a scene where renown Brazilian photographer Vik Muniz and his team discuss the ramifications of whether to bring their impoverished subjects to London for a lavish art showing. In this way, reflexivity acts as a technique that provides a visual signifier to the audience. It allows the audience to "understand both the process employed and the resultant product and to know that the revelation itself is purposive, intentional, and not merely narcissistic or accidentally revealing" (Rosenthal & Corner, 2005, p. 35). This aspect of reflexivity deals with how to translate choices and processes into the film; or, how the end-product is viewed.

Within critical and feminist approaches, however, reflexivity is not just a filmmaking technique; rather, it is a commitment to being systematically self-aware and structurally cognizant. As one of the four main principles feminist methodology (see Tickner, 2005, p. 4), reflexivity is not just an individual's investigation of identity, but also a thorough examination of the societal positions of influence and power that one holds because of their socially defined identities. Ann J. Tickner (2005) suggests, "Most feminist research insists that the inquirer be placed in the same critical plane as the subject matter" (p. 8). This stands in contrast to hegemonic scientific approaches by acknowledging that the ever-present subjective elements of one's analysis does not act as a detriment; rather, it "actually increases the objectivity of the research" (Tickner, 2005, p. 8).

This latter understanding of reflexivity, one born out of a feminist commitment to examining the embedded and inherited structures of power, is what this chapter is calling for within documentary film practice. To apply this level of critical reflexive practice is to be ever-evaluative and conscious about representational choices. It comes from the realization that no scholarship is value-free. Likewise, no film is crafted without value-laden choices being made every step of the way.

Critical reflexivity calls for filmmakers to recognize their subjectivities and social positions of power and to see them as a means to increase objectivity, or what is often referred to as strong objectivity (Harding, 1987).

> Whereas personal experience is thought by conventional social science to contaminate a project's objectivity, feminists believe one's awareness of one's personal position in the research process to be a corrective to "pseudo-objectivity." (Tickner, 2005, p. 9)

This calls for the recognition that all knowledge comes from somewhere. As such, the reflecting upon and making known the researcher's standpoint and subjectivities serves to strengthen standards of objectivity.

Critical reflection – referring to the tradition from sociology of critical theory that consists of social scientists focused on how social structures are made and remade – on representation choices (of who and how to film and why certain people are featured over others) create films that are more cognizant and open to the dignifying or dehumanizing effects of their craft. Knowing it is not possible to fully represent the multiplicity of human experience means that work produced as scholars/artists will necessarily be incomplete and inadequate. This, however, should not be a reason for inaction; rather, critical reflexivity requires action. Brazilian educator Paulo Freire (1970/2005) explains,

> The insistence that the oppressed engage in reflection on their concrete situation is not a call to armchair revolution. On the contrary, reflection – true reflection – leads to action. On the other hand, when the situation calls for action, that action will constitute an authentic praxis only if its consequences become the object of critical reflection [...] Otherwise, action is pure activism. (p. 66)

(In)dignity via (mis)representation signifies that the relationship between representation and dignity are in constant flux, a relationship mitigated by critical reflexivity. Documentary films are productive forms of power that have real-world repercussions on attitudes and policy. Those who create or engage in discourse creation must be vigilantly in their reflexive practices to ensure the portrayal of the human experience is one of complexity, reverence, and dignity. Documentary films are not only sites of misrepresentation, but they can also be sites of contestation where representations of distant peoples are negotiated and reconfigured.

Give to Live

The diversity of the *Give to Live* film team contributed significantly to our representational practices. had to be understood within the context of the diversity of the film team. The team consisted of six professionals, four of which were people of color – three women, two of which were African American, and three men, one born in Kenya (the site filming) and, myself, a Filipino-America. We also had one white female who acted as a project manager and an older white cinematographer. The age of the team ranged from 25 to 55.[17] Throughout the course of the film, the team met in person, via Skype, email, and through phone calls. We consulted extensively directly on with representational choices throughout the three stages of pre-production, production, and post-production. Three choices we decided upon were (1) to not show any images of children with flies on faces, (2) being cognizant of three "eye-levels" while filming, and (3) to not use subtitles

---

[17]I mention the demographic background of the team to illustrate the diversity of thought and experience that contributes to our reflexive practice. I am careful not to suggest professionals can be understood solely through demographic aspects. Clearly, they are much more than just these labels that they carry, but they are a marker, albeit insufficient, of diversity and differing perspectives.

with individuals speaking English. Through a consultative process, we decided to take firm stances on each of these issues.

For those who were exposed to television commercials in the 1980s, it is easy to remember charitable organizations using images of children with flies buzzing around their faces. Christian Children's Fund commercials of that era featured celebrity Sally Struthers soliciting money from audiences to address global childhood poverty. These charity efforts had used these images to evoke pity and compel people to give money and resources. It also, however, furthered the sense of separation between American audiences and distant peoples. The dehumanization and objectification of these distant peoples and children added to a sense of superiority and judgment – no caring, civilized mother would let flies buzz on their child's face. Because of this legacy, the *Give to Live* film team decided to not show any images of flies on children's faces, causing us to stop filming a few times, as well as having to alter how we went about filming and editing. There were video shots in the field that we had to redo or throw out during editing because of the desire to make sure the shots were dignifying. A few more technically difficult slider shots (through a tripod mounted slider mechanism), as well as other shots that could not be replicated had to be omitted from the final edit of the film.

Being aware of the eye-levels or eyelines refers to the eye-levels of not only the subject being filmed, but also the camera level and the interviewer's eye-level. These eyelines have subconscious impacts on the viewer. For *Give to Live*, we decided to never have the camera eye-level rise above those of subjects being filmed. Simply, we never let the camera raise above the eyes of those we were shooting. Shooting at an angle that is below the subject's eyeline, when exaggerated, evokes a feeling of grandeur and a "larger than life" quality. In contrast, shooting downward with a camera, with the eye-level of the subject noticeably lower than that of the camera, gives the viewer a feeling of superiority and inferiority of the subject. These feelings are not often consciously recognized but provide a technical camera technique to evoke grandeur or pity. This is why heroes are often shot with the camera below the character's eyeline so to give the impression of bravery and strength. When filming a staged or directed film, where every shot is craftily coordinated by Cinematographer and Director, these technical choices of eyelines are agreed upon and utilized in a manner to support the larger narrative. These technical choices can impress upon the viewer certain feelings without the use of dialog. This coordination is much more difficult in the run-and-shoot requirements of documentary film, but no less important. A non-fiction example of this effect is in the style of news reports where reporters quickly investigate poverty in a way that often includes scenes of people living in squalor or sleeping on the streets and should-mounted camera operators filming downward toward the subjects. Throughout the *Give to Live* filmmaking process, we were hyper-aware of all eyelines while filming. This led to multiple occasions where our cameraman had to lay on the ground or get on hands and knees to ensure desired camera angles.

Another choice, the film team made was regarding the usage of subtitles. We decided if a subject is English, we will not use subtitles. Though this may not seem to make much sense when seen through the audience's ability to understand the dialog being recorded, we decided early on in the pre-production stage that this was something we were committed. Through a consultative process, we viewed it as an issue of who do we, as the filmmakers, deem as intelligible or understandable. Kenya, the location of much of the overseas filming, was a former British colony and English had been widely taught in their schools for decades. We knew that if we subtitled, we would have to consider whether to subtitle all non-American subjects and how would we draw the line between those who are subtitled and those who are not?

We made the decision not to use subtitles on English-speaking subjects early in pre-production, before we carried out interviews and it proved useful to know exactly how we all felt about this representative choice. For instance, we interviewed a US college professor of economics who happens to be Kenyan and specializes in East African affairs. Yes, he had an accent, but he was also teaching in English at one of the best universities in the country. There was also an African NGO Director who spoke multiple languages and interacts daily with multiple English-speaking international organizations. Again, she had an accent but was proficient in interacting and navigating the English-and French-language non-profit world. We filmed a few interviews and segments in the US southern part of the US, would we subtitle an American with a deep southern accent? By using subtitles, we would be defining who is intelligible and, as a result, we would be reifying standards of normativity. How would it feel if you were subtitled in spite of the fact that you teach at an English-based university or run the operations of large international NGO? We decided not to subtitle anyone speaking English. As a result, certain parts of the film were more challenging to understand. Despite receiving negative feedback about this during our focus-group showings, we felt it was an important representative choice in how we represent distant cultures and peoples.

This chapter has multiple contributions, two of which are the significance of the discursive power of documentary film and the representative and (de) humanizing ramifications of filmmaking choices. More specifically, it adds to the under-theorized area of ethical ramifications of technical filmmaking choices from a feminist perspective and reinforces the importance of the practice of critical reflexivity within the conceptual and ideological considerations of filmmaking.

The documentary film possesses unique and powerful characteristics associated with the visual, the sensual, and science and objectivity. It has real-world implications on how distant peoples are conceived and rendered intelligible. The making of documentary films is not void of the political. There are choices continually being made and remade, choices which recreate and reinforce unequal and oppressive relationships. This chapter explored (in)dignity and (mis)representation through the medium of documentary film by situating its analysis at the intersection of theory and practice. It illustrated how filmmaker choices of representation can both dignify or dehumanize. This practice of critical reflexivity, which involves a constant self-awareness and the recognition that no film is value-free, would transform the discursive impact documentary has on marginalized peoples.

References

Alexander, J. (2005). *Pedagogies of crossing: Meditations on feminism, sexual politics, memory, and the sacred*. Durham, NC: Duke University Press.

Astle, R. (2012). Half the sky & social documentary transmedia. *Filmmaker Magazine*, October 1. Retrieved from http://www.filmmakermagazine.com/news/2012/10/half-the-sky-social-documentary-transmedia. Accessed on November 1, 2012.

Barnett, M., & Duvall, R. (2005). Power in international politics. *International Organization*, *59*(1), 39–75.

Cesaire, A. (1972). *Discourse on colonialism*. New York, NY: Monthly Review Press.

Chapman, J. L. (2009). *Issues in contemporary documentary*. Cambridge: Polity.

Chowdhry, G., & Nair, S. (2002). *Power, postcolonialism and international relations: Reading race, gender and class*. Abingdon: Routledge.

Class Dismissed [Film]. (2009). *Adam B. Ellick (Director)*. New York, NY: New York Times.

Dolby, N. (2012). *Rethinking multicultural education for the next generation: The new empathy and social justice*. Abingdon: Routledge.

Escobar, A. (1995). *Encountering Development: The Making and Unmaking of the Third World*. Princeton Studies in Culture/Power/History Series. Princeton, NJ: Princeton University Press.

Foucault, M. (1977). *Discipline and punish: The birth of the prison*. In A. Sheridan Smith. (Trans.), London: Allen Lane.

Fonow, M., & Cook, J. (1991). *Beyond methodology: Feminist scholarship as lived research*. Bloomington, IN: Indiana University Press.

Freire, P. (1970–2005). *Pedagogy of the oppressed*. In M. B. Ramos (Trans.), New York, NY: Continuum.

Gaines, J. M. (1999). 'Political Mimesis'. In J. M. Gaines & M. Renov (Eds.), *Collecting visible evidence* (pp. 84–102). Minneapolis, MN: University of Minnesota Press.

Ginsburg, F. (1999). The parallax effect: The impact of indigenous media on ethnographic film. In J. M. Gaines & M. Renov (Eds.), *Collecting visible evidence* (pp. 156–175). Minneapolis, MN: University of Minnesota Press.

Give to Live [Film]. (2015). Justin de Leon (Director). USA.

Gordon, A. (1997). *Ghostly matters: Haunting and the sociological imagination*. Minneapolis, MN: University of Minnesota Press.

Green, E. D. (2008). Decentralisation and Conflict in Uganda. *Conflict, Security & Development*, *8*(4), 427–450.

Half the Sky [Film]. (2012). *Maro Chermayeff (Director)*. Arlington, VA: PBS.

Half the Sky Website. (2013) Retrieved from http://www.halftheskymovement.org. Accessed on January 1, 2013.

Harding, S. G. (1987). *Feminism and methodology: Social science issues*. Bloomington, IN: Indiana University Press.

Invisible children: Rough cut [Film]. (2006). *Jason Russell, Bobby Bailey, & Laren Poole (Directors)*. San Diego, CA: Invisible Children.

Invisible Children Website. (2013). Retrieved from http://invisiblechildren.com. Accessed on June 1, 2013.

Juhasz, A. (1999). Bad girls come and go, but a lying girl can never be fenced. In D. Waldman & J. Walker (Eds.), *Feminism and documentary*. (pp. 95–116). Minneapolis, MN: University of Minnesota Press.

Kony 2012 [Film]. (2012). *Jason Russell (Director)*. San Diego, CA: Invisible Children.

Kristof, N., & WuDunn, S. (2010). *Half the sky: Turning oppression into opportunity for woman worldwide*. New York, NY: Vintage Books.

Lorde, A. (1984). *Sister outsider*. Berkeley, CA: Crossing Press.

Mackey, R. (2012). After a bullet in the head, assaults on a Pakistani schoolgirl's character follow. *The New York Times*, October 16. Retrieved from http://thelede.blogs. nytimes.com/2012/10/16/after-a-bullet-in-the-head-assaults-on-a-pakistani-school-girls-character-follow/?hp. Accessed on November 1, 2012.

Matsiko, H. (2011). Hunting Kony. *The Independent*. Uganda. Dec. 20.

Mohanty, C. T. (1991). Under western eyes. Feminist scholarship and colonial discourses. In C. T. Mohanty, A. Russo, & L. Torres (Eds.), *Third world women and the politics of feminism* (pp. 51–80). Bloomington, IN: Indiana University Press.

Mohanty, C. T. (2003). *Feminism without borders: Decolonizing theory practicing solidarity*. Durham, NC: Duke University Press.

Moreton-Robinson, A. (2015). *The white possessive: Property, power, and indigenous sovereignty*. Minneapolis, MN: Minnesota Press.

Neal, A. W. (2009). Michel Foucault. In J. Edkins & N. Vaughan-Williams (Eds.), *Critical theorists and international relations* (pp. 116–170).

Payne, Y. A. (2017). Participatory action research and social justice: Keys to freedom for street life-oriented black men. In J. Battle, M. Bennet, & A. J. Lemelle (Eds.) *Free at last: Black America in the twenty-first century* (pp. 265–280). Abingdon: Routledge.

Rabinowitz, P. (1994). *They must be represented: The politics of documentary*. Brooklyn, NY: Verso.

Renov, M. (1999). New subjectivities: Documentary and self-representation in the post-verité age. D. Waldman & J. Walker, J. (Eds.), *Feminism and documentary* (pp. 84–94). Minneapolis, MN: University of Minnesota Press.

Roger and me [Film]. (1989). Michael Moore (Director). Burbank, CA: Warner Brothers.

Rosenthal, A., & Corner, J. (2005). *New challenges for documentary* (2nd ed.). Manchester: Manchester University Press.

Said, E. (1978). *Orientalism*. New York, NY: Vintage Books.

Shepherd, L. (2008). *Gender, violence, and security: Discourse as practice*. London: Zed Books.

Shohat, E. (2006). *Taboo memories, Diasporic voices*. Durham, NC: Duke University Press.

Silvey, R. (2010). Envisioning justice: The politics and possibilities of transnational feminist film. In A. L. Swarr & R. Nagar (Eds.), *Critical transnational feminist praxis* (pp. 206–218). Albany, NY: State University of New York Press.

Smith, L. T. (2012). *Decolonizing methodologies: Research and indigenous peoples*. London: Zed Books.

Sontag, S. (2003). *Regarding the pain of others*. London: Macmillan.

Spivak, G. (1988). Can the subaltern speak?' In C. Nelson & L. Grossberg (Eds.), *Marxism and the interpretation of culture* (pp. 271–313). Basingstoke: Macmillan.

Swarr, A. L., & Nagar, R. (2012). *Critical transnational feminist praxis*. Albany, NY: SUNY Press.

Tickner, A. J. (2005). What is your research program? Some feminist answers to IR's methodological questions. *International Studies Quarterly*, *49*, 1–21.

Torchin, L. (2012). *Creating the witness: Documenting genocide on film, video, and the internet*. Minneapolis, MN: University of Minnesota Press.

Tuck, E. (2009). Suspending damage: A letter to communities. *Harvard Educational Review*, *79*(3), 409–427.

Waldman, D., & Walker, J. (1999). *Feminism and documentary*. Minneapolis, MN: University of Minnesota Press.

Walker, G. (2018). *Movie making as critical pedagogy: Conscientization through visual storytelling*. Basingstoke: Palgrave Macmillan.

Wasserman, T. (2012). "Kony 2012" tops 100 million views, becomes the most viral video in history. *Mashable.com*, 12 March. Retrieved from http://mashable.com/2012/03/12/kony-most-viral. Accessed on October 15.

Wasteland [Film]. (2010). *Lucy Walker (Director)*. USA: Midas Filmes.

Weber, M. (1918). *Science as a vocation*. Speech at Munich University, München, Germany.

White, S. A. (2003). *Participatory video: Images that transform and empower*. London: Sage Publications.

Chapter 8

Dignifying Education: The Emergence of Teachers as Transcultural Messengers

Barbara Finkelstein

Introduction

In the increasingly communicative, interconnected, and interdependent world of the twenty-first century, young people across the planet are growing up with an unprecedented awareness of their connections to one another. They are able to observe immense disparities of wealth and poverty, privilege, and power. With few exceptions, they are increasingly aware that they speak different languages, inhabit different nations, worship at different altars, respect different kinds of authority, live-in relative states of conflict and/or cooperation, and conceive of their identities in complex ways. They are awash in worlds where encounters between total strangers from around the globe are the stuff of daily life; the con-tours of community life and bonds of affiliation are trans-local, poly-vocal, and subject to negotiation; where time-honored habits of heart, mind, and association are multitudinous and deeply challenged; where the languages of instruction, communication, and daily discourse are continually shifting and fusing; where designations of insiders and outsiders are manifold and fluid; and where access to information and social media sites have expanded their networks of communication in profound and transformative ways.

What is to become of this new world of unrelenting pluralisms, complex border crossings, and de-territorialized networks of association? Will young people in possession of alternative habits of heart, mind, and association learn to honor rather than demean one another? Will they learn to trust their differences or celebrate them; to approach one another with respect rather than suspicion? Will they regard conflict as inevitable or preventable? Will they learn to celebrate rather than fear and eradicate diversity? Will they use the interconnected and virtual worlds of Facebook, Tumbler, Twitter, YouTube, and Vimeo to strengthen connections among and between them or exacerbate their differences and continue cycles of violence and hatred? Will they learn to live as inhabitants of a dystopian world of chaos, brutality, contest, and humiliation, or as members of a more

Interdisciplinary Perspectives on Human Dignity and Human Rights, 131–149
Copyright © 2020 by Emerald Publishing Limited
All rights of reproduction in any form reserved
doi:10.1108/978-1-78973-821-620191014

peaceable global kingdom where dignification informs the social and cultural practices of everyday life, and each person, has somehow learned to become an "agent of dignity?"[1]

This chapter is about the dignifying potential of an array of transcultural education practices that suffuse in the cracks and crevices of daily life where young people might learn to imagine and reimagine who they are, what they hope to become, what might be available for them in life, and where they fit in the scheme of things. It is about a million tiny moments of human interaction, transcultural encounter, and message sending that give form and shape to the meaning of dignity in sites of teaching and learning. Specifically, the chapter centers on the cultural, social, and educational practices of four individuals who, in the conduct of their daily lives as educators, have labored to mute the force of adverse circumstances for generations of dispossessed, status degraded, impoverished, and physically assaulted young people whom they encounter in their professional lives each day.[2]

Each individual has grown up, lived, and worked in the company of strangers in communities of unprecedented cultural congestion. Two are the children of immigrants to the United States – one who grew up in a family of asylum seekers from Congo; another as a cultural and linguistic double and the offspring of an intercultural, interethnic marriage between her Irish father and Nicaraguan mother. Two others, whom I have chosen to pair, are perpetual border crossers and gradually evolving cultural hybrids who have, over the course of their lives, acquired and cultivated a highly tutored and experiential understanding of the world as a moving hub of transcultural connection. One grew up in possession of a complex transcultural heritage as a Canadian-born Chinese, the daughter, and granddaughter of Chinese Hakka, and a legatee of Asian-Indian cultural roots; the other as a Japanese who has shuttled between Japan and the United States all of her life. Both have inhabited and transgressed a multitude of cultural and political worlds and, in the process, have acquired a vision of the world as a seedbed of opportunity for the construction of more inclusive global communities, more permeable boundaries of nation-state, and more expansive and culturally empowering transcultural educational worlds.

Each individual represents a distinct type of dignity worker. Sonia O'Connell is one of an evolving generation of bilingual and bicultural classroom teachers, who has spent a professional lifetime teaching English to speakers of other languages

---

[1] Nelson Mandela in Donna Hicks (2011).

[2] Each of these individuals has been a student at the University of Maryland, College Park. Each has taken my courses in "Transcultural Education Policies and Practices" and "The Art and Craft of Oral History." Each has also taken "Independent Studies" focusing on the contours of "Transcultural Education Theory" and the intersections of context and voice as a narrative form. For two students – Tomoko Tokunaga and Omékongo Dibinga – I have served as both PhD advisor and dissertation chair. Sonia O'Connell is a participating oral historian for the University of Maryland Center for New American History's "Voices of Migrants" project, for which I served as senior advisor. All are voluntary participants.

in transculturally congested localities in the United States, Equatorial Guinea, and Central America. Out of the burdens of her lived experience as a bilingual and bicultural citizen of the United States, Sonia, like other ESOL (English for Speakers of Other Languages) educators, has developed and deployed an array of cross-cultural repertoires and teaching practices that privilege linguistic diversity and multilingual capacities as the ultimate outcome of a worthy educational system.

Omékongo Dibinga, a second generation Congolese-American, is a trilingual poet, musician, and a positive rapper who writes, raps, and performs in English, French, and Swahili. He is a community activist, a motivational speaker – a consummate performance educator. For Omékongo, the stage is a pulpit, a platform, and a staging ground for the distribution of politically and culturally empowering messages and dignifying forms of political and social critique.

Li Fong Koo and Tomoko Tokunaga have grown up in cross-cultural crucibles of unprecedented complexity. Both have struggled to fashion dignifying identities in shifting school and community settings. Both carry vestiges of their original homeland cultures but have learned to loosen the weight of tradition that has bound them into rigid constructions of who they ought to be, what they should believe, and what they could hope for in life. For Li and Tomoko, their affiliated loyalties attach to multiple places. They speak in multiple tongues. They celebrate multi-ethnicity. They claim hybrid identities. They own plural personalities. They celebrate inclusion and live happily with cultural ambiguity. Both are crafting professional careers that place the dignity of children, youth, and cultural minorities on center stage – Tomoko as a rising academic scholar-teacher; Li as an arts and international development educator, curriculum planner, communication strategist, and architect of global cross-cultural education networks. Both are master chroniclers of border-crossing experiences. Both regard borderland worlds as important and sustained sites of cultural transmission, worthy of close study and inclusion.

No matter what the precise contours of their teaching repertoires, communicative styles, or experiences, each of the four has found ways to amplify the voices of the previously unheard, expand the scope of imagined communities, and nurture hope for a gentler and kinder, more dignifying world. Their stories and their work could be dismissed as eccentric, particular, exceptional, or simply anecdotal. But if we put them together, we can see their lives as successive acts in a grand and evolving dignity narrative worthy of our closest attention.

Sonia[3]

Sonia O'Connell was born in San Francisco in 1953 and has spent a lifetime in the company of strangers. She has been an inhabitant of multiple linguistic and cultural universes for all of her life. She grew up as a cultural and linguistic double

---

[3]Sonia's mini-bio is based on oral history testimony gathered with her over many hours, on personal correspondence, and a series of reflective essays on the work of post-colonial theorists. There is also Sonia's meditation on the history and lives of three Nigerian students from three different tribes: Yoruba, Igbo, and Hausa; and an oral history of an eight year-child émigré from Sierra Leone. See Sonia O'Connell (2010, 2012).

in a San Francisco barrio – the daughter of a dark-skinned Nicaraguan mother and an Irish father in an extended bilingual family and with the company of a gregarious close-knit Spanish speaking community with 17 aunts and uncles living nearby. She remained in close touch with her extended family – even after her parents climbed an economic ladder and moved to a white middle-class neighborhood close to the ocean in San Francisco.

No longer geographically enclosed within the protective community of the barrio, she began to learn what it meant to be a cultural double and to live in a pigmentocracy – to use Nelson Mandela's extraordinary concept. She attended English-only elementary and secondary Catholic schools, where she encountered a phalanx of language police who demeaned, dismissed, and prohibited the use of Spanish, dishonored her linguistic versatility, and transmitted a message that the language and cultural habits of her household and community were inferior, un-American, and culturally unacceptable. In fact, she did not learn to read or write Spanish until after she had graduated from high school and double majored at the University of California, Berkeley, in French and Spanish literature.

As she grew up, Sonia was also the recipient of an array of dignity violations that complicated her sense of identity and pride of place. On a bus with her dark-skinned mother, Sonia was reprimanded by a stranger for calling her "mommy," based on an apparently mistaken notion that her mother had to be her babysitter. She heard a parent describe her "as one of them …" when they were waiting in line to register for kindergarten. In high school, she says, "I was a Spic." "I was too white in one context" and "too Hispanic in the next." "I tried to figure out where I fit in." "I didn't know who I was." "I was always on the edge."

Sonia's early experiences as a cultural and linguistic double initiated a lifelong struggle to fashion empowering sites of belonging for young people who, like her, did not quite "fit in." She entered the teaching profession in 1992, at a time when the numbers of new immigrants were growing exponentially, the landscapes of diversity in the United States were becoming ever more complex, and school districts around the country were scrambling to find linguistically versatile, culturally bifocal, and well-trained teachers.

Sonia was recruited into the Houston, Texas, Independent School district, enrolled in an alternative teacher certification program, and discovered what she describes as "whole new worlds of multicultural education practice that would transform the contours of second language teaching and the organization of group work as [she] had known them." She took charge of Spanish immersion classes for monolingual Spanish speaking students. She used Spanish language instructional materials. She created a family-like face-to-face informal education environment that "meshed in" with the ways that children communicated at home. She eliminated competition between students and substituted group learning approaches instead. She combined speaking, listening, reading, and writing across the disciplines, and created whole units with everything integrated. She explained it all to me in this way: "You had to teach ecologically, cooperatively and collaboratively in order to do well in mainstream classes." The method worked with her students (Sonia O'Connell, email message to author, April 2011).

Sonia emerged from the Houston school system in 2005 as a dedicated advocate of bilingual education, family-like school environments, cooperative learning instructional strategies, and culturally responsive pedagogies. She took off for Equatorial Guinea for a year, taught physics in Spanish, and adopted an innovative transcultural dimension into her evolving repertoire as an ESOL teacher: the need to understand the habits of heart, mind, and association that students had learned before they arrived in the United States.

She found the most challenging school imaginable to embark on such a journey. Since 2005, Sonia has taught at the Catherine T. Reed Elementary School in Prince George's County. C. T. Reed is a dazzling site of cross-cultural encounter where students and teachers from different parts of the world have to navigate the boundaries of race, class, gender, ethnicity, tribe, nation, generation, and belief on a daily basis. It is a poly-vocal school site – a place where the language of instruction is English – but the sounds of the playground, cafeteria, the gymnasium, the hallway, or the bathroom are Somali, Hausa, Ibo, Yoruba, Eritrean, and Ethiopian; Spanish, Portuguese, and Tagalog; Vietnamese, Arabic, Urdu, Hindi, and the English of the Indian subcontinent and the Caribbean. It is a site of new global communities in the making.

Sonia is one of two ESOL specialists with a room of her own and, as it has happened, a unique perch to apply her newly minted skills as an oral historian to learn about the habits of heart, mind, and association that students have brought from far distant homes. More than 100 students walk through her doors each day. The four walls insulate each child from the relentless pressures of test taking, the travails of learning a new language, the bullying that might punctuate each day, and the sense of outsider-ness that the school commonly presents to them. Sonia, in keeping with her commitment to the discovery of homeland cultures, listens so deeply to their stories about home that she can tailor her English language responses and teaching practices to the needs of each of them. "I visit the children's countries as often as [I] can." She studies their countries of origin, their mother tongues, their lives as border crossers, their hopes, their opportunities, their struggles, and their dreams. She makes home visits. She relives her own childhood experiences as she hears her students talk in multiple tongues. She knows that students occupy multiple homelands simultaneously. "They make weekly Skype and video calls to their mom in the village." They travel between homes "here and there." "Things are no longer forgotten and left back home." "My students embody a new cultural hybridity." "They dwell in the in-between of two [or more] worlds." Sonia O'Connell (2010, College Park, Maryland, 2009) knows that she has become a transcultural messenger.

Sonia is, as she always has been, a cultural sensitive and bridge builder for immigrant parents and their children. She is their port in a storm. If there is trouble, "Go to Ms. Okana." [sic]. She is a cultural broker who creates in-between spaces, so-called borderland worlds, where students can fashion complex identities, construct terrains of freedom, and work around the regulatory universes of home and school. She tries to make a home and be at home in dignity-conferring spaces where speakers of "other languages," and dislocated young people can thrive.

Omékongo[4]

Omékongo Dibinga was born in Cambridge, Massachusetts, in 1979 – the seventh of nine children descended from a long line of Congolese warriors on his father's side and proud, educated royalty on his mother's. His parents entered the United States in 1968, as student asylum seekers and exiles from the Central Republic of Congo. They were heir to generations of imperial domination and witnesses to serial atrocities during their time in Congo. They were also lifelong, impassioned carriers of Congolese social, cultural, and spiritual traditions, which they reproduced, as best they could, in the daily rituals and routines of their Roxbury household.

"The New Dibinga Generation in America," as their father liked to call them, jogged together in perfect chronological order around the neighborhood. They ate together. They learned Swahili and Swahili songs from both parents. They shared food with trusted neighbors and friends. They learned that elder children cared for younger ones when their parents, graduates of the Sorbonne and Harvard doctoral programs, were professing at Boston College, or, as his father was to do in 1987–1988, risking his life and making common cause with freedom fighters in Zaire. They worked for and with one another in a variety of family-owned small business enterprises and, to this day, regard the businesses of each of the children as "family business." "My house was my best zone growing up," Omékongo recalled. It was a haven from an assortment of dignity-sapping degradations, brutalities, and name-calling, which punctuated life growing up on the violent streets of Roxbury, Massachusetts, in the 1970s and 1980s.

"We were brought up having to switch up – out of the places where they call me nigger, or African bush boogie, or African booty scratcher"; out of cultural invisibility at the Boston Latin School where Ralph Ellison's *Invisible Man* was the only officially sanctioned black-authored literary work required by his teachers, and where a classmate at his school prom asked if he could "leave Africa behind for just one night"; out of a then ethnocentric Morehouse College where he learned that African spirituality and non-Christian forms of belief had no place and no history during "Religious Emphasis Week." "I grew up encountering new groups not to trust, and new groups to whom not to belong." All the while, Omékongo was also growing into as well as out of things; into poetry and the discovery of Maya Angelou and Nikki Giovanni; into black power, into Africa first, and an activist class presidency at Boston Latin; into the School of Foreign Service at Georgetown University, a year of study abroad in Senegal; into the Fletcher School of Law and International Diplomacy Master's program at Tufts University. Forged in a transnational and transcultural crucible

---

[4]This portrait of Omékongo is part of a larger transgenerational oral history of his family. It emerged from many hours of oral history testimonies; his own oral histories of the Dibinga Family; observations of his performances; the contents of his signature motivation book entitled *Grow into Your Greatness,* his poetry, both spoken and recorded; and other work that can be found on his web-site, omekongo.omekongo. com.

of profound complexities, Omékongo has emerged as an institutionally unbound dignity educator, a stereotype buster, a practitioner of non-violence.

Like the young people he seeks to reach, Omékongo is a person in possession of a diasporic identity – a tightly knit connection to multiple communities and to his family's homeland that he has visited only once, in 2002, when he worked in a refugee camp in the capital city of Kinshasa. Omékongo has stitched together a vision of education and cultural possibility designed to bring hope, dignity, and inspiration to rising generations of disempowered young people in schools and communities in sixteen countries and three continents.

"I put black history in my poems so that I can remember it." "My job is to put historical things together, to connect the dots." "I think of history as therapy an antidote to hate, and a place to find a name." "My poems are memory in the present."

> I write hip-hop poems for my daughters so that they can say their
> names … I write poems about my wife and my mother, and create
> CDs and inspirational books. I take poetry to people where they are.

"I proudly use my name and my experiences as a tool to teach about diversity." "I want people to feel they belong. You can call me African, Congolese, American, Bostonian. I am …."
OMEKONGO

> Some people desire to inquire
> What my name means because it sounds so "powerful:"
> Like I need to play some drums when I say it
> Others ask if it's my "birth name"
> As if it's any of their business
> But short of the intrinsic inclination to input inhabitants in
> Pre-determined non-pensive packages
> Few people ask me what it's actually like
> To be an American in Africa,
> And an African in America
> 'Cause for real,
> I feel like I need to relocate
> To the center of the Atlantic Ocean
> Because I am truly caught in the middle
> The African, the American …
> I'm remixing Angie Palmer's words
> From "I've been rich and I've been poor"
> To "I've been dissed and I've been torn"
> Because I've been torn between being
> Called the American nigga and the African bushboogie
> I'm torn between having to speak "African"
> To prove I'm African in America
> And speaking French

> To prove that I'm African
> In francophone African countries
> What???!!!
> Because I will never fit into your box
> Whether I got a fade or some locks
> So when you're trying to figure out who I am,
> And which stereotypical categories I cover,
> I'll be covered in content
> If you just called me, "That brother"

He shares stories of adversity and inequality. He speaks for those who have no voice. Like an array of human rights theorists, scholars, community activists, and dignity workers, he broadens and deepens the concept of human rights to include dignity as a first principle.

Li and Tomoko

Li Fong Koo and Tomoko Tokunaga have discovered a distinct way of making sense of their thirty-something years as border crossers, inhabitants and chroniclers of multiple transcultural worlds, and architects of plural identities. Drawing deeply on their own experiences as cultural shapeshifters, they have fashioned innovative ethnographic, oral historical, and artistically rendered transcultural chronicles that reveal the ways in which rising generations of Asian girls and women in Japan, the Philippines, Vietnam, Indonesia, India, China, and the United States have made sense of their lives in contested borderland zones. Both have also become builders of transcultural communities: Li as she conceives, convenes, and sustains international networks of communication; Tomoko as she fashions international sites of teaching and learning for and with students in schools and universities in Japan and the United States.

Li Fong Koo (Ancient Red Lily)[5], was born in Toronto, Ontario, Canada. As the first daughter of a first son, she was called Gee Gee, which means older sister. With this title, she inherited powerful traditions of family responsibility – as caretaker, role model, and protector of traditional notions of face, family, and gender-defined social responsibilities – a challenging task for an occupant of a "second-class" gender status. She has described herself as a first-generation Chinese Canadian who learned about her mixed Chinese and Indian heritages as she

---

[5]This portrait of Li is part of a larger and evolving oral history that focuses on teachers as transcultural educators and mediators of culture, which has been generously supported by a University of Maryland General Research Board grant. This mini-biography has been importantly shaped by Li Koo's (2009) auto-ethnography, by an extensive two-hour Skype conversation (June 2013), many hours of conversation about her work as a PhD candidate, by close study of five videos that she filmed and edited, an array of documents that describe the trajectory and substance of her professional life and career, and some of her publications.

grew up in a multilingual household where Hakka Chinese was the main language of communication, and Hindi and Bollywood movies informed the speaking universe of her daily home life. Li tells a family story of her grandparents who fled to Calcutta, India, in an attempt to keep themselves and their future family safe from the ravages of the Japanese invasion and occupation of Manchuria that began in 1931. Like a myriad other Hakka merchant families before them, Li's grandparents hoped to prosper and thrive in a safer and more promising world of business and re-located to Calcutta, India. Li's parents were born and raised in Calcutta. Her mother became familiar with western literary and artistic canons and aesthetic forms, adapted local Indian cultural customs, but remained true to her migratory Hakka heritage, and took advantage of an opportunity to move to the prosperous, more invitingly cosmopolitan, industrially developing English-speaking world of Toronto, Canada.

Li carried the multiple weights of both Chinese and Indian cultural habits and traditions into the schools of suburban Toronto and, in the process, underwent a fundamental status transformation that she has inscribed in two moving vignettes. The first, which she reports – not without shame – is that she had once denied her Indian roots and her Hakka ethnicity in order to protect the family from the shame of being born into a so-called developing world – a strategy which her mother had learned well as an Asian national working in a Canadian world:

SHAUNA: Li! Li! It's not true [Li's given name, Li Fong, was shortened in grade school to be more Western]
LI FONG: What?
SHAUNA: You're not from India are you? You're not Indian?
LI FONG: What? What are you talking about?
SHAUNA: Your cousin just told me that your family is from India.
LI FONG: Of course not! We're Chinese. We're from Hong Kong. Why would we come from India? That's silly.
SHAUNA: [Speaking to Li's cousin, Fung Fung] You're lying. I knew you were lying. You're not from India – you're Chinese! [The girls split off and Fung-Fung runs up to Li Fong.]
FUNG FUNG: Why did you say we're not from India, Gee Gee?
LI FONG: Because I'm trying to protect us. I don't want people to look down at us or make fun of us. They don't understand. Didn't your mother ever tell you that? People look down at you if you come from a third world country. And we shouldn't say China – they are still developing. Hong Kong or Taiwan is better.
FUNG FUNG: No Gee Gee, mommy never said that before. We're from India – why would I lie about that? That's where we come from. That's who we are.

In an effort to avoid humiliation and to protect her family's honor, Li, as her mother had taught her, publicly denied both her cultural inheritance and her family history. She invented an alternative group self, and only later began to understand that her sense of cultural inferiority was a colonial relic. Without quite knowing or understanding it at the time, Li had invented a cultural history in an attempt to preserve dignity, but did so, as she reflected "... at the cost of erasing the heroic, courageous, and successful accomplishments of my family history."

At a later point in her school career, when she was a high school junior, Li had learned to embrace her hybridity, deflect status assaults, and transform a potential humiliation into a teachable moment – an education habit that she relishes and deploys regularly to this day. She described an event that occurred in an 11th grade English literature class when Ian, a tall, gangly red-headed student of Irish descent, called her a liar when she was trying to finish a sentence "... something about how my parents came from India and that Indian heritage was as much a part of our identity as our Chinese heritage." "He approached me and stood towering over me and said:"

IAN: What are you talking about?

[I took the question in stride and said that my parents are from India. He promptly refuted my statement.]

IAN: "That's not possible – you're Chinese."
LI: "Yes it is. I'm living proof."
IAN: "But you don't look Indian. You're lying."

[I was shocked. How could this classmate tell me who I was or where I came from? I took a deep breath, stepped forward and said:]

LI: "I am, just because my parents are from India doesn't mean they are
         Indian – much like how I'm born in Canada, but that doesn't make
         me white. My parents are of Indian and Chinese descent .... So Indian
         culture, Indian heritage, and Indian food is as much a part of my life as
         Chinese chopsticks and rice."

Li, by the time she was 18, had constituted ways to protect the dignity of her family – not by obscuring the traditional subaltern status of her Chinese and Indian cultural roots as she had done when she was younger, but by discovering, recognizing, outing, and insisting on her multicultural ancestry as a mark of privilege rather than cultural inferiority. Li had struggled to take account of her multicultural inheritance by fusing her multiple group selves together. "It's not whether [I] fit into a dominant culture, but how [I] can negotiate a complementary existence that brings together all of the various elements of [my]'minority cultures.'" What is more, she had learned that it was "... important and healthy, to challenge stereotypes, confirm the multiplicity of identity, and create a space for conversation."

As an undergraduate student at York University, Li deepened her transcultural consciousness. A chance encounter in Professor Richard Perry's Introduction to Asian Art class, with a poem of Lao Tzu in the Tao Te Ching, changed her life. Through deep and informed study and contemplation, she discovered that the

ways of the world were fluid, ever changing, and suffused with multiple possibilities. Li's thoughtful self-reflection reveals a breathtaking discovery of history as a
form of cultural enlightenment and a beacon of light for persons in possession of
hybrid identities and less privileged social status.

She learned about Asian history and Asian culture. A western man taught her
how to appreciate her own culture – and if he could see value in it, why could
not she? She learned that her perceived "otherness" was actually something that
could be seen as unique, special, and steeped in history. Her feeling of rootlessness
had been misplaced. Contrary to her original belief, she did have roots. She had
a history. She had a tradition and philosophy … difference could be good. The
polarities of east and west could be brought together without losing the inherent
characteristics that defined them.

From this transformative moment forward, Li began to cross geographic, as
well as, imagined boundaries of nation, region, and globe – all the while refining
her knowledge of her Asian cultures and western cultural roots. She expanded her
linguistic and cultural reach to include Danish and western European social forms
and practices and acquired a highly tutored grasp of cultural hybridity as a way
of being in a globalizing world. As a graduate student at the Ontario Institute of
Educational Studies and the University of Maryland, College Park's Education
Policy and Leadership program, Li cultivated an understanding of cultural minority and the workings of status degradation in multiple education settings.

Simultaneously, she worked at the Smithsonian Institution's National Museum
of Asian Art in Washington, DC. As a museum educator, Li became an Asian Arts
specialist, curriculum developer, and outreach coordinator who helped to fashion
culturally responsive Asian art program for students and teachers in underserved
and educationally challenged schools in the Washington, DC, metropolitan area.
In the process, she would also discover the power of informal learning communities to promote knowledge, counteract negative stereotyping, and equalize the life
chances of rising generations of children, youth, and dispossessed minorities.

Thus endowed and empowered, Li took a position with World Literacy Canada (WLC) as an India-based Community Library Programming Associate, and
thus returned to her parent's native India. She re-located to Varanasi City, in
the State of Uttar Pradesh in Northern India.[6] Varanasi is an ancient city and
the holiest of seven sacred cities for Hinduism and Jainism. It is also a place
of extreme poverty and extreme wealth. Li's task was to build more libraries in
remote villages and the heartland of the slums. She would become a live-in resi-
dent photographer, filmmaker, and mentor in the palace of a former Maharaja,
which had been refitted to accommodate a development education program serving relatively unschooled young Indian girls and boys.

She transformed her work by producing and editing a series of five videos
that documented the stories and impact of WLC's small grant programs on girl
and women grantees. Intended to encourage donors and investors to support this
effort, the videos went much further. All five reveal the hand of an artistically and

---

[6]Varanasi is also known as Barnares or Kashi.

analytically skilled filmmaker and passionate polemicist. Li created a narrative line in each film that presented the facts of poverty, illiteracy, and inequality in stark relief. The films also portrayed each child, parent, and woman in the fullness of their humanity as well as their need.[7] One of Li's finest personal moments occurred when a group of jubilant, newly literate women entrepreneurs were able to push away the stamp pads that were offered to make a thumbprint that would seal a deal, for those who were illiterate. Instead, they signed their names to contracts and disentangled themselves from the predatory practices of loan sharks who charged exorbitant interest rates and pocketed most of the profits when the women could not read (Skype conversation with author, June 25, 2013).

As an associate of WLC, Li was able to facilitate deep connections between previously far distant groups of people. She had learned to fashion a platform and a foundation that transcended space, time, and religious preferences. And, along the way she reflected on the roads she might take and the work she might undertake to make the world a more dignifying and empowering place, especially for those who struggle the most and are the most endangered.

Li returned to Canada as an accomplished development educator and political activist, with flares for community building and the uses of social media. She had found a calling and a strategy: to constitute, join, and sustain international communication networks that connect government agencies, non-profits, and for-profit institutions in collective efforts to advance global literacy, eradicate poverty, undergird corporate social responsibility, and otherwise contribute fundamentally to the advancement of dignity and prosperity among and between children, women, and youth in South Asia and North America.

More recently, as a senior communications advisor to Canadian provincial ministers and as a senior communications executive in the public and private sector, she has functioned as a master communicator, conflict resolver, public relations professional, media specialist, transcultural networker, and a sensitive reader of multicultural perspectives. For Li, dignity resides in the fair and equal distribution of status, respect, and material well-being, and in the elimination of status-degrading labels and traditions of association that demean, diminish, and dishonor the value and importance of cultural diversity and prevent inclusive representations of history.

Tomoko Tokunaga's[8] evolution, on the other hand, as a transcultural scholar, educator, and dignity worker, emerged in a different crucible from Li's. While

---

[7]See videos: "Voices of Future Graduates," http://youtu.be/Eq6TQE2v6ww; "Seeds for a sustainable Income," http://youtu.be/b9Qs0AuDt-k; "The Power of Community Libraries," http://youtu.be/Ej55lxV1P54; "Literacy for Life," http://youtu.be/jFudOQnNdSk; and "A Healthy Vision for Tomorrow," http://youtu.be/KpCH40PIKug.
[8]This portrait of Tomoko is part of an evolving exploration of teachers as transcultural mediators in Japan and the United States. Her personal story of border crossing has rolled out gradually over the time when I was her program advisor and doctoral dissertation chair at the University of Maryland, College Park. Beyond scores of conversations and opportunities to observe her evolving understandings of border crossing

Li was shaped by the multiple crossings of her ancestors and by her status as a cultural minority in Canada, Tomoko was born in Japan into a more thoroughly mainstream Japanese family. Ironically, the circumstances of Tomoko's life would become less bounded within a single nation-state, and less deeply rooted in place than Li's had been in her early life growing up.

Tomoko was born as a Japanese national in the 1980s in Yamagata Prefecture at the foot of majestic mountains, close to her family's orchards, and away from the hustle-bustle of Japan's larger cities. Like most little Japanese girls of her age and station, she grew up in circles of like-mindedness – safe, comfortable, close-knit, enmeshed in an interlocking circle of family, friends, and community:

> I remember having so much fun playing outside with my friends, my brother and kids living in the neighborhood. (I was like a big sister and always took care of small kids.) I had three pretty close childhood girlfriends and we all went to the same kindergarten and often played together. We would play at a park, find some bushes to hide in, and play hide and seek. I guess we also hung out at each other's homes .... I also loved singing so would always sing so loudly at performances in my kindergarten.

Her life after five would thrust her out of her original circle of protection in Japan. She would become entangled in a continuing series of dislocations, attachments, and reattachments, struggles and hardships that mobilized a yearning for a place to belong. It was also a life that would require and nurture a capacity for cultural shape-shifting and improvisation, a nuanced understanding of the power of memory, a highly reflective disposition, and an ability to explore and reveal the worlds that border-crossing young people could fashion. Her story, as she narrates it, is a "struggle for being, belonging, believing" and a hope that it would become possible to inhabit multiple places and still belong to a land of your birth. Her search is a search for a dignifying identity,

> a secure place in an unsecure world. It is a story of the challenges of border crossing and the discovery of belonging for a person who has crossed borders, migrated from place to place, nation to nation, setting to setting. It is the story of a transborder migrant. (Tokunaga, 2009)

Each move was a step along the way. The first step required that young Tomoko leave her first elementary school after only two weeks, to accompany her

---

and ethnographic techniques, this mini-biography is deeply informed by her auto-ethnography (Tokunaga, 2009), as well as an array of her conference presentations, a corpus of already published scholarly work and her doctoral dissertation, (Tokunaga 2012)," which received the American Education Research Association, Asia-Pacific special interest group's Best Dissertation of the Year Award (2013).

parents and two younger brothers across a continent to Pennsylvania, transport her belongings, and take up a life in the United States as a non-speaker of English. She carried to school a

> pink color Mickey Mouse book bag, a Japanese square shape pen case full of writing utensils, brand new clothes ... *shitajiki* [a plastic board to write on], *onigiri* [a rice ball lunch], etc.

She sometimes "taught origami and Japanese language to her school mates." Carrying a bag full of Japanese artifacts on her back, she was able to preserve and reveal fragments of her Japanese cultural landscape. As the only Japanese person in a multicultural public elementary school, she helped others to learn about her original homeland, a challenge which she relished and which deepened over time.

All the while, she was crossing a linguistic divide – in the classroom and in the corridors hanging out with friends. She "acquired English rapidly." She loved to write stories and read books in English. She loved music class where she could wear fancy American dresses with accessories and sing and dance with friends. She made friends with Americans and became close to students with diverse ethnic backgrounds – young girls from Vietnam, Korea, Pakistan, and Greece with whom she played outside of school. Every Saturday, Tomoko, like other children of Japanese corporate internationalists and diplomats, went to Japanese school in order to keep up with her language skills and participate in typical Japanese educational events and cultural festivals. She had her first encounter with Japanese Americans who spoke Japanese with an American accent and English without a Japanese accent. For Tomoko, they were a novel type of Japanese – whom she kept at a small distance, preferring the company of native-born Japanese students who had arrived in the United States at the same time as she.

In a second border crossing – from the United States back to Japan – Tomoko reentered Japan in possession of habits of heart, mind, and association that had been made in America. She had expanded her networks of association with culturally diverse friends. She was excited to return to Japan. As a Japanese "returnee," however, her newfound persona would eventually go undercover. Colorful clothes, English language fluency, self-assurance, hope to become a class leader, and share her knowledge of the United States were driven underground by her fear that her eight-year-old classmates might reject her because she did not fit in. In order not to stick out, Tomoko dumb-downed her English, changed the way she talked, lowered her public profile, lengthened her skirts, and carried traditional dark-colored school bags. She refashioned her public appearance and relearned the rules of deportment for Japanese girls.

> At home, she stored her American toys, books, textbooks, articles, journals, tapes, pictures, clothes in a safe place and often took them out and reminisced about her days in the United States. She kept in close contact with her friends from America.

Tomoko had learned to enjoy the company of ethnically diverse friends in the United States and had a difficult time re-adapting to life in Japan. Nonetheless, she remained a dedicated student and a full participant in a wide range of school and community activities. At the same time, she stockpiled and nurtured memories of and connections to friends in the United States. She had, without quite knowing it at the time, adapted a particular, not fully culturally prescribed way of being – grounded in cultural hybridity. She had acquired a borderland consciousness and a lifelong disposition to observe, reflect, and survive in culturally ambiguous situations. She became skilled at cultural camouflage, carving out private and public identities, and selectively picking and choosing ways of being, thinking, and feeling. Indeed, the circumstances of her early life had prepared her to negotiate multiple worlds of difference, and imagine her way through a series of cultural ruptures.

There were almost two years living in Indonesia in a protected Japanese bubble and avoiding contact with the local community; completing Japanese middle school, and attending a culturally congested international high school with schoolmates from sixty countries. In this apparently multicultural institution, she encountered a status hierarchy and near-impenetrable cultural divides separating students from different nation-states and militating against mixing between Asian and White students. A fellow Korean student would hold her responsible for the Japanese colonization of Korea and she would acquire yet another perspective on the particularities of being Japanese. She often had a "strange feeling" toward many of her Japanese classmates who seemed to be more interested in passing entrance exams in Japan than learning about Indonesian cultures and society. And once again, because she lived in a racially and culturally charged crucible, she often kept her American memories and experience under wraps, while at the same time playing at being strange, but not too strange, and funny but not outrageous.

By the time of her next border cross – from Jakarta back to Japan, she had mastered the art of cultural shape-shifting and had improvised her way through a transcultural thicket by fashioning a secret hybridity, a plural personality, and a borderland consciousness which she kept to herself. Tomoko, like all Japanese returnees who had been away from Japan for less than two years, could not take the high school qualifying exams for returnees. Rather, she took the regular high school exam and entered a private school close to home. As she had done before, she worked very hard to make up for time lost and was accepted to the University of Tsukuba – a high-status Japanese public university, where she was pleased to study international development and follow her dream of contributing to the education of young people in developing countries.

For Tomoko, the transition from high school to college was a liberating, empowering, and transformative experience. She felt a kinship with Japanese returnees who, like herself, had spent time in English speaking countries and followed offbeat educational pathways. Tomoko became friendly with Japanese speaking international students who had struggled and failed to form close ties to Japanese students. They turned to Tomoko, a different sort of Japanese, with whom they could share their struggle of belonging.

Tomoko continued to refine her borderland consciousness further in a study abroad year in the United States living in an International House at the University of California, San Diego, where she discovered a pan-Asian identity and a like-minded community of students from Taiwan, Korea, Hong Kong, the Philippines, Burma, China, and Vietnam, with whom she felt a strong connection, a cultural affinity, and a linguistic comfort zone.

As a graduate student in Japan, she studied the fate of Filipina girls living in Japan. She was encouraged to go to the United States to complete her doctoral degree and continue her studies at the University of Maryland – a university that privileged cultural and transcultural study and research. It was there that Tomoko became deeply conversant with cultural and transcultural theories and practices. She discovered "a transcultural language and a lens to capture her own and other's lives in-between various cultures, ideas, nation-states, and more."[9] Together with a trusted friend, Beth Douthirt-Cohen, she co-created a robust learning community that, for all members of the group, was so much more than a dissertation support group. It was a place where friendships blossomed and rigorous critique occurred. It was a place where combinations of them wrote together, taught together, prepared presentations for scholarly societies together, and shared their networks.[10] It was also a place where Tomoko learned an important transcultural lesson: that "we all inhabit the in-between in different ways." Somehow, this insight

> allowed [her] to appreciate [her] hybrid identity as a Japanese American, American Japanese, Asian American, American Asian, and explore who [she] is and what she "wants her life to be. (E-mail correspondence with author, July 2013)"

She is so deeply connected to the group that she feels as though she has another home in the United States – "a nurturing and welcoming home where she could always come back."

Tomoko's corpus of scholarly work reveals and honors the many ways in which diverse groups of border-crossing Asian girls have constructed sites of belonging in the cultural worlds of the United States, Japan, the Philippines, Vietnam, China, and India (see e.g., Tokunaga, 2011a, 2011b, 2012; Tokunaga & Douhirt-Cohen, 2012). As Li had done in Varanasi, Tomoko entered into the small corners of their everyday lives, listened deeply to their voices, captured the contours of their aesthetic and communicative worlds, and generated a sensitive portrait of their hopes, dreams, and community building powers. They emerge as transnational

---

[9]Tomoko Tokunaga and Beth Douthirt-Cohen, "Dear Dr. Finkelstein ... Two letters, many pictures, and our thanks on the occasion of our finishing," booklet put together in honor of the author, December 2012.

[10]Beth Douthirt-Cohen and Tomoko Tokunaga, "Culture, identity and experience in education," a syllabus created and prepared for an undergraduate class at the University of Maryland, College Park. Copies are available from Drs Douthirt-Cohen and Tokunaga.

shapeshifters who have imagined and remained loyal to multiple homelands, nurtured hybrid identities, cultivated a pan-Asian consciousness, and built a diverse community in worlds of their own making. No longer imaginatively bound within the borders of single nation-states, these girls, like Li and Tomoko, are becoming new-age actors on a world stage. Like Li and Tomoko, they are cultural brokers, global citizens, community builders, and diasporic agents who connect one world to another and invent new ways of knowing, being, learning, and communicating.

Both Li and Tomoko continue to struggle with the complex work of building borderland worlds. Both have become master chroniclers of the border-crossing experience: Tomoko as a creative ethnographer, an already respected and rewarded rising scholar-educator, mentor to rising generations of border-crossing Asian girls, and a creator of networks of belonging in multiple communities in Japan and the United States; Li, as a sophisticated and creative arts and development educator, a transcultural broker, an inventive architect of innovative and integrated global forms of networking, and an astute advisor to influential provincial governors, government agencies, non-profit transnational advocacy groups, and for-profit CEOs seeking to internationalize their companies and work productively and harmoniously in culturally congested spaces around the world.

Conclusion

Sonia, Omékongo, Li, and Tomoko inscribe principles of dignity deeply into their daily work as scholars, educators, network builders, and transcultural messengers. Each aims to correct asymmetries of power and status – Sonia by honoring heritage languages as well as English; Omékongo, by giving voice to young people who live uneasily as cultural minorities in a discriminatory world; Tomoko by legitimizing the study of young people in borderland worlds; Li by calling attention to the inevitability of cultural hybridity for a world continually in motion. Each aims to combat aversive stereotypes – Sonia by assigning instructional materials that fit in with and honor the cultural practices in the daily lives of her students; Omékongo, by elevating the importance of a name; Li by honoring the dignity and status of cultural hybridity; Tomoko by finding value and beauty in her in-between-ness. Each promotes non-violence: Sonia by nurturing cooperative rather than competitive modes of teaching and learning; Omékongo, by creating rap music that honors rather than demeans; Li and Tomoko, by reconciling wisdom, knowledge, and professional careers that cross generations and boundaries of race, class, nation, ethnicity, generation, and gender.

Each celebrates and nurtures human solidarity;[11] Sonia by dwelling in the experience of others every single day; Omékongo as he invents language that

---

[11]I am grateful to Beth Douthirt-Cohen for her extraordinary work on the meaning of solidarity as a rising generation of contemporary young people have constructed and enacted it across boundaries of difference. Were it not for her work, I would not have thought to identify solidarity as form of dignity thinking and action. See Douthirt-Cohen (2012).

inspires: "Be an Upstander, not a bystander"; "Go with your Greatness"; "Free your Mind"; Tomoko, as she studies and constructs sites of belonging in multiple spaces. Li and Tomoko as they refuse labels that pin them into spaces of non-belonging and level critiques of regimes of knowledge that limit the exercise of the human imagination and the search for common ground.

No matter, whether they are school teachers like Sonia, performance educators like Omékongo, chroniclers of the border-crossing experience and network builders like Li and Tomoko, all are dignity exemplars and change agents who seek an equal distribution of dignity across boundaries of race, class, gender, ethnicity, generation, and spiritual belief.

For each of them, dignity is a first principle, a birthright, a form of human capital, an economic strategy, a political principle, a fundamental driver of human capability, and a foundation for a dignifying education.[12] Their appearance on the world scene signals the emergence of a new generation of experienced education border crossers who are culturally and media-savvy educators, performers, community builders, policy makers, and entrepreneurs. They have mobilized innovative transcultural education forms and social practices. In short, they are masters of dignification who deserve our closest attention – because their lives reveal and catch glimpses of dignity as it can unfold in the margins of possibility, the fine lines of social change, and the intersections of the past and the future.

References

Bontekoe, R. (2008). *The nature of dignity*. Lanham, MD: Lexington Books.

Douthirt-Cohen, B. (2012). *Altering the borders between you and me: The culture, politics, and practice of solidarity across difference in high school*. Doctoral dissertation, University of Maryland, College Park.

Hicks, D. (2011). *Dignity: Its essential role in resolving conflict (p. ix)*. New Haven, CT: Yale University Press.

Kateb, G. (2011). *Human dignity*. Cambridge, MA: The Belknap Press of the Harvard University Press.

Koo, L. (2009). *Negotiating identity*. Unpublished data. College of Education, University of Maryland, College Park, MD.

Lindner, E. (2006). *Making enemies: Humiliation and international conflict*. Westport, CT: Praeger Security International.

Lindner, E. (2012). *A dignity economy: Creating an economy that serves human dignity and preserves our planet*. Lake Oswego, OR: World Dignity University Press.

Nussbaum, M. C. (2011). *Creating capabilities: The human development approach*. Cambridge, MA: Harvard University Press.

---

[12]I am deeply grateful to a series of brilliant dignity scholars who have invented an extraordinary and innovative dignity lexicon on which I have relied repeatedly. For examples, see: Bontekoe (2008), Hicks (2011), Kateb (2011), Lindner (2006, 2012), Nussbaum (2011, 2012), and Rosen (2012).

Nussbaum, M. C. (2012). *The new religious intolerance: Overcoming the politics of fear in an anxious age.* Cambridge, MA: The Belknap Press of Harvard University Press.

O'Connell, S. (2010). *Opening the window.* Unpublished paper.

O'Connell, S. (2012). *I wish I was back in Africa: An oral history of Mattu Amari.*

Rosen, M. (2012). *Dignity: Its history and meaning.* Cambridge, MA: Harvard University Press.

Tokunaga, T. (2009). *The continuing discovery of places 'in-between': Tomoko's pathways to a 'borderland consciousness'.* College Park, MD: University of Maryland.

Tokunaga, T. (2011a). 'I'm not going to be in Japan forever': How Filipina immigrant youth in Japan construct the meaning of home. *Ethnography and Education, 6*(2), 179–193.

Tokunaga, T. (2011b). Learning from the in-between spaces of Filipina immigrant youth in Japan. *Research Connections, (Spring),* 12–14.

Tokunaga, T. (2012). *Sites of belonging – Sites of empowerment: How Asian American girls construct home in a borderland world.* Unpublished doctoral dissertation, University of Maryland, College Park.

Tokunaga, T., & Douhirt-Cohen, B. (2012). The ongoing pursuit of educational equity in Japan: The accreditation of ethnic high schools. *Equity and Excellence in Education, 45*(2), 320–333.

Chapter 9

Cultivating Human Rights by Nurturing Altruism and a Life of Service: Integrating UN Sustainable Development Goals into School Curricula

Michael J. Haslip and Michael L. Penn

Introduction

Decades of research and diplomacy designed to promote human rights and protection of the environment have culminated in two monumental international accords – the 2030 Sustainable Development Agenda and the Paris Agreement for Climate Change. These documents establish a common framework for action that expresses concern for human rights by involving the vast majority of countries and peoples in a common vision for social, economic, and environmental development. Within this framework can be perceived the early signs of the emergence of a global moral identity[1] which represents the collective will of humanity to uphold respect for the natural world and the equality and dignity of all people.

However, if these sustainable development agreements are to achieve full fruition, what will be required is a global approach to education from early childhood onward which develops in young people the moral identity that will empower them to contribute to the framework for sustainable development in villages, neighborhoods, and cities around the globe. The mission of schooling itself will need to evolve so that the process of learning can provide regular opportunities for young people to contribute directly to the advancement of human rights and protection of the environment in their own communities. Here, we explore

---

[1]*Moral identify formation* is described as internalizing a moral standard either as an act of will or an act of insight, which then reinforces our "focus and practice" around that standard. This is a "deep identity" which motivates the self toward fairness and caring behavior and is not simply a "claim" to such principles and behaviors (Peterson & Seligman, 2004, p. 402).

Interdisciplinary Perspectives on Human Dignity and Human Rights, 151–173
Copyright © 2020 by Emerald Publishing Limited
doi:10.1108/978-1-78973-821-620191015

an educational framework focused on moral development for sustainability. We begin with a brief review of the context of sustainable development and the recent global agreements that seek to mobilize world endeavor around the peace and prosperity of both people and the planet.

We propose that the movement for sustainable development, and the principles it embodies, can only be realized universally if educators at all levels focus intentionally on every child shifting to a consciousness of cooperation and collaboration worldwide. Such a shift, which, as we envision it, would be reflected in a shift away from the competitive struggle for existence and toward a spirit of compassion and altruism that is global in its reach, will require the development of a much more mature form of moral agency than is currently achieved during schooling today. Indeed, we suggest that the cultivation of moral agency among children be measured as an essential feedback mechanism for curriculum reform. Absent the focus on moral development, which elevates consciousness beyond selfishness, dishonesty, and expediency motivation, the clash between competing interests, identities, and ideologies within and among cultures and countries will continue to retard achievement of sustainable development outcomes and arrest achievement of the values that are embodied in the effort to protect human rights. In short, if succeeding generations are not focused on altruistic service to humanity as a whole, we will continue to entangle ourselves in environment destroying competition for material resources and society destroying conflicts that embody gross violations of human rights. Our educational systems need urgently to inculcate both the desire and the capacity to mobilize the talents and capacities of the young toward promoting the collective prosperity of all humankind.

At present, educational reform plans rarely focus on children's moral development. Yet, a peaceful future depends upon the full character and intellectual development of each generation. Similarly, technology only becomes "good" to the extent that it is used in pursuit of morally desirable ends. Only by teaching children how to live an *altruistic life of service* can the world's educational systems serve as the moral bridge between a potentially sustainable and ethical society, on the one hand, and the children and youth who are needed to create such a society on the other.

What follows is a framework for shaping childhood and youth education around three interrelated processes: (1) promoting moral development, particularly the capacity for moral engagement and other-oriented altruism. (2) empower children and youth to serve their communities in ways that advance UN sustainable development goals; and (3) academic and technical preparation of young people designed to assist them to contribute to processes of civilization building. In summary, then, the educational system envisioned here seeks to empower young people to devote their talents to advancing the sustainable development goals (SDGs) while also helping to create more peaceful and prosperous communities. Achieving this three-fold educational purpose will, we believe, contribute significantly to freeing humanity from the struggle for basic survival.

In the sections that follow, we review the global agreements that bind humanity into a common framework for sustainable development and human rights.

We then relate this set of agreements to the emergence of a world embracing a sense of moral identity. We then briefly contextualize altruistic development historically and presently and describe the role of education in developing an altruistic life of service that begins with teaching children about their *service related purpose* and extends to using the UN Global Goals in the construction and delivery of curricula. We end with examples and recommendations for research and practice.

Global Agreements

In September, 2015, the UN General Assembly affirmed:

> We are announcing today 17 Sustainable Development Goals with 169 associated targets which are integrated and indivisible. Never before have world leaders pledged common action and endeavour across such a broad and universal policy agenda. We are setting out together on the path towards sustainable development, devoting ourselves collectively to the pursuit of global development and of "win–win" cooperation which can bring huge gains to all countries and all parts of the world.[2]

This global development agenda was adopted by all UN member states and is part of a larger process of global development that is guided in sequential 15-year plans. The previous plan from 2000 to 2015 was organized to meet the Millennium Development Goals, while the current plan is more inclusive and broad, as evidenced by the 17 goals, 169 tasks, and 304 indicators for compliance which inform thinking, policy, and accountability from 2015 to 2030. All people are meant to be included, in all locales from areas that are both urban and rural.

Following swiftly after the adoption of the Global Goals came the news of a global climate change agreement reached on December 12, 2015, which was designed to address the problem of global warming. The agreement went into effect on November 4, 2016, after sufficient country ratification. The breakthrough came after the convergence of several propitious conditions: a continuous message of optimism, recent technological advancements which rendered sustainable energy cheaper than fossil fuels for electric generation, provisions that allowed countries to submit personalized energy plans rather than hold each country to pre-determined goals, and, among other components, the creation of a global Fund to help propel energy transformation in developing countries.[3]

---

[2]2030 Sustainable Development Agenda. Retrieved from https://sustainabledevelopment.un.org/post2015/transformingourworld.

[3]Christiana Figueres led the UN's multi-year agreement process and describes these ingredients in her "inside story" TED Talk. Retrieved from https://www.youtube.com/watch?v=MIA_1xQc7x8.

> The Paris Agreement … for the first time brings all nations into a
> common cause to undertake ambitious efforts to combat climate
> change and adapt to its effects, with enhanced support to assist
> developing countries to do so.[4]

Emergence of a Global Moral Identity

Implicit in this human and ecological development agenda is the recognition
that all people are inherently valuable and deserve to live in dignity and that
all of life depends on a healthy environment. Human and ecological rights, and
the principles they embody, are thus enshrined in the conception of the sustainable development agenda. Without the active presence of these values and
principles, sustainable development for "people, planet, prosperity, peace and
partnership" could not be consistently pursued. Thus a moral framework which
has been steadily articulated over previous decades in such instruments as the
Universal Declaration of Human Rights, the UN Charter, the Convention on
the Rights of the Child, and many other Conventions guides this universal
policy agenda.

Most particularly, the Earth Charter, which was launched in 2000, serves as a
universally acceptable ethical framework to guide sustainable development:

> The Earth Charter is centrally concerned with the transition to
> sustainable ways of living and sustainable human development.
> Ecological integrity is one major theme. However, the Earth Char-
> ter recognizes that the goals of ecological protection, the eradi-
> cation of poverty, equitable economic development, respect for
> human rights, democracy, and peace are interdependent and indi-
> visible. It provides, therefore, a new, inclusive, integrated ethical
> framework to guide the transition to a sustainable future.[5]

Upon this foundation of widely disseminated and accepted ethical principles
(e.g., sanctity of knowledge; the imperative need for justice; equality of women
and men; the right to universal education; freedom of conscience; the oneness of
the human family; and the importance of the pursuit of peace[6]), the development
agenda is organized around putting these ethical principles into action.

---

[4]UN Framework Convention on Climate Change, the Paris Agreement. Retrieved
from http://unfccc.int/essential_background/convention/items/6036.php.
[5]From "What is the Earth Charter? Retrieved from http://earthcharter.org/discover/
what-is-the-earth-charter/.
[6]There are numerous statements of moral principle binding humanity into a framework for cooperation. These principles are codified in related conventions ratified by
member states. Other examples include protection of the environment; protection
of children from harm; preservation of indigenous peoples; responsibility to protect
through collective security, and so on.

The application of this moral framework has become increasingly tangible as global development plans are established, renewed, and expanded, such as occurred with the launching of Agenda 21[7] in 1992, the Millennium Development Goals framework for 2000–2015 and Agenda 2030 for 2015–2030. By pursuing the Millennium Development Goals, significant progress in reducing global poverty rates, increasing global vaccinations, expanding access to universal education, empowering women and girls, developing renewable technologies, and other progress was made between 2000 and 2015.[8] Although the Millennium Development Goals remained mostly focused on developing countries, the expanded development agenda for 2015–2030 is now inclusive of nations that are both rich and poor. Taken together, we can clearly observe a comprehensive and systematic plan for advancing human welfare beginning to embrace the whole planet.

Achieving sustainable development for all requires that each succeeding generation be educated in the underlying moral framework that is at the heart of the process. Having adopted the values that animate this moral framework, they must also become academically and technically prepared to do the work that would bring these values into the formation of sustainable economies that promote the prosperity of all humankind, rather than a privileged few.[9] In the sections that follow, we articulate the questions and terms that are central to the development of the educational framework being articulated here.

Guiding Questions

Two questions are at the heart of the effort to achieve widespread, sustainable development:

(1) How do we raise and educate each generation to meet the moral challenges framed by the UN Global Goals, knowing that trends point to a climax of economic, environmental, and social problems in the coming decades?

---

[7]In 1992, the UN Conference on Environment and Development (the Earth Summit) produced a 40-chapter action plan for sustainable development called Agenda 21, for the twenty-first century. The plan was reaffirmed in 2002 at the World Summit on Sustainable Development. Retrieved from https://sustainabledevelopment.un.org/outcomedocuments/agenda21.

[8]See the Millennium Development Goals Report, 2015. Retrieved from https://www.un.org/millenniumgoals/2015_MDG_Report/pdf/MDG%202015%20 rev%20(July%201).pdf.

[9]In Bangladesh, the Grameen Bank and its related projects revolve around a conception of economics and capitalism for the social good. Muhammad Yunus (2007), Nobel Peace Prize Laurette, founder of the Grameen Bank and the micro-credit revolution, describes how *social business* transforms capitalism. For example, the Grameen-Danon company provides nutrient-rich yogurt to children and Grameen Shakti has installed 1.5 million solar power systems providing electricity to homes for the first time. Retrieved from http://www.greeneconomycoalition.org/glimpses/grameen-shakti-bangladesh.

(2) How can we use school curricula to inspire young people to work, altruistically, in the interest of the sustainable development goals over significant periods of time?

Terms

Altruism. Altruism is characterized by the tendency to act in the service of others without a hidden motivation to benefit oneself. It thus implies selfless service that is animated by the spirit of kindness and benevolence. Altruism is "considered the highest form of social competence" (Benard, 2004, p. 16) as it promotes the common good.

Life of Service. A life of service is manifested in a coherent and balanced approach to serve the well-being of people and the planet, and it is embodied in everyday efforts that transcend part-time civic engagement. Indeed, "solidarity" with others is implied, and not just "service to" them. Such a life requires a balanced approach to sustaining one's own emotional, psychological, and physical health while promoting the health of others. It requires that all concerned strive to align personal goals with ethical principles. The allures of wealth, fame, and power as motivating purposes for action are avoided and in exchange, one is encouraged to pursue the highest forms of self-actualization and moral authenticity.

Global Citizenship Education. Global citizenship education, defined by UNESCO as "nurturing respect for all, building a sense of belonging to a common humanity and helping learners become responsible and active global citizens,"[10] is integrated into every aspect of the educational enterprise.

Global Moral Identity. Invites adherence to the totality of virtues and principles across all international charters, conventions, and agreements promoting international peace, human and ecological rights, and sustainable development. Living an altruistic life of service is viewed as closely related to constructing a strong global moral identity.

Sustainable Development Goals. A total of 17 major goals, 169 related tasks and 304 indicators for compliance to inform thinking, policy, and accountability from 2015 to 2030. They address the following objectives:

- End poverty, reduce inequality, and provide decent work for all.
- Food security, nutrition, and sustainable agriculture.
- Health and well-being.
- Education (inclusive and equitable).
- Gender equality and empowerment of women and girls.
- Sustainable energy.
- Resilient infrastructure, sustainable industrialization, and innovation.
- Inclusive, safe housing, and cities.

---

[10]UNESCO. (2018). *Global citizenship education.* Retrieved from https://en.unesco.org/themes/gced

- Sustainable consumption.
- Combating climate change, conserving oceans and ecosystems.
- Peaceful societies through access to justice and accountable institutions.
- Global partnerships to meet these objectives.

Altruistic Development: Context and Need

As young children express empathy in compassionate behaviors, the altruistic capabilities and inclinations of the human spirit develop.[11] Altruism implies the ability to serve the needs of others, rather than pursuing what we might want to do for them (Vaillant, 2002). As noted earlier, altruism has been described as the "highest form of social competence" and is central to resilience (Benard, 2004, p. 16). Lacking an altruistic motivation, human beings struggle in competitive, winner-takes-all relationships that produce and reinforce inequality, conflict, and environmental destruction. In its most extreme forms, "lack of empathy is seen in criminal psychopaths, rapists, and child molesters" (Goleman, 1995, p. 97).

The human capacity for love and creative altruism can be developed when caregivers focus on the cultivation of children's innate capacity for moral development by developing loving and secure relationships with them, guiding them in the development of moral reasoning, and encouraging them to recognize the influence of conscience which counteracts tendencies toward selfish, hurtful, and divisive attitudes and behaviors.[12]

The twentieth century witnessed the most horrific acts of genocide and bloodshed in human history. Preventing a repeat of these horrors requires that we help people heal from hatred and trauma. The key value which is at the heart of the promise of peaceful coexistence, regardless of cultural heritage, is altruistic or creative love (Sorokin, 1954). Transforming aggression or selfishness into loving and self-sacrificing behavior is possible; building humanity's capacity for good, rather than only preventing or coping with the bad can be consciously pursued. Indeed, since the 1990s this "strength-based" thinking has been applied in community and youth development work (Benard, 2004) around the world. It is also supported, most notably, by research in "positive psychology" which seeks to explore and develop universal "character strengths and virtues" (e.g., love, curiosity, humility, honesty, creativity, spirituality, among others) (Peterson & Seligman, 2004).

---

[11]"Empathy is the ability to understand another person's feelings by experiencing the same emotion oneself. Empathic behavior is demonstrated through caring, compassion, and altruism" (Epstein, 2009, p. 35).

[12]"Moral development, also called having a conscience or a superego, is a long process. It begins in toddlerhood, with concrete ideas such as that it is wrong to hurt others, and extends well into adolescence and even adulthood as people form abstract moral values, such as the concept of equality and how it should govern our behavior. (Epstein, 2009, p. 101)"

Scholarship that explores the development of positive attitudes and behaviors is now interdisciplinary and draws insight from neuroscience, anthropology, philosophy, psychology, and related fields in order to understand and extend the reach of humanity's capacity for moral responsiveness (Narvaez, 2014). Unfortunately, in the United States, conservative versus liberal ideological warfare has politicized and stunted character education efforts. However, as the scientific evidence related to its impact continues to emerge, we can expect that greater receptivity across the political spectrum can be anticipated.

The institutions historically responsible for moral development have been the major world religions. Families consciously implementing moral principles and virtues were usually informed by a religious tradition. Yet, at the individual and family level, several factors appear to be contributing to a loss of focus on human moral identity: (1) distrust of traditional sources of moral authority, (2) a tenuous and pernicious philosophy of *moral relativism*,[13] and (3) overwhelming preoccupation with material development and economic gain, enshrined in ideologies related to consumerism and profit-maximization for shareholders.[14] The responsibility to ensure the moral development of each generation has thus not found a universal institutional home through which it can operate.

There are, of course, many volunteer-based organizations involving young people in altruistic acts, such as the Peace Corp in the United States. But unlike the National Institute of Health or the World Trade Organization which execute a health or economic mission, there is no similar Moral Development Organization to guide peoples and succeeding generations to the altruistic orientation to life that is necessary to sustain increasingly complex and interdependent human relationships.[15] In the absence of a responsible global institution created to guide and

---

[13] *Moral relativism* states that moral judgements are determined by a particular perspective, whether historical, cultural, individual or otherwise and is "often associated" with "the denial that there are universal moral values." See the Internet Encyclopedia of Philosophy (IEP). Retrieved from http://www.iep.utm.edu/moral-re/ Moral relativism, of course, ignores the human capacity to identify, co-construct and/ or agree upon a universal set of values and principles which is precisely the process that has been underway for at least 70 years as the *global moral identity,* described in this chapter, has emerged and is catalyzed into global actions through the sustainable development agenda, an agenda which progressively renews universally adopted and shared principles for moral judgement and action as it evolves.

[14] Many states in the US have now passed laws allowing for the legal creation of "benefit corporations" as an alternative to the profit-maximizing corporation. When legally incorporated as a benefit corporation, the officers of the company are not legally limited in their decision-making to profit-maximization for shareholders as the sole purpose of the organization. The movement to introduce legislation permitting the creation of benefit corporations began around 2010 in the US and is accelerating.

[15] An international or national Moral Development Organization might be charged with promoting the widespread development of a *global moral identity,* and measuring change in terms of altruistic commitment and action. Such an identity would embrace universal principles and virtues necessary to sustain human-ecological well-being.

help execute moral development education worldwide, a tapestry of voices serve at various times to fill the void.[16] We are, however, encouraged by UNESCO's effort to build a worldwide movement for global citizenship education.

Education for a Life of Service

We place education for sustainable development (ESD) in a wider context of preparing each child to live a coherent life of service. By doing so, we seek to balance the twin needs for altruistic development (inner change) and sustainable development (outer change). We doubt that altruism can fully develop without active engagement of children and youth in projects that serve others and the environment. Combining the character strengths associated with altruism, such as compassion and empathy, with the skills and knowledge needed for sustainability, can shape the broader framework of education for a life of service.

Indeed, scholars have advocated a paradigm shift in education from "transmissive" to transformative (Sterling, 2001). In 2002, the Ubuntu Declaration on Education called for "mainstreaming of sustainable development into school curricula at every level of education."[17] Toolkits for educators to promote sustainable development began emerging in the early 2000s (McKeown, Hopkins, Rizi, & Chrystalbridge, 2002). From 2005 to 2014, the Decade of ESD was promoted by the United Nations in order to advocate the concept (Wals, 2012). This decade-long effort culminated in the UNESCO World Conference on Education for Sustainable Development held in Japan in 2014.[18] More recently, the Brookings Institution (2017) published a toolkit of practices for measuring global citizenship education, as it relates to the Sustainable Development Goals.

The need to shift education toward student accomplishment in real-world projects that improve the community is central to educational reform (Prensky, 2016, p. 15 and 38). Aligning student projects with the UN Global Goals creates a coherent and universal "curriculum" (or framework for action) so that all children can enjoy opportunities to participate in improving their community and world. Such a framework for action allows for infinite local adaptation and

---

The totality of international human rights instruments would guide identification and application of the global moral identity.

[16]Sources of moral authority range widely: street protesters, social activists, rare heads of state respected for morality, individual scholars and university institutes investigating moral development and character traits scientifically, traditional religious institutions, and their leaders, humanitarian-oriented organizations and institutions, including the United Nations.

[17]Press conference on "Ubuntu Declaration" on education. World Summit on Sustainable Development. Retrieved from https://www.un.org/events/wssd/pressconf/020901conf1.htm.

[18]UNESCO. World conference on education for sustainable development. Retrieved from http://www.unesco.org/new/en/unesco-world-conference-on-esd-2014/

lowers the barrier between schooling and the needs of society. Schools themselves become agents for social change. As such, schooling becomes central to the development of both society and each child's *global moral identity*. The stronger a child's moral identity becomes, the more committed she becomes to living an altruistic life of service. This dynamic interplay between the cultivation of moral identity and altruistic action represents the heart of the concept of education for a life of service.

Teaching Children that the Purpose is Service

As noted above, a life of service requires internalization of universal principles and virtues which are applied in altruistic actions. In the context of loving and caring adult–child relationships, we recommend explicitly teaching children that each of us has a core purpose to live a life of service. Developing in children the understanding that service is an overarching life purpose requires concrete exploration of one's capacities in an altruistic context.

Young children are just learning about the many parts of their body and the various powers and capacities that exist within them. Early childhood educators, teaching children from birth to age 8, can help develop a child's emerging *service purpose* by mapping these principles and virtues onto the body, as "actions" to be taken by each part of the body. As young children learn how each part of their body, or self, contributes to a service purpose these connections are integrated by the mind into a more coherent understanding of one's whole self and the service purpose of "life" as a whole. Teachers, therefore, can be taught to "map" for children the connection between body parts, corresponding capacities, and service. The goal is to ensure that children consciously integrate each part of themselves into the core purpose of altruistic service and that they be given opportunities to practice expressing their multitude of capacities toward altruistic ends.

Visual and exploratory activities (lesson plans) for young children can be designed to explicitly teach children about each part of the "whole self" as it relates to living an altruistic life of service. We call these lessons "purpose mapping" and recommend that all early childhood teachers (up to age 8) conduct regular purpose mapping lessons starting with concrete body-to-purpose activities, discussions and reflections. Table 1 provides a framework for early childhood teachers to begin purpose mapping with the children in their classes. For older grades just transitioning to an altruism-sustainability curriculum, purpose mapping may help "reset" for the learner the focus of schooling itself as practicing to live a life of meaningful contribution.

The rest of the curriculum, and at all ages, must also be grounded in these purposes to ensure that schooling remains meaningful and coherent for each person. An altruistic purpose approach to teaching and learning will help avoid the dichotomies created by single subject-matter study (e.g., high school chemistry or calculus taught without connection to one's purpose to serve through application to solving problems related to the sustainable development goals).

Table 1: A Lesson Plan Framework for Purpose Mapping.[19]

Body Part	Purpose	Service Connections
Body	Be healthy	Be alert, strong, and clean By extension, care for the environment which is the "outer" body that our physical body depends upon and is a part of
Hands	To help	To serve, share, and give
Head	To learn	To plan, reflect, consult, and understand. To solve a problem and to resolve a conflict
Heart	To love	To care for, protect, forgive, empathize, befriend, console, encourage, sacrifice, persist, and so on. We relate virtue development to the core human relationship with authentic or unconditional love because children can understand that love expresses itself as all the other virtues, depending on the need. Justice is also taught to children as "in the heart" with a relationship to love. We do not wish to cheat or be dishonest to those we love. Without love, justice cannot be established. But also conversely, it is not fair to cheat one who loves you. Justice requires also loving the one who loves us. It becomes understandable to young children, and everyone, that all "good" comes from the "heart"
Whole self, life	Service	With the purpose of life being to serve, the purpose of each body part also becomes clear, and service is understood comprehensively as including being healthy, helping, learning, and loving

Integrating the UN Global Goals into Curricula

The goal of the educational framework described here is to form in the learner a complete *global moral identity* through study of universal virtues and principles that are codified in human rights instruments and international conventions, as well as study of the agreements themselves, while also beginning to explore their application through the sustainable development agenda. This is to be accomplished in the context of local academic standards. Connection between virtues

---

[19]A visual map of a whole child would be placed in front of the classroom with labels for *body, hands, head, heart* and *whole self.* Teachers would then explore the main purpose of each part of the self in ongoing lessons, with activities and child discussion and reflection.

Table 2:   UN Sustainable Development Goals in School Curricula

Goal	Theme[20]	Curricular Examples
1	End all poverty	(1) Involve students in advocacy campaigns for fair resource allocation.
		(2) Improve moral reasoning through justice education, beyond history and civics education, to include the concepts of taxation systems and government transparency.
		(3) Students study "societal protection programs."
		(4) More sustained introductions to career opportunities and requirements.
		(5) Introduce and investigate economic policy and consequences beyond introductory "government" lessons. Partner with college students to help facilitate these investigations.
		(6) Create a student-to-nonprofit partnership to learn about local needs, consequences, and solutions related to poverty.
2	Nutritious food	(1) Teach nutrition, including vitamin nutrients.
		(2) Change school lunch menus to healthy foods.
		(3) Students run fruit and vegetable distribution program.
		(4) Students participate in school menu and meal preparation.
3	Healthy lives and well-being	(1) Students involved in monitoring their own and other's health at the classroom/school level.
		(2) Older children work as an assistant to the school nurse to establish an individual health monitoring program.
		(3) Rigorous exercise, sport, and outdoor activities.
		(4) Knowledge of body science, strength training, healing, and physical therapy.
		(5) Teach relationship between physical and mental health.
4	Quality education and lifelong learning	(1) Opportunities for technical and project-based learning are regularly available.
		(2) Curriculum teaches all 17 of the sustainable development goals through projects and investigations.
		(3) The development of altruism is monitored along with meeting academic standards.
		(4) Highly qualified teachers maintain high academic standards and differentiate instruction as needed.

---

[20]Goals, targets, and indicators can be explored in detail at the UN Sustainable Development Knowledge Platform. Retrieved from https://sustainabledevelopment.un.org/sdgs.

Table 2: (*Continued*)

Goal	Theme	Curricular Examples
		(5) Holistic education (embracing complete human well-being) is emphasized
5	Gender equality; empower all women and girls	(1) Challenge gender stereotypes emerging in young children (e.g., types of play, color usage and friendship selection).
		(2) Teach for integrated personality traits (e.g., sensitive men).
		(3) Introduce practical expressions of gender equality: women's equal access to land and property ownership, financial services, inheritance, positions of leadership, and freedom from sexual or gender harassment.
		(4) Is the culture of the school gender neutral or reflective of dominating social norms? (e.g., schools that are punishment-oriented and tolerate verbal bullying would be reflective of an overly aggressive US culture and, therefore, not gender balanced)
6	Access to clean water and protection of water	(1) Science lessons on water purification.
		(2) Create water purifiers at increasing levels of complexity depending on student capacity.
		(3) Investigate local water cleanliness, sources, treatment, and distribution
7	Clean energy for all	(1) Explore wind and solar power generation.
		(2) Build energy generation systems.
		(3) Study of the local power grid and its inefficiencies.
		(4) Introduce energy and clean power policy
8	Decent work for all and economic growth	(1) Classroom jobs.
		(2) Team member assignments. Understanding team dynamics and responsibilities, as they relate to social and emotional skill development. The ability to create teams, set common vision, goals, objectives, and project management skills are all related.
		(3) Students as active agents in classroom rule and procedure formation as introduction to policy-making and preparation for entrepreneurship.
		(4) See also examples in Goal 1
9	Industry, innovation, and infrastructure	(1) Introduce younger children to diverse materials, building usages, and types and scale of infrastructure.
		(2) Teach concept of sustainable/responsible business practices (formation of "benefit corporation").
		(3) Regularly review new and emerging technologies and innovations

Table 2: (*Continued*)

Goal	Theme	Curricular Examples
10	Reduce inequalities	(1) Teach the concepts of equality, justice, and human rights. (2) Children investigate inequalities related to disability, race, nationality, religion, income, political preference, and social status. (3) Investigate trade agreements and duty-free market access. (4) Investigate financial inequalities between and within countries.
11	Safe habitations and cities	(1) Positive classroom climate. (2) Beautify and organize the classroom, school, and grounds. (3) Friendship-building project with neighboring residents.
12	Sustainable consumption	(1) Teach sustainable consumption and economics with a focus on reducing material consumption. (2) Classroom reuse and recycling procedures. (3) Share common materials. (4) Analyze product life cycles including supply chains, disassembly, and reuse.
13	Climate change	(1) Adjust K-2 weather explorations from the typical "what is the weather today?" to "how is the weather changing?" (2) Topical investigations: desertification, deforestation, land use, clean power innovation, related investment funds, climate policy, and international agreements (COP21).
14 and 15	Marine and terrestrial ecosystems (preserve biodiversity)	(1) Maintain a fish tank. (2) Maintain a class or school garden. (3) Related investigations: local land use, mapping, local development projects, environmental assessment policies, and procedures prior to development, conservation, and advocacy for conservation.
16	Peaceful societies sustained by justice and accountable institutions	(1) Introduce methods of active citizenship. (2) Introduce procedures and mechanisms that sustain accountable institutions: appeal, public comment and documentation, press access, financial transparency, recourse to courts, and democratic organizations. (3) Introduce rule of law through student-informed classroom rules and procedures; team participation rules, etc. (4) Create student-involved school courts (e.g., conduct committee) to teach wisdom and justice. (5) Teach conflict-resolution. (6) Focus on student relationship building. (7) Teach character strengths (compassion, honesty, etc.)

Table 2: (*Continued*)

Goal	Theme		Curricular Examples
17	Partnerships for sustainable development	(1)	Community and civic engagement.
		(2)	Traditional schools transition to "community-school" model.
		(3)	Students serve as community mentors or ambassadors with related outreach campaigns to neighborhoods and organizations to build partnership skills.

[a]The 17 Sustainable Development Goals are from Agenda 2030 of the United Nations. Associated themes and curricular examples presented.

and principles and the sustainable development goals must be made explicit to increase moral reasoning and prepare children to be active problem-solvers by engaging them in relevant projects. Table 2, above, aligns the 17 sustainable development goals with actionable curricular examples to help prepare learners to live an altruistic life of service.

Education Examples

Immediately following the acceptance of the UN Global Goals in 2015, a campaign to raise awareness about them was initiated and remains ongoing. The campaign is called Project Everyone[21]. Likewise, lesson plans to teach children about the SDGs are continuously being written for teachers under the name World's Largest Lesson[22], along with accompanying videos for children[23]. Through this campaign, lessons, videos, and resources are emerging steadily to inspire children and youth to innovate for change.

There are many examples of schools organizing aspects of their mission and curricula to teach the values associated with human rights and problem-solving for sustainable development. A catalog of global citizenship education programs, practices, and assessment tools has been published in a toolkit by the Center for Universal Education at the Brookings Institution (Brookings Institution, 2017). Examples can also be found through the Global Citizenship Education hub organized under the auspices of UNESCO.[24] We introduce a few salient examples below that represent primary, secondary, and higher education, as well as research centers.

---

[21]Project Everyone. Retrieved from http://www.project-everyone.org/.
[22]World's Largest Lesson. Retrieved from http://worldslargestlesson.globalgoals.org/.
[23]The Road to the SDGs: A Discussion with Students. Retrieved from https://www.youtube.com/watch?v=ZZzBbO6Y0uc.
[24]United Nations Educational, Scientific and Cultural Organization (UNESCO). Global Citizenship Education. Retrieved from https://en.unesco.org/themes/gced.

Avonwood Primary, the first UK Earth Charter school

A 2002 UN press statement called for sustainable development to be widely adopted in education, with additional advocacy for the Earth Charter[25] as providing "the principles and guidelines that should permeate all education."[26] In 2014, the UK opened its first Earth Charter school, the Avonwood Primary School,[27] currently serving approximately 130 children aged 4–6. By 2020 the school will serve children up to age 11. Avonwood Primary adopted the Earth Charter as the "moral compass for all that it does" by teaching children the principles it contains. Children learn to "care for all living creatures," go on a "daily journey around the world," to learn about religions and festivals, are rewarded for practicing "acts of peace," and participate in "school council" to learn about decision-making and democracy (Godfrey-Phaure, 2016).

> The children are learning that to make the world a better place it must all start with them. We begin by making them responsible for the tidiness of their own classroom, and then we broaden that to the whole school and eventually get them thinking about what they can do to make things better for their street, their town, their country and even the globe. (Godfrey-Phaure, 2016)

Avonwood Primary seeks to "convey the universal principles of the Earth Charter to our children" by following eight principles related to caring for life and the human family, practicing peace and love, understanding the wisdom of the past, and promoting a healthy and harmonious future.[28]

The World Course, Interdisciplinary K-12 Curriculum

Scholar Fernando Reimers (2016) of the Harvard Graduate School of Education writes:

> [...] as an institution of the Enlightenment, public education is, at its core, an institution created to advance the cosmopolitan idea of humanity as one and human rights as a shared responsibility. (p. xxix)

---

[25]Earth Charter Initiative. Retrieved from http://earthcharter.org/.
[26]Press conference on "Ubuntu Declaration" on education. World Summit on Sustainable Development. Retrieved from https://www.un.org/events/wssd/pressconf/020901conf1.htm.
[27]Avonwood Primary School. Retrieved from http://www.avonbournetrust.org/Avonwood-Primary-School.
[28]Avonwood Primary School, Earth Charter. Retrieved from http://www.avonbourne trust.org/Avonwood-Earth-Charter.

Toward this end, Reimers and colleagues have written a full K-12 curriculum:

> We demonstrate what these principles look like in practice in an
> integrated, interdisciplinary, problem and project based curricu-
> lum aligned with Human Rights, the Sustainable Development
> Goals and the Global Risk Assessment Framework developed by
> the World Economic Forum. (Reimers et al., 2016)

The curriculum draws on the Sustainable Development Goals providing "unit-based sample lessons that teachers can customize" (Doyle, 2017). The World Course curriculum emphasizes various themes as children grow. For example, by 4th grade, children explore the *evolution of civilization*, and then learn about *the power of ordinary citizens to improve society and the world*.

> Each year ends with a capstone project; students might make a book,
> create a documentary, or create a social enterprise. (Doyle, 2017)

The World Course high school themes emphasize student agency with courses on the environment, society and public health, global conflicts and resolutions, development economics, innovation and globalization. Across the four years of high school, students conduct an independent research project on a challenge of their choice, which includes an "internship with a mentor organization, develop-ment and implementation of a plan to address the issue and a senior-year pres-entation." Peer coaching to help younger students is also included (Doyle, 2017).

The World Course K-12 curriculum has been published as a book: *Empowering Global Citizens: A World Course*, under a Creative Commons license so that edu-cators can customize the lessons and expand the curriculum (Reimers et al., 2016). The World Course curriculum has been adopted by Avenues: The World School, described as an "innovative elite school" in New York City with global expansion plans.[29] For educators interested in adopting the World Course in their schools, and exploring global citizenship education, a program called the Think Tank on Global Education was created at Harvard in 2011 and convenes annually.[30]

UN University: Institute for the Advanced Study of Sustainability

Based in Tokyo, the United Nations University: Institute for the Advanced Study of Sustainability (UNU-IAS) pursues "policy-oriented research and capacity development focused on sustainability and its social, economic and environmental

---

[29]Avenues: The World School. Retrieved from http://www.avenues.org/en/. A video about the Avenues World Course is available at http://www.avenues.org/en/the-world-course/.

[30]Think Tank on Global Education: Empowering Global Citizens. Harvard Graduate School of Education. Retrieved from http://www.gse.harvard.edu/ppe/program/think-tank-global-education.

dimensions" in "three thematic areas: sustainable societies, natural capital and biodiversity, and global change and resilience" (UNU-IAS, 2019). Students can earn masters and doctoral degrees in sustainability and postdoctoral fellowships.

The UNU, operating as a research think tank and graduate school, has 13 affiliated institutes in 12 countries exploring subjects related to sustainable development, such as the UNU Institute for Environment and Human Security (Germany), the UNU Institute on Globalization, Culture, and Mobility (Spain), the UNU Institute for Global Health (Malaysia), the UNU Institute for Water, Environment, and Health (Canada), among others.[31]

Learning System Tutorial in Latin America – Sistema De Aprendizaje Tutorial

We will review the salient features of a case study conducted by the Brookings Institute summarizing the Sistema De Aprendizaje Tutorial (SAT) program (Kwauk & Robinson, 2016). SAT provides secondary education to 300,000 rural youth in Columbia, Honduras, Guatemala, Nicaragua, Ecuador, and Brazil. SAT education is holistic in nature, emphasizing knowledge integration that embraces economic and community development.[32]

> The program's trained tutors use a "learning-by-doing" methodology, such as learning mathematics and science in the context of agricultural innovation, to promote rural education and community development in marginalized communities. SAT is grounded in Baha'i principles, and it emphasizes civic engagement, social justice, and female empowerment, in addition to academic skills. (Kwauk & Robinson, 2016)

While SAT measures literacy and numeracy growth in learners, it also uses qualitative studies to measure women's empowerment and civic responsibility. "A central tenant of SAT is to prepare rural youth to participate effectively in the sustainable development of their communities" (Kwauk & Robinson, 2016, p. 8). Therefore, the eighty textbooks organically created for the program over the past 30 years emphasize capacity development needed for rural life by teaching "mathematics, science, language and communication, technology, and community service" (p. 8) from the standpoint of *capabilities* needed for application, rather than just academic proficiency (e.g., the capability to make thoughtful life decisions, or the capability to use mathematics in managing and expanding an entrepreneurial enterprise such as a chicken farm). Paid tutors are co-learners, working with groups of 15–25 students and remaining with the group for six years. These groups progress together as a cohort meeting for about 20 hours a week. During

---

[31] United Nations University: UNU System. Retrieved from https://unu.edu/about/unu-system.

[32] To read more about the SAT program, see the work of the Foundation for the Application and Teaching of the Sciences. Retrieved from http://www.fundaec.org/en/.

this time, students are involved in numerous applied learning projects sustaining rural life (e.g., poultry, fish and agricultural farming, providing childhood education, public health and sanitation campaigns, and creating income-generating initiatives). The program is implemented through a network of partner institutions who all adhere to a common vision.

By "educating a generation of young leaders committed to serving their communities," SAT is a powerful example of organizing education for community empowerment that develops in the learner an altruistic life of service and meets challenges of sustainable development.

School Lunch in Japan

Japanese children are healthy with one of the lowest child obesity rates and longest life expectancies. For 40 years, schools across Japan have taken a unique service-learning approach to organizing school lunch. Children help prepare and serve the meals to one another, and clean up. Children also learn about nutrition as healthy meals are made from scratch. Food is locally grown, sometimes by the children in a school garden, and each meal is balanced. Nutritionists work with children in the schools (Harlan, 2013). Lunchtime and nutrition are fully integrated into the educational system, teaching cooperation, self-sufficiency, and service. The 45-minute lunch period is seen as an educational period like math or science (CafCu Media, 2015).

Examining Japan's service-learning approach to lunch provides a good illustration of meeting the sustainable development goals (Goal 2, nutritious food; Goal 3, healthy lives and well-being) in the context of altruistic service as the children themselves do the cleaning and serving. This is highly significant because the entire country follows this system, not just a school or two. No other country has yet adopted such a holistic approach to combining nutrition education, character building, and serving balanced, healthy meals from locally grown produce. Meals cost just $3.00 per day, with free and reduced prices for low-income families. Other countries could certainly benefit from following such an example.

Center for Compassion and Altruism Research and Education, Stanford University School of Medicine

Center for Compassion and Altruism Research and Education (CCARE) is conducting neurological and medical research on the effect of practicing compassion and altruism in various contexts.[33] This research explores the transition to service-minded virtues and action as opposed to self-interested determinism. CCARE has piloted Compassion Cultivation Training, an eight-week course "designed to develop the qualities of compassion, empathy, and kindness."[34] In a related

---

[33]Stanford Medicine, Center for Compassion and Altruism Research and Education. Retrieved from http://ccare.stanford.edu/.

[34]About Compassion Cultivation Training. Retrieved from http://ccare.stanford.edu/education/about-compassion-cultivation-training-cct/.

study, compassion meditation twice a day was shown to reduce mind wandering and increase pleasant thoughts "both of which were related to increases in caring behaviors for oneself and others" (Jazaieri et al., 2015, p. 1). Another study found that 10 minutes of *loving kindness meditation* increased well-being, both implicitly and explicitly, increased feelings of social connection and reduced focus on the self (Seppala et al., 2014).

As scientific research increasingly reveals how compassion, altruism, and related positive psychological traits facilitate biological and psychological health, educators can increasingly invent or adopt related methods (e.g., classroom meditation breaks) into educational programing. Such research is essential to support the wider mission described here: developing an altruistic life of service in the context of meeting the UN Sustainable Development Goals.

Recommendations

In summary, we advocate the creation of curricula and experiences from early childhood through the college years that revolve around the cultivation of moral agency for global sustainable development.[35] Such an approach begins with loving relationships and teaching children about their core purpose to love, learn, and serve. We have suggested that all people can live an altruistic life of service. As children become adults they should be guided to use their talents and skills in choosing career paths that contribute to human and ecological well-being. Such consciousness, and preparation to meaningfully contribute to society, requires an educational system that has made a significant shift away from placing academics at the center of discourse. Educators must learn how to measure altruistic development across the school years, guard children against the development of egotism and selfishness, and engage them in community-based projects where academic skills are learned in the context of contributing to sustainable development goals. Altruistic education would ensure that academic endeavors are meaningful and relevant to the learner, thereby increasing motivation for schooling. Practices, such as loving-kindness mediation, would regularly refocus the mind on caring feelings and behaviors (Jazaieri et al., 2015). As children and youth learn to connect the UN Sustainable Development Goals with their future career and consumer choices they express an emerging global moral identity.

To achieve this vision we recommend:

(1) Scholarship into the hypothesized interdependent linkages between developing altruism in the individual and promoting and achieving sustainable development across society. An integrated scientific framework capable of carrying on the mission of altruism for sustainable development should

---

[35]Examples include the World Course K-12 curriculum and the Learning System Tutorial (SAT) for rural secondary students, described in the Education Examples section.

gradually emerge. This may be best situated within the interdisciplinary field of human ecology.[36]

(2) Research into the development and assessment of altruism across all childhood ages.[37]

(3) Creation of a project-based learning curriculum which involves children working on all 17 of the UN Sustainable Development Goals through 2030. Such projects would emphasize local adaptation and student contribution.

(4) The principles and values contained in the Earth Charter and international human rights instruments would be explicitly connected to all sustainable development/global citizenship education curricula. Schools at all levels will increasingly align their mission statements with the principles and values contained in these documents and related global agreements, and transition from traditional educational institutions into agents of social change and centers for community well-being.

Conclusion

A profound change in thinking about education is underway as the imperatives for global sustainable development are increasingly recognized as inseparable from the ethical principles sustaining integration and human rights (Reimers et al., 2016). The human being embodies altruistic and cooperative capabilities which are collectively sufficient to solve existing and future problems, whether environmental, economic, or social. While subject-specific academic training remains essential, this can be accomplished by revitalizing education within a wider framework for human-ecological development.

The educational systems of the future need to be designed from within a human-ecological development framework that conveys universal principles and virtues to all learners while deeply involving children and youth in working toward the sustainable development goals. Such an approach would not only be holistic for the individual, but also holistic for the species, the planet, and an emerging global civilization. In such a context, educators create and sustain deep commitment to learning that is grounded in moral purpose.

Such a vision can begin to be achieved by pursuing the creation of educational systems and curricula that measure altruistic development alongside the implementation of projects for sustainable development. More than academic or technical knowledge, we need each generation to develop a *global moral identity* rooted in the shared principles and virtues contained in the Earth Charter and

---

[36]The Cornell University College of Human Ecology is a good example of pursuing a multidisciplinary approach to human development aligned with sustainability. Retrieved from https://www.human.cornell.edu/.

[37]For an example, see the Center for Compassion and Altruism Research and Education, School of Medicine, Stanford University, investigating the "neuroscience of compassion." Retrieved from http://ccare.stanford.edu/.

human rights documents, and exemplified in related global compacts, such as Agenda 2030 and the Paris Agreement.

The 17 UN Sustainable Development Goals provide an extensive framework of potential learning activities, when considering the hundreds of related tasks and indicators, ready-made for exploration by children, youth and college students if educational systems can be so designed. Conceptualizing all schools as agents for social change and community development will inspire experimentation needed to guide each generation to live out its core purpose of altruism for a life of service.

References

Batson, C., Ahmad, N., Lishner, D., & Tsang, J. (2002). Empathy and altruism. In C. Snyder & S. Lopez (Eds.), *Handbook of positive psychology* (pp. 485-498). New York, NY: Oxford University Press.

Benard, B. (2004). *Resiliency: What we have learned.* San Francisco, CA: WestEd.

Brookings Institution (2017, April). *Measuring global citizenship education: A collection of practices and tools.* Washington, D.C. Retrieved from https://www.brookings.edu/wp-content/uploads/2017/04/global_20170411_measuring-global-citizenship.pdf .

CafCu Media. (2015, April 19). *School lunch in Japan – Its not just about eating* [Video Ffile]. Retrieved from https://www.youtube.com/watch?v=hL5mKE4e4uU

Doyle, H. (2017, May 8). *A curriculum for changing the world: Preparing students for an interconnected, global society – Starting in Kindergarten.* Harvard Graduate School of Education Usable Knowledge. Retrieved from http://www.gse.harvard.edu/news/uk/17/05/curriculum-changing-world

Epstein, A. S. (2009). *Me, you, us: Social-emotional learning in preschool.* Ypsilanti, MI: Highscope Press.

Godfrey-Phaure, D. (2016, July 5). *UK's first earth charter school.* Earth Charter Initiative. Retrieved from http://earthcharter.org/news-post/uks-first-earth-charter-school/

Goleman, D. (1995). *Emotional intelligence: Why it can matter more than I.Q.* New York, NY: Bantam Books.

Harlan, C. (2013, January 26). On Japan's school lunch menu: A healthy meal, made from scratch. *The Washington Post.* Retrieved from https://www.washingtonpost.com/world/on-japans-school-lunch-menu-a-healthy-meal-made-from-scratch/2013/01/26/5f31d208-63a2-11e2-85f5-a8a9228e55e7_story.html?utm_term=.cd8eae495cf7

Jazaieri, H., Lee, I. A., McGonigal, K., Jinpa, T., Doty, J. R., Gross, J. J., & Goldin, P. (2015). A wandering mind is a less caring mind: Daily experience sampling during compassion meditation training. *Journal of Positive Psychology.* Doi:10.1080/1743 9760.2015.1025418

Kwauk, C. & Robinson, J. P., (2016). *Sistema de aprendizaje tutorial: Redefining rural secondary education in Latin America.* Retrieved from the Center for Universal Education at the Brookings Institute Website: https://www.brookings.edu/wp-content/uploads/2016/07/FINAL-SAT-Case-Study.pdf

McKeown, R., Hopkins, C. A., Rizi, R., & Chrystalbridge, M. (2002). *Education for sustainable development toolkit.* Knoxville: Energy, Environment and Resources Center, University of Tennessee. Retrieved from http://www.esdtoolkit.org/

Narvaez, D. (2014). *Neurobiology and the Development of Human Morality: Evolution, Culture, and Wisdom* (Norton Series on Interpersonal Neurobiology). New York, NY: WW Norton & Company.

Peterson, C., & Seligman, M. (2004). *Character strengths and virtues: A Handbook and classification.* New York, NY: Oxford University Press.

Prensky, M. (2016). *Education to better their world: Unleashing the power of 21st century kids.* New York, NY: Teachers College Press.

Seppala, E. M., Hutcherson, C. A., Nguyen, D. T. H., Doty, J. R., & Gross, J. J. (2014). Loving-kindness meditation: A tool to improve healthcare provider compassion, resilience, and patient care. Journal of *Compassionate Healthcare.* DOI:10.1186/s40639-014-0005-9

Sorokin, P. A. (2015). *Ways & power of love: Techniques of moral transformation.* West Conshohocken, PA: Templeton Foundation Press.

Sterling, S. (2001). Sustainable Education: Re-Visioning Learning and Change. Schumacher Briefings. Schumacher UK: CREATE Environment Centre.

United Nations. (n.d.). *Sustainable development goals: 17 goals to transform our world.* Retrieved from http://www.un.org/sustainabledevelopment/sustainable-development-goals/

UNU-IAS. (2019). United Nations University - Institute for the Advanced Study of Sustainability. Retrieved from https://unu.edu/about/unu-system/ias#overview

Vaillant, G. (2002). Aging well: *Surprising guideposts to a happier life from the landmark harvard study of adult development.* Boston, MA: Little, Brown, and Company.

Wals, A. E. (2012). *Shaping the education of tomorrow: 2012 full-length report on the UN decade of education for sustainable development.* United Nations Economic and Social Council.

Yunus, M. (2007). *Creating a world without poverty: Social business and the future of capitalism.* New York, NY: PublicAffairs.

Afterword

Michael L. Penn

Recurring threats to the world's peace and security and a resurgence of virulent forms of racism, nationalism, and authoritarianism have reminded us of how very fragile human rights and human dignity continue to be. Events suggest that these forms of human capital can be as easily trampled upon today as they were in earlier periods of history when we had not yet developed the words and concepts that capture something of what we might mean when we endeavor to protect human beings from unnecessary suffering, deprivation, and death brought on by humanity's inhumanity to itself.

Realizing our responsibility to protect it, this volume has sought to survey the many ways that concern for human dignity may be articulated and operationalized. And although a range of themes have been explored here, each of the authors has situated the concept of dignity at the foundation of the discourse on human rights; each has suggested, in their own ways, that without concern for human dignity – however, dimly understood the construct may be – much of what we pursue when we pursue human rights may be lost in the fog of competing interests, dubious cultural or political claims, and/or centuries-old traditions that are invoked in order to deny to some that which is justly the birthright of all.

As these essays suggest, human dignity embodies the notion of a desire, not just to protect against brutality, but to create conditions that can permit the human race to flourish. Every civilization on earth has had something to say about these conditions, and many cultures have contributed to the reservoir of understandings that illuminate what it might mean to honor and respect the dignity and rights of others. These accumulated insights can continue to nourish us, even as we draw upon fresh insights resulting from the work of men and women in a variety of fields.

Twenty-five hundred years ago, Mencius, a Chinese sage, noted that when life is properly lived and the state is wisely ordered, a humanizing process unfolds. The primary responsibility of government, he suggested, was to create the conditions necessary for the excellent qualities that adorn the human reality to be realized. At the heart of Mencius's philosophy was an understanding of humanity's capacity for *moral responsiveness* and the conviction that what matters most in human interactions is the motivation of the actors and their capacity for mutual respect and regard based on recognition of their common humanity (Bloom, 1987).

It is interesting to note that in Mencius's defense of the good qualities and capacities that define humanity, and in his insistence that the state's primary responsibility is to nourish and protect these qualities, he proved to be among the very earliest defenders of human dignity and human rights. Mencius insisted that there is no moral principle that precludes the ousting of a ruler who "mutilates humaneness and cripples rights" (Bloom, 1987, p. 262). He argued that the overthrow of the last ruler of the Shang by the Chou founders was not regicide but was morally justified punishment of a ruler who had done violence against others and his own humanity by relying on force, failing to cultivate the people, and being overly concerned with profits over all other values.

As Mencius's writings reveal, concern for protecting humanity's well-being from abuses imposed by private and state-centered interests has been at the heart of governance problems for millennia. Indeed, in the twentieth century, many government-originated ideologies invited us to value only the sensual aspects of reality. From these perspectives, the value of a human person had little to rest upon except his or her social address (e.g., one's race, gender, social class, party affiliation, and so forth). In their grossest forms – such as was seen in Nazi Germany, Stalinist Russia, Maoist China, and Apartheid South Africa – defenders of such ideologies proved willing to sacrifice human lives in order to advance the government's political, material, or "cultural" interests. These systems, which valued ideas over human lives, became manifestations of the problem of idolatry. We continue to struggle with the same problem today.

Yet these destructive trends are also concomitant with one of the most significant concepts of the twentieth century – the notion that just as crimes against humanity were within the scope of human possibilities, so also was a love for humanity – expressible in the arts, philanthropy, volunteerism, social action, scholarly endeavors, environmental activism, and other undertakings. These expressions sought pathways that would promote the best interests of all people. Indeed, the twentieth century saw the emergence of many remarkable thinkers, artists, and activists whose life and work was animated by a world-embracing vision and by a desire to promote human dignity in the fullest sense of the term. Among these were Nelson Mandela, Mother Theresa, Albert Schweitzer, Mahatma Gandhi, Paulo Freire, Miriam Makeba, Erich Fromm, Karl Jaspers, Pitirim Sorokin, Bob Marley, Nina Simone, Amartya Sen, Bill and Melinda Gates, Muhammad Yunus, Albert Einstein, Louis Gregory, Dag Hammarskjöld, Thich Nhat Hanh, Eleanor Roosevelt – and many others too numerous to name.

Over the course of the century, a concern for dignity also began to express itself in a range of declarations, covenants, and charters designed to safeguard the best interests of the human community. One document of this sort was the Earth Charter, launched on June 29, 2000 at the Peace Palace in The Hague. Its Preamble reads:

> We stand at a critical moment in Earth's history, a time when humanity must choose its future. As the world becomes increasingly interdependent and fragile, the future at once holds great peril and great promise. To move forward, we must recognize that in the midst of magnificent diversity of cultures and life forms we are one human family and one Earth community with a common destiny. We must join together to bring forth a sustainable global society founded on respect for nature, universal human rights, economic justice, and a culture of peace. Towards this end, it is imperative that we, the peoples of the Earth, declare our responsibility to one another, to the greater community of life, and to future generations.[142]

---

[142]See Earth Charter at earthcharter.org.

Many similar covenants, declarations, and conventions were written over the course of the twentieth century. These documents should not be dismissed as mere platitudes; they embody expressions of humanity's most noble aspirations and represent the gradual emergence of a developing consensus. Since aspirations precede actions, these works can influence individuals, organizations, and nations in their struggle to transform ideals into action. A greater emphasis on shaping values and attitudes can pay social and humanitarian dividends in the centuries ahead. The war for better humanity is fought one battle at a time. By defining the terms of engagement, we empower ourselves as well as those to come. Books such as these – interdisciplinary, academic, rigorous – enumerate possibilities of engagement, new futures available to those who will build them. By establishing a grammar of possibilities, this book adds to the cannon of principled approaches to one of humanity's most pressing problems. Two short decades into the twenty first century, the memory of the inhumanity of the twentieth century remains cogent. The fundamental questions – what the human species must know and believe in order to endure – remain the same as they ever have been. What must we do to live well? How do we live with one another? How do we establish a peace that endures? The success of human achievement first and foremost lies within the scope of what it means to be human. In defining and making a claim for human dignity, we are defining the best possibilities for our collective lives. In mapping out a series of principles and practices, we are suggesting a broad moral cartography fitting for our time, and fitting for the time to come.

Reference

Bloom, I. (1987). A note on Mencius. In M. Adler (Ed.), *The great ideas today* (pp. 259–267). Chicago, IL: Britannica.

Index

www.ingramcontent.com/pod-product-compliance
Lightning Source LLC
Chambersburg PA
CBHW052007270326
41929CB00015B/2819